NORTH CAROLINA
THE YEARS BEFORE MAN

NORTH CAROLINA
THE YEARS BEFORE MAN

A GEOLOGIC HISTORY

FRED BEYER

CAROLINA ACADEMIC PRESS
DURHAM, NORTH CAROLINA

ISBN: 0-89089-400-0
LCC Number: 91-70197
Printed in the United States of America

Carolina Academic Press
700 Kent St.
Durham, NC 27701
(919) 489-7486

Table of Contents

Introduction

At one time or another, I suppose each of us looks at the earth and wonders about its past. Some people are curious about the ancient plants and animals that once lived on the earth's surface. Others want to know how King's Mountain, the Blue Ridge Escarpment, or the barrier islands were created. If you are one of those individuals—whether a student, a teacher, or an interested citizen—this book was written for you.

Until the last three hundred years, the history of the earth was told in myth and fable. During the past two hundred years, the study of the earth developed into a science called **geology** . As a result, the last century has witnessed an explosion of information about the geology and geologic history of North Carolina. Even with the birth of the science of geology, little progress was made until the last few decades. Today dozens of scientists, each pursuing a seemingly minor problem, are assembling the evidence that will reveal the earth's past.

Today's understanding of the earth's history bears little resemblance to earlier ideas. Many old theories have been revised and new theories developed. As research continues, the story of the earth's history as we presently understand it will continue to change. Every day discoveries raise new questions and result in the elimination or revision of old ideas. Much of the earth's history has yet to be deciphered and the farther back one goes in time, the less clear the evidence becomes.

I believe you will find North Carolina's story interesting and exciting. Even if you think the story is only a curiosity, it is important that you understand our state's geologic history because in one way or another your life has been, and is, affected by the events of the past. Some of the effects are tangible, such as water and mineral resources, the character of the soil, or the shape of the land. But in more intangible terms, understanding the earth's past can help us as we strive to understand man's relation to time and the planet on which we live. In each case, the answers can be found in the rocks because the earth's history is preserved in their layers.

This recounting of North Carolina's past is not a collection of research papers. Every effort has been made to relate events to one another in a way that will present an understandable story. You may wish to begin by simply skimming through the book. The previews at the beginning of each unit, along with the geologic time charts, are designed to help you construct your own picture of events.

With these things in mind, I must caution you that this story of the events that formed the earth, the Appalachians, and North Carolina in particular, represents only one version of the evidence. What follows is an interpretation of continuing investigations by many working scientists. In coming days and years, some of the theories used in this book to explain the evidence in the rocks may be proven wrong. Many chapters contain statements that reflect the current differences of opinion among dedicated scientists concerning what actually happened at a particular place or point in time. Yet no matter how muddled the picture may appear, it still offers us an opportunity to consider ourselves as products of an evolving planet, one with a past so lengthy that human history is diminished to insignificance.

A Word Of Thanks

No book of this kind could be written without the assistance of many people. I am indebted to dozens of people who have given willingly of their time and expertise. I owe them more than I can ever repay for tolerating stupid questions and correcting obvious errors. Special thanks go to Dr. Walter H. Wheeler, Professor Emeritus at the University of North Carolina at Chapel Hill for consistent encouragement and tireless editing of the Mesozoic and Cenozoic portions of the manuscript, and to Dr. J. Robert Butler, Dr. Edward F. Stoddard, Dr. Duncan Herron, Dr. Robert

Hatcher Jr., Mr. Edward Burt, Mr. Eldon P. Allen and many other geologists who contributed ideas, discussed various theories, or suggested sources for information. I am grateful to my wife and children who tolerated hundreds of hours in libraries, days visiting outcrops, and innumerable evenings spent with a word processor.

Finally, I wish to thank Dr. Henry Brown of North Carolina State University for overseeing the final assembly of the manuscript. His ability to see our state's history as a whole has helped make the book a lucid picture of the events that produced the rocks beneath our feet.

Some Notes On Organization

The organization of any story as complex as the geologic history of our state involves the correlation of a number of different themes. The following notes are intended to help you keep several major ideas in mind as you read.

The book is divided into units that correspond to the major events in North Carolina's history. Each unit begins with a brief overview of the most important events discussed in the unit. The story then moves into two separate and distinct areas. The first relates the history of the rocks, while the second deals with the evolution and development of life. Generally, each part is treated separately within each chapter. However, occasional references may be made in a chapter on the rock record, for example, to the fossil record or vice versa.

It is important to keep a sense of location in terms of time. Appendix A contains a simplified geologic timetable. The table follows the standards established by the American Geological Institute. The era, period, and epoch names, time spans, and dates used in this book follow the standards set forth in that chart. In addition, you will find pertinent portions of the time chart placed in the text at the beginning of major time periods or where their insertion seemed necessary to help fix an event in time. Numerous specific dates or time spans have been inserted in the text using the abbreviations [Ma] for millions of years and [Ma-BP] for millions of years before the present. The symbol [Ma] is an abbreviation of the term mega-annum which represents one million years.

This book is based on the research of thousands of geologists in dozens of specialties. Their work is credited in the bibliography. The bibliography is organized to reflect the chronology of geologic history. References to specific citations are noted in the text by numbers that correspond to the numbers of the citations in the bibliography. The references are noted in brackets, as shown here [   ]. Readers who wish to pursue a specific point in greater detail will find the cited publications in a number of libraries. North Carolina libraries with special geologic collections include the Geology Library located in Mitchell Hall at the University of North Carolina at Chapel Hill and the D. H. Hill Library on the campus of North Carolina State University at Raleigh. Many of the publications are also available in other college and university libraries around North Carolina. The reference librarian at your local public library should also be able to assist you in securing specific publications through the interlibrary loan service.

Finally, the events in North Carolina's history did not respect the artificial, and very recent, political boundaries established by humans. Many events occurred in areas which are now referred to as other states or countries. As you read, you should try to develop an aerial view of the region surrounding North Carolina. Think of yourself as being seated comfortably in a chair far above the earth's surface. From that chair you will be able to watch events occur as time passes not only in North Carolina, but also in Virginia, West Virginia, Tennessee, Kentucky, Georgia, and South Carolina. Occasionally your vision will turn to New England, Europe, Africa, or the entire Appalachian mountain chain. With such a mental perspective, you will be better able to understand the story of our state as it unfolds in the chapters that follow.

NORTH CAROLINA
THE YEARS BEFORE MAN

Part
1
The Shrouded Past

North Carolina has not always existed as we know it today. In the distant past, there was water where our state now stands. The North American continent was formed far from the present-day location of North Carolina. As millions of years passed, erosion destroyed the newly formed continent. The resulting debris formed new land in the surrounding ancestral oceans. Periodic mountain-building events changed the sedimentary deposits into metamorphic and igneous rocks, and created regions of high land. Erosion then carved the newly raised land, creating another belt of sedimentary deposits in the sea.

The first deposits in what is now North Carolina followed a mountain-building episode about 1,700 million years ago. Those sediments were changed during the next mountain-building event that we know as the Grenville Orogeny. The Grenville Mountains were created by the collision of the ancient African and North American crustal plates and became a major mountain system. Erosion began attacking the new mountains even as they were being formed. Debris created by weathering was carried away by streams as the newly formed mountain range was systematically destroyed. Today, the remnants of the ancient Grenville Mountains form the deep core of the Appalachian Blue Ridge.

1
BEGINNINGS

In order to recount the history of North Carolina, one must consider the history of our planet. The story of our state begins far back in time. Our journey will take us to a point so long ago that it is almost impossible to imagine.

Astronomers tell us that our solar system began as a cloud of gas and dust far out on one arm of the large spiral galaxy we call the Milky Way. For reasons we shall probably never know, the cloud began contracting as one particle attracted another. Trillions of dust particles began moving toward one another as the cloud slowly collapsed. Some of the energy generated by the cloud's contraction caused it to begin to turn and flatten into a disk-like shape.

Within the disk, clumps of dust and gas formed masses that began orbiting around the sun, which was forming at the cloud's center. As the clumps swept through space they collided with more dust, causing them to grow in size and mass. (The same process continues today as the earth collides with dust and other objects in its path.) As the masses that would become planets grew, their increasing mass produced an ever-larger gravitational field which pulled the particles more tightly together. [12]

In the clump of matter that would eventually become the earth, gravity slowly pulled immense numbers of particles toward one another. The compression of the gases and dust particles concentrated increasing amounts of heat energy in a small area. As a result, the temperature began to rise. While the compression of the gas and dust produced most of the heat, decaying atoms of radioactive elements were also beginning to produce significant amounts of heat energy. As the temperature increased, portions of the developing planet slowly melted. The little evidence available suggests that the developing planet did not melt completely, but that the increasingly **plastic**[1] nature of the sphere allowed molecules to begin moving from one place to another within the forming planet.

The increasing force of gravity pulled heavier substances, such as nickel and iron, toward the planet's center forming its **core**. Lighter materials, such as silicon and aluminum, were displaced and slowly rose toward the surface.

This sorting of minerals within the rock mass resulted in the development of distinct zones, or layers. Within the earth, heat and pressure combined to maintain rocks in a nearly molten, plastic condition. The interior zone, called the **mantle**, began moving with a flowing motion that slowly transferred heat from the planet's interior to its surface. The outermost layer of the planet cooled, forming a thin but rigid **crust**. Since the crust was made up of less dense minerals it "floated" on the denser plastic rocks of the underlying mantle. [13]

Movement within the plastic mantle caused the crust to break into plates. The movement within the mantle and the resulting shifting of crustal plates continues to the present. This movement is responsible for the shape of our continents, seas, and mountain ranges. [14]

One interesting exception in the sorting process involved the heavier radioactive elements. Uranium and thorium atoms are much more massive than atoms of more common elements. Logic suggests that they should have been pulled inward and concentrated deep in the planet's core. But their chemical characteristics caused them to form compounds with silicon, oxygen, and aluminum. As a result, uranium and thorium are concentrated in the earth's crust. Gold and platinum, on the other hand, did not form such chemical compounds, therefore scientists believe they are concentrated in the earth's core.

Elements were not only sorted between the core and mantle while the planet was molten, but also within the mantle and crust. In cooling crustal rocks, the lighter elements, such as silicon and aluminum, combined in minerals forming light-colored (**felsic**) rocks near the surface. At the same time, dark-colored (**mafic**) rocks were formed deep in the crust as iron and magne-

---

1. Tremendous pressure deep within the earth prevents rock from melting. While the rock appears to be solid, it actually moves, or "flows," very slowly while molecules change position within the rock mass.

sium minerals were sorted out of the upper mantle (figure 1–1).
[15]

Heat, concentrated within the crust by moving mantle rock,
resulted in volcanic activity. Masses of rock melted in response to
reduced pressure near the surface. The molten rock, called
magma, worked its way up to the earth's surface by melting the
overlying crust or by migrating along cracks in the crust. When
the magma reached the earth's surface it erupted forming volcanoes. Gases escaping from the erupting lavas blanketed the
land, forming the beginnings of a primitive atmosphere.

Some of the oldest rocks on the earth's surface are found in
eastern Greenland. They have been dated using radiometric
techniques and found to be 3,800 million years old. [16] The
rocks were altered by heat and pressure, causing their minerals
to change into different forms. This changing of rocks by heat
and pressure is known as **metamorphism**. Since the metamorphic processes which altered the rocks could only have taken
place in the presence of water in the liquid state, it seems fairly

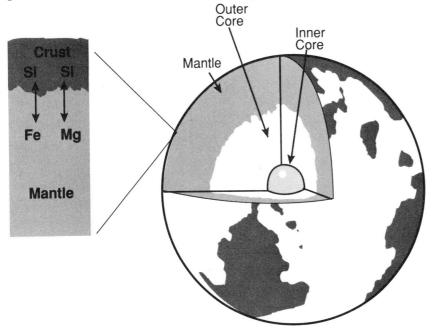

Figure 1–1: This model of the earth shows the general relationship of the
planet's core, mantle, and crust. The enlarged view of the crust illustrates the
approximate relation between the crust and the mantle. It also suggests how the
elements were sorted relative to their mass.

certain that by about 4,000 million years ago, the earth had a relatively stable crust with oceans and a primitive atmosphere.

The early atmosphere probably consisted of a great deal of water vapor with lesser amounts of methane, ammonia, carbon dioxide and very little oxygen. Yet with an atmosphere, free water, and a semistable crust, the earth had reached a stage where most of the processes that would later shape its surface had begun to work in the same ways they are working today.

By about 3,500 million years ago, the rock fragments and dust which had been thrown from earlier volcanoes were being consolidated and cemented, forming the first surface rocks. In remnants of those early deposits there is evidence that glaciers were carving valleys and grinding rocks. Other evidence indicates that rock was being broken down by physical and chemical means in a process called **weathering**. [12]

As the next hundred million years passed, the crust shifted and moved across the mantle's surface. Heat moving upward from the earth's interior produced **convection currents** in the mantle. These currents in turn generated forces that began shifting the crust. The shifting crust broke into plates that moved over the earth's surface in response to the currents in the mantle. Where plates separated, new crust was formed by upwellings of basaltic magma from the mantle. Collisions between plates compressed rock units over large areas. The resulting metamorphism, folding, faulting, and volcanic activity raised the land, forming mountain ranges. The newly uplifted surface was immediately subjected to weathering and erosional forces which worked to reduce the newly raised land to sea level. Together, the processes of uplift and erosion began writing the geologic record that we now read in the rocks.

2
THE CONTINENTS APPEAR

Geologists know very little about the formation of the early continents. Every major continental land mass contains central stable areas of ancient rock called **cratons**. Over thousands of millions of years, belts of younger rock have been added around these cratons, slowly building today's continents.

One of several possible models suggests that those earliest rocks were formed by chains of volcanic islands created when ancient crustal plates collided. The sheet-like plates collided with one another as they were moved about by the shifting plastic rocks in the mantle.

Where crustal blocks collided, one oceanic plate often plunged downward under another creating a **subduction zone**. As the plunging plate moved downward it carried ocean sediment and material from the oceanic crust deep into the mantle. There the increasing heat and pressure caused the rocks and sediments to melt, forming magma. The molten masses of minerals moved upward forming volcanoes. Where molten rock poured out through these volcanoes onto the surface, islands of new land formed in the sea.

Some geologists think that the land masses which formed in subduction zones may have slowly collided with one another. This process pressed several island chains together until they formed one single land mass or "continent." Today such a system may be seen in the northwestern Pacific. The arc of island volcanoes known as the Marianas and the plunging oceanic crustal plate marked by the Marianas Trench are slowly moving toward the subduction zone marked by the Ryukyu Trench and the Philippine Islands. If the present trend continues, the Philippine Sea will eventually disappear as the oceanic crust beneath it plunges into the Ryukyu Trench. The two chains of islands being carried on the moving crust may then collide, forming one larger chain of islands (figure 2–1). [8]

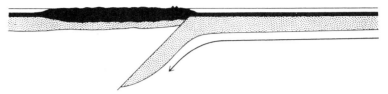

Stage 1: Two or more subduction zones produce island arc land masses

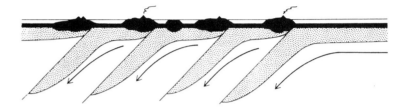

Stage 2: Island arcs collide producing larger land masses

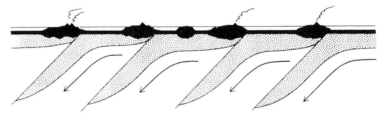

Stage 3: Later subducting plates add to growing continental land mass

Figure 2–1:   Subduction zones involving oceanic crust produced chains of volcanic islands that eventually formed land masses. Where two island arc subduction systems formed near one another, the resulting island chains could have been carried toward one another by the moving plates. Some evidence suggests that collisions of several such systems may have formed the early land masses that now form the stable cores of the continents. [8]

The model of colliding island arcs is only one of several ways to explain continent formation. Today, rocks which suggest such an origin may be seen in the Beartooth and Big Horn mountains of the western United States where they were formed about 3,400 million years ago. Similar groups of rocks dating back about 2,500 million years cover areas in today's Great Slave Lake region in eastern Canada and Labrador (figure 2–2). [18,19]

During the great span of time in which the ancient continental cratons were forming, other processes were operating on the earth's surface. Those processes probably led to the beginning of life.

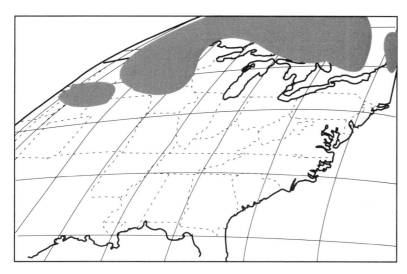

Figure 2–2:   Some 2,500 million years ago, land masses had formed in the northwestern United States, the Great Slave Lake region of Canada, and over an area stretching from the Great Lakes through eastern Canada and Labrador.

Life Begins

The exact process by which life began may never be known. Little evidence has been found because the rocks surviving from those ancient days have been greatly changed. Outside forces acting on the rocks have destroyed much evidence of the ancient climate. In addition, the fragile nature of the earliest single-celled plants and animals resulted in a sparse fossil record. Nevertheless, the earliest traces of primitive life appear in rocks about 3,400 million years old. Slightly younger rocks contain the fossils of more complex plants much like today's blue-green algae. The algae built complex layered structures that reflected an advance to colonial life forms. [21]

As the Proterozoic era began about 2,600 million years ago (figure 2–3), an episode of metamorphic activity seems to have occurred throughout the world. The episode is thought to reflect the collisions of a number of different island arcs and land masses that had been forming for at least fifty million years.

In North America, major metamorphic events occurred in eastern Canada, in the area around what is now Lake Superior, and in the state of Wyoming. The collisions resulted in the for-

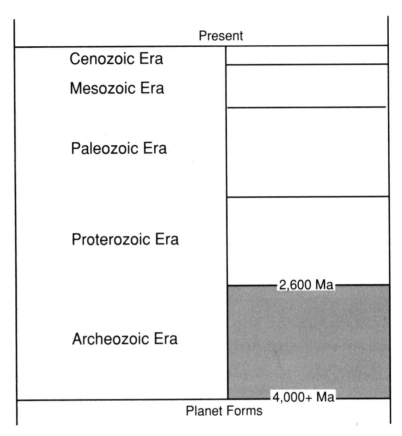

Figure 2—3:   Geologic time column showing the Archeozoic era in relation to the span of earth history (Ma-1 million years ago or 1 mega-annum). For complete geologic time scale, see Appendix A.

mation of a single land mass which stretched from eastern Idaho and Northern Wyoming to the Lake Superior region and then northward to Labrador. [19,20]

Erosional processes began working on the newly raised land, and streams carried sands and muds into a shallow sea along the southeastern edge of the continent. [8] The earliest layers took the form of sediment deposited on an ocean floor. Later, on three different occasions, ice sheets moved over the land. The moving ice deposited layers of unsorted boulders, rocks, sand, and finely ground rock called **glacial till**. [22,23] When the climate finally warmed, the sea level rose as the glaciers melted. Layers of limestone and siltstone were laid down over the older beds. Within the upper layers of silt and lime, occasional beds of iron ore and or-

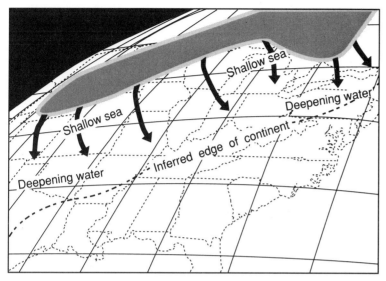

Figure 2–4: The ancient North American continent as it may have appeared following the metamorphic event about 2,400 million years ago. Erosion reduced the land mass and deposited the resulting material in the surrounding sea, building a new belt of sedimentary rock around the continent.

ganic-rich mud were formed by the remains of early plants and animals that lived in the warm shallow seas. [20,25] As each new layer was added, the continent was being built out toward the area that would become today's eastern United States (figure 2–4).

3

NORTH CAROLINA: THE BEGINNING

Another 700 million years passed during which the edge of the ancient land mass was slowly built eastward. Shifting crustal plates then caused a major mountain-building episode that once again raised the land. The event, which took place some 1,700 million years ago, built a chain of mountains across central Canada, south to Nevada and California, and east through northern Kansas and Nebraska (figure 3–1). The Vishnu Schist, located in the lowest levels of the Grand Canyon, is one of the best-known rock units dating from that time. The rock was formed from sediments and volcanic deposits which have since been altered by numerous metamorphic events. These events formed a **schistose** rock in which the mineral grains were changed and realigned to form nearly parallel bands of mineral crystals such as mica. [1,26,27]

Land in the Carolinas

During the next 400 million years streams wore down the newly raised land. Rivers flowed eastward into the sea and, for the first time, sediment from a landmass was deposited in the area that would become North Carolina (figure 3–2).

Since that time, the sediments have been transformed by recurring episodes of metamorphism and mountain building. Today they form the basement of the Appalachian mountain chain, stretching from the provinces of Quebec and New Brunswick in Canada through New England and the states of New York, Pennsylvania, and Virginia and into the Carolinas. The rocks con-

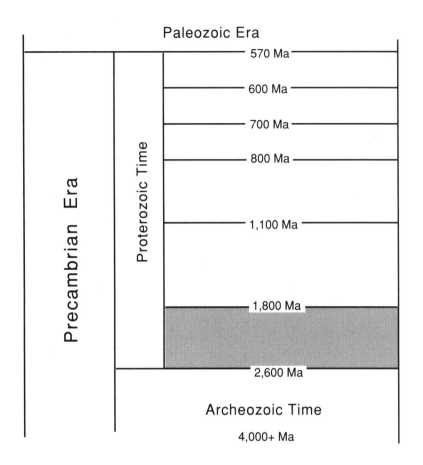

Figure 3-1: Geologic time column showing Proterozoic time in relation to the Precambrian era (Ma-Million years ago).

tinue southward until they finally disappear beneath younger rocks in Georgia and Alabama.

Salt deposits in the New England states have been interpreted as evidence that the ancient continent was probably located close to the equator. They also suggest that the climate was hot and dry. [28] In the area that is now the southeastern United States, later events destroyed any evidence that might have revealed the nature of the ancient climate.

Sedimentary units deposited in those ancient seas are now part of the oldest metamorphic rocks in the Carolinas. The Cranberry Gneiss, a series of younger intrusive rocks, and the Crossnore Suite compose the massive structural feature known as the

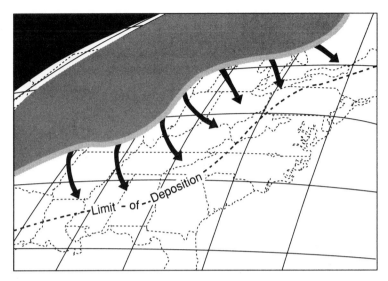

Figure 3−2:   The approximate size and extent of the landmass that had developed about 1,700 million years ago. Erosion carried materials from the land and deposited them in the sea. For the first time, significant amounts of sediment were deposited in what would become North Carolina.

Elk Park **Massif**. Today they form a series of rocks in the very core of the Blue Ridge.

The rocks of the Elk Park Massif are layered biotite gneisses with lesser amounts of muscovite gneiss and schist and hornblende gneiss. **Gneisses** are metamorphic rocks in which the altered bands of granular minerals, such as quartz and feldspar, alternate with layers of schistose minerals such as biotite and muscovite mica. **Schists** tend to be composed primarily of mica with minor amounts of feldspar, quartz, and other minerals. The gneisses and schists of the Elk Park Massif are thought to have been formed from unsorted quartz-poor sandstones and a variety of volcanic deposits including layers of ash. [29,30]

The first major mountain-building event that directly affected the Carolinas began about 1,300 million years ago. There is little evidence available to explain the cause of the 200 million-year-long surge of mountain building. However, geologists generally agree that a major collision of crustal plates was responsible for this event, which they call the **Grenville Orogeny**[1](figure 3–3).

As the plates collided, the sedimentary and igneous rocks on the eastern edge of the continent were pressed together and pushed upward. Large folds developed when layers of rock bent in response to the tremendous pressure produced as the plates pressed against one another. Some rocks were refolded several times. Heat and pressure changed the sedimentary rocks to gneisses, and schists, along with quartzites, formed when grains of quartz sand were welded together. In today's Blue Ridge,

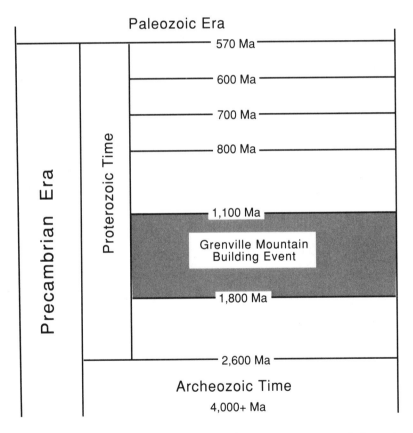

Figure 3–3:   Geologic time column showing Proterozoic time in relation to the Precambrian era (Ma = Million years ago).

1. The Grenville Orogeny is named for a unit of metamorphosed sediments located in the province of Quebec, Canada.

series of older layered gneisses and schists may reflect ancient sedimentary or volcanic bedding but they have been so completely metamorphosed that much of their present structure was probably caused by the effects of heat and pressure. [29]

During several phases of the mountain-building process, molten masses of magma invaded overlying rocks. The granites which formed as the magmas cooled have since been changed to granite gneisses by metamorphism. Most of the Grenville granites have ages of between 1,100 and 1,200 million years old. The ancient rocks may be seen near Bryson City, in Toxaway Gorge, and as far east as Surry County where they have been raised in the cores of large open folds and exposed by erosion. [32–33]

The metamorphosed schists and gneisses of the Elk Park Massif were intruded by igneous rocks that formed far beneath the surface in the roots of the Grenville mountains. The granitic magmas which formed the **pluton**[2] intruded the gneisses and schists some 1,100 million years ago. Since the magma invaded the surrounding rock, the sediments which today form the gneisses and schists must be older than the granite. [30]

The Grenville mountain-building event came to an end between 1,000 and 800 million years ago. The mountain-building event, also called an **orogeny**, had produced a major mountain range that stretched from Canada to Georgia. The new mountains ran along the eastern edge of the continent for nearly 5,000 kilometers (3,100 miles) and in places were almost 1,000 kilometers (600 miles) wide (figure 3–4).

In North Carolina, Grenville-age rocks are exposed from the very edge of the Coastal Plain in Wake County to Watauga County on the Tennessee Border. The Grenville-age rocks are known to extend westward beneath the overlying younger sediments in Tennessee. There is every reason to expect that the rocks also extend eastward beneath the Coastal Plain sediments in North Carolina.

Today, all the rocks which were formed during this time of mountain building are said to be of Grenville age. When they are combined with those formed during earlier periods of the earth's history, they are called the Precambrian Shield and are considered to be the lowest exposed units or, "basement rocks," of the Appalachians.

---

2. A pluton is a mass of igneous rock formed deep in the earth's crust.

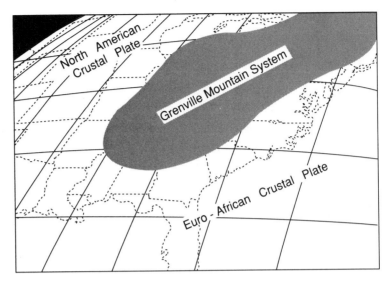

Figure 3–4:   The Grenville mountain-building event created a belt of high mountains similar to today's Alps or Rockies. The mountain system may have stretched from Nova Scotia south and west into Texas and Arizona, but today its rocks are exposed only as far south as Georgia and Alabama.

The mountains produced by the Grenville Orogeny were perhaps as high as many modern mountain ranges. As a result, erosion became the dominant process along the eastern margin of the continent for the next 150 million years. Running water and other erosional processes stripped away the overlying rocks exposing the metamorphic core of the new mountain belt. As they carved and removed the rocks, the erosional forces reduced the mountains nearly to sea level. In the process, most of the evidence for what may have been the greatest mountain-building event eastern North America would ever experience was destroyed. [7]

Part 2
Appalachian Beginnings

The Grenville mountain-building event raised the land surface from Canada to Georgia. The newly raised mountains were subjected to the accelerated weathering and erosion typical of all mountainous areas. For tens of millions of years the land mass seems to have been relatively stable. Then forces within the earth's mantle began pulling the ancient continent apart. As these forces increased, the zone of weakness between what were to become the North American and the Euro-African continents fractured. The continental masses split apart, forming a major ocean and leaving numerous fragments of continental material, called terranes, in the widening rift.

Basins developed between the continent and the terranes as the fragments were pulled apart. Magma, moving upward along crustal fractures, intruded beneath the land surface and caused volcanic eruptions both on land and in the ocean basins. Continued erosion of the land surface produced sediments that covered the ocean floor and filled the tectonic basins between the terranes.

For almost 300 million years the crustal plates moved away from one another. Then, about 750 million years ago, changing conditions in the mantle caused the plates to reverse directions. The crustal plates began moving toward one another and the

Euro-African plate plunged beneath the plate carrying the North American continent. Ocean sediments carried downward on the surface of the subducting plate melted, producing a chain of volcanic islands far to the east of the continent. The erupting volcanoes produced large volumes of ash, dust, and lava which settled to the floor of the surrounding ocean.

About 600 million years ago the eruptions stopped for a time and then resumed their earlier pattern of island building. Fossil remains confirm the presence of animals in the shallow ocean waters. Erosional processes continued, destroying the continental land mass while streams and glaciers deposited the eroded material east and west of today's Blue Ridge.

The volcanic eruptions of lavas and ash lasted for nearly 100 million years as the crustal plates continued moving closer to one another. The colliding plates set the stage for the raising of the Appalachians.

4

A NEW OCEAN

It seems likely that the Grenville Orogeny was followed by a long period during which the crustal plates carrying the ancient North American and Euro-African continents were essentially at rest. Then, between 850 and 800 million years ago, new forces

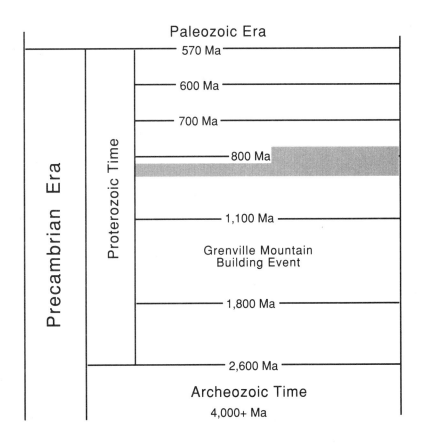

Figure 4–1: Geologic time column showing the Late Precambrian era in relation to the Paleozoic era (Ma = Million years ago).

began affecting the Carolinas. Movement in the plastic rocks of the mantle began pulling the crustal plates apart. [7] The forces which were acting on the plates created tremendous stresses in the crustal rocks. As the stress increased, the rocks finally fractured. The breaks developed in two series referred to as "sets." One set of fractures ran northeast, nearly parallel to the trend of today's Appalachian mountain chain. The second set of fractures cut across the first in a northwesterly direction (figure 4–2). Along some of the fractures the crust sank, forming large depressed regions called **rifts**. The changes caused by the shifting and fracturing of the crust were destined to have a profound effect on later events in the region. [34]

In the area of today's Blue Ridge, fluid magmas moved up along the newly opened fractures. Where magma moved along vertical fractures and cooled within the earth, the resulting igneous rocks formed sheet-like features called **dikes**. In other places, magma spread horizontally between rock layers and cooled, forming flat sheets of igneous rock called **sills**. Where magma reached the surface, lava flowed over the land or across the sea floor. Near the modern towns of Linville and Beech Mountain, in Avery County, the intruding igneous rocks make up more than 50 percent of the ancient terrain known as the Elk

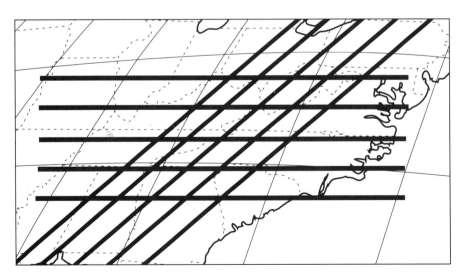

Figure 4–2: This map shows the orientation of the fractures that formed as the ancient North American and Euro-African continents separated between 850 and 800 million years ago.

Park Massif. Geologists have mapped the dikes and sills along with several bodies of granitic rock. They have concluded that the larger bodies of granite may have been the source of the magmas that produced the dikes and sills. This entire collection of igneous and volcanic rocks is called the Crossnore Plutonic-Volcanic Group.

As the crustal plates separated, a rift developed east of today's Blue Ridge Mountains. The exact location of the break will probably never be known, but in North Carolina the rift was probably just east of a belt of rocks known as the Brevard Zone. [1,29,31,33–38] The Brevard Zone is a belt of severely deformed rock that runs through the town of Brevard in Transylvania County and generally follows the eastern trend of today's Blue Ridge Mountain belt.

As the space between the two plates widened, a new ocean formed in the developing rift. Geologists call that ancient ocean the **Theic-Rheic Ocean**[1] (figure 4–3). This name refers to the Greek goddess Rhea who was the mother of Poseidon, the god of the oceans. [6]

Erosion carved the ancient land surface of the lands bordering the new ocean basin. [24] Weathering processes worked on the exposed rocks. The resulting soil was as much as 50 meters (164 feet) deep in some areas. Streams eroded the soft, weathered rock material, cutting deep channels in the land. The running water carved the land surface, producing a relief of as much as 300 meters (984 feet) from hilltop to valley bottom. [29] Rivers carried the resulting sand and mud to the Theic-Rheic Ocean. There the water slowed, depositing thick layers of sediment.

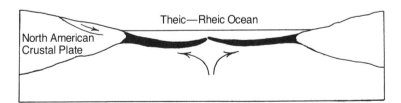

Figure 4–3:   Forces in the mantle pulled the ancient continent apart, creating fractures. Eventually a rift developed between the ancient North American and Euro-African continents. Magma moved up and filled the developing rift while water filled the developing basin. These actions formed the Theic-Rheic Ocean. [6]

---

1. Pronounced THAE-ick RAE-ick.

As millions of years passed, the eastern margin of the continent sank, allowing ocean waters to move westward over the eroded surface. At that time the shoreline was located roughly near the center of today's Ridge and Valley Province[2] in northwestern Georgia, eastern Tennessee, and southwestern Virginia.

The rift between the two great continental crustal plates was not a simple break. Instead, a series of relatively small crustal blocks appear to have separated from the North American and the Euro-African continental plates. By late Precambrian time the space between the continents included several "micro" continental fragments separated by shallow seas. Geologists refer to these crustal fragments as **terranes** (figure 4–4).

As the two great land masses moved apart, stress within the oceanic crust between them caused a second ocean basin to develop west of the Theic-Rheic Ocean. The new ocean was known as the **Iapetus Sea**[3] and was separated from the Theic-Rheic Ocean by the Avalon Terrane. The name, Iapetus, refers to the hero of Greek mythology whose son's name, Atlantis, has been given to the modern-day Atlantic Ocean. [6]

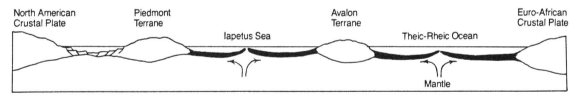

Figure 4–4:   As the ancient North American and Euro-African crustal plates continued moving away from each other, fragments of the ancient land mass appear to have been pulled away from both continents, producing island-like terranes separated by shallow seas. [6]

2. A province, such as the Ridge and Valley Province, is an area which is characterized by similar features. In the southeastern United States several areas including the Coastal Plain, Piedmont, Blue Ridge, Ridge and Valley, and Appalachian Plateau have distinctive features and are referred to as provinces.

3. Pronounced eye-A-pet-us.

Sediments on the Ocean Floor

By about 840–800 million years ago, sediments were being deposited in the Theic-Rheic Ocean on the eastern side of the Avalon Terrane. Some geologists believe the Avalon Terrane was far away from the North American continent when these deposits formed. Such an origin would have placed the deposits in the deeper waters of the Theic-Rheic Ocean and isolated them from events nearer the North American continent.

Recent research has also suggested that the sediments may have actually been deposited to the north and east in what is now Virginia. This suggestion is based on evidence which indicates that the rock units may have been shifted south to their present locations. The movement is believed to have occurred about 280 million years ago during the last major mountain-building event of the Appalachian Orogeny. [40]

Today these rocks are known as the "Raleigh Belt" (figure 4–5). The quartzites, schists, and gneisses stretch from northeastern Virginia through the eastern Piedmont of North Carolina and southwest into South Carolina and Georgia. In places, the former sediments reach thicknesses of almost 2,700 meters (8,858 feet).

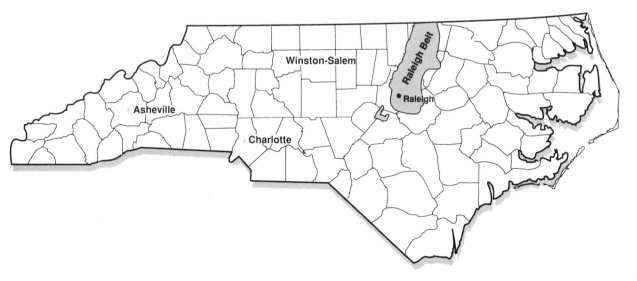

Figure 4–5:   Today the rocks of the Raleigh Belt are located in Vance, Warren, Franklin, Wake, and Harnett counties.

Careful study of the structures and features preserved in the rocks of the Raleigh Belt has revealed evidence of alternating mud flats and sandy bottoms. Layers of volcanic ash were also deposited on the ocean floor. Some of the gneiss units contain small lens-shaped grains of quartz that have been flattened by metamorphism. The resulting quartz-disk gneiss suggests that the rocks were formed from ancient pebble beaches or streams with pebbly bottoms.

Of all the rocks in the Raleigh Belt, perhaps the most intriguing are the layers of graphite schist which run through the center of Wake County. The graphite-bearing unit stretches nearly 47 kilometers (29 miles) from the Bayleaf community on the north to Panther Lake on the south. In places the unit is as much as three kilometers (1.9 miles) wide. Because the rocks have been folded several times there is no way to tell how wide an area the muddy layers covered when they were being deposited.

The graphite schist can be generally divided into two long narrow bodies. Each, in turn, is composed of many smaller units. Each individual unit is generally long and narrow with a lens-like shape. Some geologists believe that the schists formed from black mud which was deposited in shallow troughs between sand bars or large current-formed depressions on the ocean floor. While the actual origin of the graphite may never be known, one theory suggests that single-celled organisms lived in the protected areas of shallow water or on the muddy bottoms. When the organisms died their remains collected along with the mud, forming a carbon-rich ooze. Later, the heat and pressure of metamorphism compressed the mud layers, changing them to a metamorphic rock called schist. The same process converted the organic remains to a form of carbon called **graphite**. There is no way to prove that the process outlined here actually happened. However, the presently available evidence suggests that these graphite-bearing schists may be the oldest evidence of life in North Carolina (plate 1). [3,40,43,44]

The Raleigh Belt is typical of many of the ancient deposits in North Carolina because of the problems it presents for geologists. A lack of fossil evidence, coupled with the changes caused by several later mountain-building events, make determination of the exact time and conditions of deposition virtually impossible. The best geologists can do at present is to draw conclusions based on the little evidence that is available where the rocks are exposed at the earth's surface.

Sediment and Lava on the Sea Floor

Far to the west of the Avalon Terrane, in the shallow waters of the Iapetus Sea, layers of sediment accumulated on the ocean floor. Today, the resulting rocks may be seen in Stokes and Surry counties where they form the Sauratown Mountains.[4] The interbedded layers of mud and sand deposited during that time have since been changed into schists and quartzites by metamorphism. One thick layer of clean white sand is preserved as quartzite. These rocks cap Pilot Mountain, Cooke's Wall, and Hanging Rock in Stokes and Surry counties (figure 4–6). The crossbedded sandy layers reflect the presence of currents flowing over the ancient ocean floor. The clay-rich layers have been changed to schists by metamorphism, which suggests that the layers may have been deposited in relatively quiet and shallow waters. In places, the beds of sandstone thin out and disappear, only to reappear not far away. The variable nature of these deposits suggests that the sands may have been deposited as sand bars on the shallow ocean floor. [45–53]

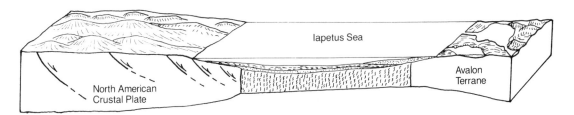

Figure 4–6: The quartzites and schists which form the rocks of the Sauratown Mountains were originally deposited as layers of sand and mud on the ocean floor.

---

4. Many features in the North Carolina Piedmont are locally known as "mountains" when, in fact, they are neither tall enough nor large enough to meet the definition of mountains.

Between the Sauratown region and the beaches farther west, the Iapetus Sea was slowly deepening. To the north and east, in Virginia, a great wedge of sediment called the Lynchburg Formation was being deposited in the deepening sea. Swiftly flowing streams running off the low, but rugged, land surface of the Piedmont Terrane to the west deposited loads of sand, gravel, and large, fist-sized, fragments called **cobbles**. The new deposits buried the formerly eroded, but now flooded, land surface. Later, the fragments were cemented together, forming solid rocks called **conglomerates**.

As the water deepened, the character of the sediment being deposited changed to clay-rich muds and coarse sands. Features preserved in the resulting shales and sandstones reveal that the material was moving out into the ocean basin as thick **slurries** composed of mud, fine sand, and water. This suggests that the slope was gradually steepening, allowing these slurries of sediment to flow farther east. Near the modern city of Lynchburg, Virginia, geologists have measured more than 4,000 meters (13,123 feet) of these rocks. Like all the other deposits of this time, the sediments were later metamorphosed into schists and gneisses. [11,29,54]

In the southwestern portion of the Iapetus Sea, lava flows and volcanic ash deposits were laid down in somewhat shallower water. The Ashe Formation is composed of volcanic material interbedded with layers of mud and sand (figure 4−7). The deposits stretch from Ashe and Watauga counties in North Carolina to

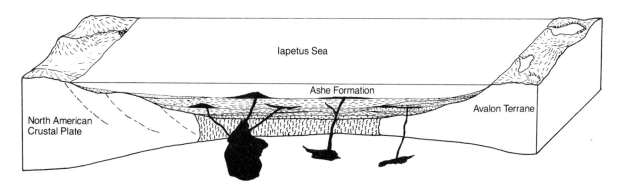

Figure 4−7:   The layers of sediment mixed with volcanic ash and lava flows which were deposited on the ocean floor between the Piedmont and Avalon Terranes now are part of the Ashe, Lynchburg, and Catoctin formations.

Franklin County in Virginia. Farther north, similar volcanic eruptions produced flows and ash deposits which geologists named the Catoctin Formation. The character and composition of the magma that formed the Catoctin Formation are typical of those being produced today where crustal plates are being pulled apart by forces within the earth's mantle.

The volcanic rocks of the Ashe, Lynchburg, and Catoctin formations merge with one another, indicating that the events which formed the three formations were occurring at nearly the same time in different parts of the Iapetus Sea. It is very common for one group of rocks to be mapped in different states or by different people and given different names. Thus, the Ashe, Lynchburg, and Catoctin formations probably represent a single unit formed from sediment and volcanic debris and now exposed in three states. [11,54—56]

Volcanoes Erupt on Land

Little is known about the nature of life in the early oceans. Some layers of schist containing graphite occur in the beds of the Ashe Formation. The graphite might represent the carbonaceous remains of plants or animals. Unfortunately, as in the case of the Raleigh Belt, metamorphism destroyed any evidence that would have verified the existence of plant or animal life.

Volcanic activity in this area decreased with the passage of time, and beds of sedimentary rock were deposited on top of the volcanic layers. These newer deposits are known as the Alligator Back Formation. The rocks include impure **marbles** formed by the metamorphism of limestone. These layers suggest that the climate was moderate and that deposition was taking place in fairly shallow water. [29]

While the volcanic layers of the Ashe Formation were being deposited, a major center of volcanic activity developed farther north and west on the land surface of the Piedmont Terrane. The first eruptions occurred about 820 million years ago, along the North Carolina—Virginia border (figure 4—8), in the area of to-

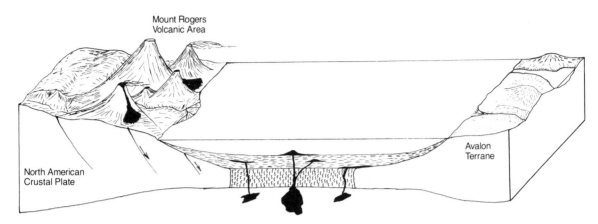

Mount Rogers
Volcanic Area

Avalon
Terrane

North American
Crustal Plate

Figure 4–8:   A large volcanic center developed near what is now the North Carolina–Virginia border. Over 220 million years, more than 3,000 meters (9,840 feet) of ash, sediment, and lava were deposited in an area near the town of West Jefferson in Ashe County.

day's Mount Rogers.[5] The eruptions continued for at least 220 million years. Early lava flows, like those of the Ashe and Catoctin formations, were deposited on an erosional surface carved in older rocks. The continuing eruptions deposited more than 3,000 meters (9,842 feet) of volcanic and sedimentary rocks. The volcanoes, which may have been as large as California's Mount Lassen (3,135 meters or 10,466 feet high), poured out basaltic[6] lavas and spewed clouds of ash and dust into the air. As they settled to the ground, the hot volcanic dust fragments welded themselves to one another, forming solid masses known as volcanic **tuffs**. Other eruptions of larger, angular fragments produced welded rock layers that geologists classify as **breccias**. Granitic magmas were also erupted from at least three separate centers producing between 500 and 1,000 cubic kilometers (120–240 cubic miles) of **rhyolitic**[7] lava. [2,29,54–59]

5. The name Mount Rogers is used here in the same sense in which a formation name is used for a typical locality. The name only indicates a location. The modern topographic feature referred to as Mount Rogers was produced in the recent geologic past, by the erosion of ancient rocks, not volcanic activity.

6. Basalt is a general term applied to very fine-grained, dark-colored, mafic igneous rock. Basalt is commonly found in the form of lava on the earth's surface, however it also occurs in dikes.

7. The term rhyolite is used for a group of very fine-grained, felsic, extrusive igneous rocks.

The rocks in today's mountains reveal little information about the nature of the ancient land surface. However, the character of the shoreline *is* revealed just south of the Mount Rogers area near Grandfather Mountain. Evidence there suggests that the rocks of the Grandfather Mountain Formation must have been deposited near a shoreline which rose rapidly toward the west. Ancient channels were formed by fast-flowing streams that rolled boulders and bounced cobbles and pebbles downhill. The rocks accumulated in the stream channels forming conglomerates. Ripple marks in crossbedded sandstones mark the channels of other ancient streams that wandered over gentler surfaces. The combination of features preserved in the ancient sediments indicates that the streams were building a large, fan-shaped delta. [54]

With the passage of time, erosion progressed and the shoreline moved farther west. As water deepened, layers of silt, mud, and lime settled to the ocean floor. Occasionally, beds of coarser material were left behind when streams rose to flood stage and washed finer sands far out to sea. A few layers of volcanic material are also interlayered with the sediments, suggesting that volcanoes in the Mount Rogers area were still erupting when the delta formed (figure 4–9). [55]

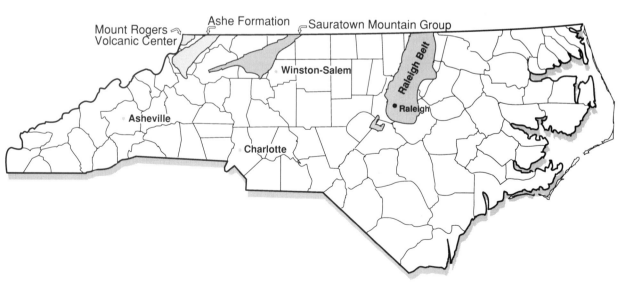

Figure 4–9:   The Raleigh Belt, Ashe Formation, rocks of the Sauratown Mountains, and earliest deposits of the Mount Rogers Group formed in different areas of what is now North Carolina.

Farther south and west, another rift basin was developing near the western edge of modern-day North Carolina. The basin formed between the ancient North American continent and the fragment of continental crust called the Piedmont Terrane. Across what are now Cherokee, Graham, Clay, and Swain counties, in the area of the Great Smoky Mountains National Park, the land slowly sank. The movement took place along fractures that developed as the crustal plates were pulled apart farther east. [2,4,35–39]

Streams flowing into the subsiding basin from the northeast began depositing a wedge of sediment. The muds and sands flowing over the bottom in the form of slurries of muddy water moved downward in the basin until the sediment finally settled, building layer upon layer on the basin floor.

The rocks which formed in this basin are known as the Ocoee Series (figure 4–10). They have been divided by geologists into three major groups and a number of formations. The oldest unit, called the Snowbird Group, was deposited on the eroded surface of Grenville-age rocks. [60] The generally thin beds of these oldest rocks are primarily fine sandstones, siltstones, and mudstones. In places the beds disappear, and a younger unit, the Great Smoky Group, lies on the eroded surface. This middle

Figure 4–10:   Today, the rocks of the Ocoee Series stretch through the western-most counties of North Carolina in the region referred to as the Blue Ridge Province. [2]

group is the thickest in the basin. In places its rocks reach thicknesses of 3,300 meters (10,800 feet). Together with the rocks of the third and uppermost unit, the Walden Creek Group, these rocks form a thick slab of material ranging from fine conglomerates to sand, silt, and mudstones.

The sediments of the Ocoee Series have been metamorphosed, welding the sandstones into quartzites and compacting the shales and mudstones into hard sedimentary rocks. The metamorphism destroyed evidence of the conditions that existed during deposition. As a result, the rocks reflect only the filling of a fault-formed basin near the edge of the continent (figure 4–11). [3,50–62]

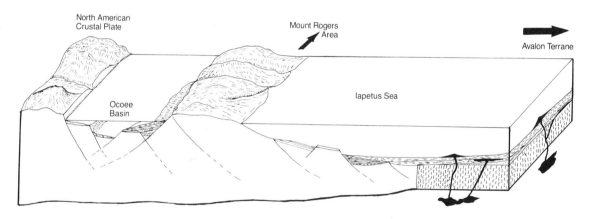

Figure 4–11: A large tectonic basin formed south and west of the Mount Rogers area when several crustal blocks dropped down along fractures created by the forces pulling on the continent. Streams flowing into the rifted basin deposited a thick sequence of sediments now know as the Ocoee Series.

5

CHANGES BENEATH THE SEA

For almost 300 million years, the crustal plates of the ancient Euro-African and North American landmasses had been moving away from one another. Then, about 750 million years ago, the forces within the mantle that were driving the plates caused

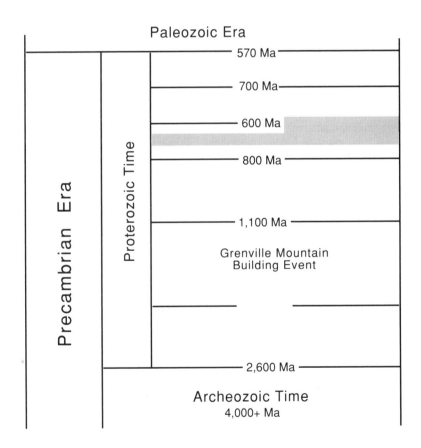

Figure 5–1: Geologic time column showing the Late Precambrian era in relation to the Paleozoic era (Ma = Million years ago).

them to change direction. The reversal took place some distance to the east of the sands and muds of the Raleigh Belt. Far out in the Theic-Rheic Ocean, what had been a rift zone became a zone of collision.

As the two plates were pushed toward one another, tremendous pressure developed. The pressure increased until the eastern plate slipped downward and plunged beneath the western plate on which the Avalon Terrane was riding. As the eastern plate moved downward, friction between the rocks created a trench at the boundary on the ocean floor (figure 5-2).

Similar trenches exist today along several plate boundaries around the world. The Aleutian Islands, Tonga Islands, and Philippine Islands are modern examples of plate boundaries that are active today in the Pacific Ocean basin. The ancient trench has since been buried beneath thousands of meters of sediment. While no direct observation is possible, geophysical evidence suggests that the ancient subduction zone was located somewhere east of our modern coastline and today lies under the continental shelf. [4-6]

Earthquakes marked the downward movement of the subducting plate. Sediments that had been deposited on the ocean floor were slowly buried and carried down on the plate surface. As the sediments were carried down toward the mantle, the temperature and pressure increased. As the temperature rose, a portion of the buried material became plastic and finally melted, forming magma. The newly created magma began working its way back toward the earth's surface. Some magma cooled and hardened beneath the surface. The remainder moved along fractures until it reached the surface and erupted, building a chain of island volcanoes (figure 5-3). Today, similar trenches and chains of island volcanoes may be seen in the Pacific Ocean. Like

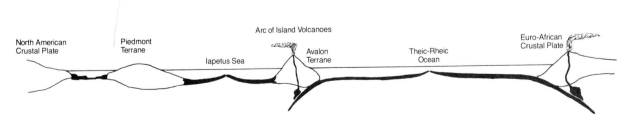

Figure 5-2: The forces that had been pulling the crust apart changed direction and caused the crustal plate east of the Avalon Terrane to plunge downward and westward, forming a subduction zone. [6]

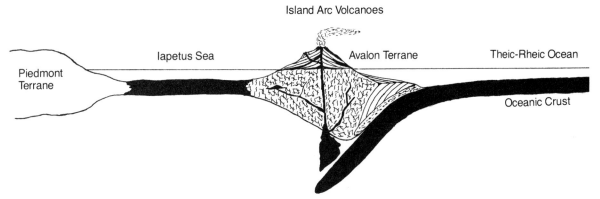

Figure 5-3: Sediment carried downward on the oceanic plate melted, producing bodies of magma that moved up through cracks in the crust. Where magma reached the surface it erupted, forming an arc of island volcanoes.

their ancient counterparts, the modern-day **island arcs** also mark subduction zones where one crustal plate plunges beneath another, causing earthquakes and creating volcanoes. [63–66]

During the next 340 million years the arc of island volcanoes grew in size as lava flows were piled on one another. Violent eruptions blew great clouds of ash and dust into the air. With the passage of time, some volcanoes became extinct and others were born. Erosion rapidly destroyed old cones, and streams deposited the resulting debris in the shallow seas.

Today, the remains of the ancient island arc stretch from northern Virginia to an area near Milledgeville in Georgia. In North Carolina, the rock units produced by the volcanic eruptions extend over a wide area of the Piedmont. In the east, the units extend for an undetermined distance beneath the sediments of the Coastal Plain. The western edge of the volcanic rock units cross the Virginia border near Roxboro and Virgilina and can be traced southwestward across the state. The boundary passes near the communities of Greensboro, Thomasville, Lexington, Salisbury, and Charlotte before crossing the South Carolina border.

Intense folding and metamorphism have destroyed much evidence concerning the nature of life and the history of eruptions along the island arc. However, the rocks known as the Carolina Slate Belt have revealed part of their story to the probing of geologists (figure 5–4). [67–71]

Near Chapel Hill, a large mass of igneous rock marks one early center of volcanic activity. The body of rock has been dated and is about 700 million years old. Such centers are thought to

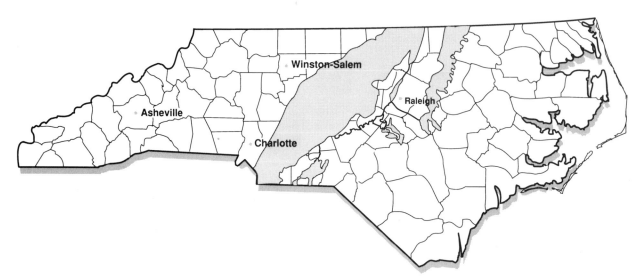

Figure 5–4:   Today, the Carolina Slate Belt forms a belt of complexly folded and metamorphosed volcanic rocks and related sediments that stretches from northeast Virginia to southwestern Georgia. [2]

have served as magma chambers. Conduits, called **pipes**, carried the magma upward to one or more volcanoes. Later events—including metamorphism, folding, and extensive erosion—destroyed much evidence including the volcanoes. However, the large igneous body, along with thick layers of erupted debris, provides clear evidence of their existence.[1]

Another large volcanic center developed in the area near Hillsborough some 50 million years later. During 30 million years of eruptions the area developed into a large **caldera**. The caldera formed when a large volume of magma erupted, causing the overlying rocks to collapse into the emptied magma chamber. Mapping has shown that the collapsed area was elliptical with a length of 45 kilometers (28 miles) and a width of 14 kilometers (8.7 miles). After the collapse, other magmas intruded into the

1. While the rocks of the Carolina Slate Belt have been studied extensively, the complex folding, faulting, and metamorphism have made the correlation of rock units very difficult. As a result, the geologic sequences—while understood in relatively small areas such as those near Roxboro or Asheboro—are not well correlated to one another across North Carolina. For that reason, no formation names have been used in this discussion. Readers who wish to learn more about the geology of a particular area should consult the references cited in the Bibliography.

broken rocks and erupted, building new volcanoes. The resulting igneous rocks filled some portions of the caldera (figure 5–5).
Throughout much of the eruptive sequence, some or all of the
caldera was under water. Where the lava entered the sea the flows
broke apart, forming pillow-like masses. The remains of pillow
lava flows related to this caldera can be seen today along the
banks of the New Hope River between Chapel Hill and Hillsborough. Modern examples of such collapsed calderas include the
Jemez volcanic field in New Mexico, Yellowstone National Park,
and Crater Lake in Oregon. [71–74]

Eruptions varied across the island arc both from place to
place and with the passage of time. A single volcanic center
might experience a series of relatively quiet eruptions in which
lava flowed down the flanks of a growing cone or out onto the
ocean floor. Later, eruptions of less fluid magmas would result in
explosive violence. The explosive eruptions blew gigantic clouds
of dust and fragments into the air. Some of the fragments settled

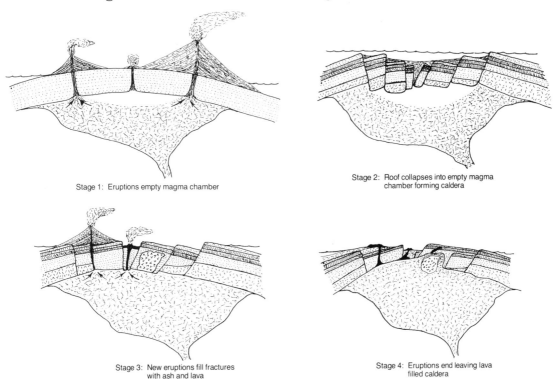

Stage 1: Eruptions empty magma chamber

Stage 2: Roof collapses into empty magma chamber forming caldera

Stage 3: New eruptions fill fractures with ash and lava

Stage 4: Eruptions end leaving lava filled caldera

Figure 5–5: Extensive eruptions emptied a large magma chamber causing the overlying crust to collapse. The resulting caldera was later partially filled with lava. [72]

on land and were welded into tuffs and breccias. In other cases, wind carried the ash and dust out over the ocean where the debris settled, forming very fine muds.

Millions of years later, the heat and pressure of metamorphism converted the muds into **slates**[2] and **phyllites**[3]. The slates are quarried today near Hillsborough. The quarried slabs are flat and make excellent building stone. As a result they have been used in the construction of many buildings across the Piedmont, including the Chapel and other buildings on the west campus at Duke University in Durham. A different slate near Jacobs Creek in Davidson County splits into very thin, wide, flat plates. It, too, is quarried, and used throughout the country for flooring and other building purposes (plate 2). [75]

Elsewhere in the Carolina Slate Belt, companies are mining mineral deposits that were formed in ancient hydrothermal areas. Such deposits occur near Glendon (in Moore County) and Hillsborough (Orange County). The rocks (originally **geyserites**) mark localities where geysers and hot springs filled the air with steam when ground water came into contact with molten rock below the earth's surface. The chemical activity of heated waters and later metamorphism combined to alter the layers of volcanic ash, changing them into the mineral known as **pyrophyllite** (plates 3a & 3b). [76,77]

Scattered Signs of Life

By about 620 million years ago, the oldest known worms in North America were living in the muddy bottoms around the island volcanoes. Near Durham, their trails are preserved in the ancient volcanic slates. The rocks were formed when ocean cur-

---

2. Slate is formed when increasing pressure aligns the minerals in a shale. Slate is said to exhibit slaty clevage because the alignment of mineral grains within the rock allows it to be split into thin plates or slabs.

3. Phyllite is a metamorphic rock that forms when slate is subjected to increasing heat and pressure. Minute flakes of the minerals sericite mica and chlorite form when clay minerals in the slate are transformed. Cleavage faces of the resulting rock exhibit a silky sheen which varies from silvery gray to greenish in color.

rents carried slurries of mud down the sloping sides of island volcanoes.

The fossil trails were discovered by a geologist working along the banks of the Little River in Durham County. The strange curved trails he discovered that day provide a rare view of life during the Precambrian era in the Carolinas (plate 4).

In Australia and other locations around the world, the last decade has witnessed the discovery of a few sites where the rare fossils of Precambrian life are preserved. In nearly every case the evidence points to a varied array of marine plants and animals. The worm impressions preserved along the banks of the Little River suggest that similar varieties of animals and plants were living in North Carolina. Yet because they lacked shells or hard parts nearly all the evidence of their existence has been destroyed. [78–80]

In spite of extensive searches, only a handful of other Precambrian fossils have been discovered in the Carolina Slate Belt of North Carolina. John Bratten, then a student at West Stanly High School, found the first two fossils in a slab of shale. The shale forms the floor of Island Creek in southwestern Stanly County. The fossils were at first believed to be badly deformed specimens of a trilobite called *Parodoxides*. [81]

Several years later, an earth science teacher discovered a third specimen while tearing down an old chimney. The volcanic siltstone from which the chimney was constructed came from Little Bear Creek near Albemarle, also in Stanly County. Additional information provided by the new specimen revealed that the three fossils were probably members of a group known as Pteridinium (plate 5).

While there is much disagreement about how Pteridinium actually looked, most paleontologists agree that the animal lived a solitary existence on the sea floor. *Pteridinium* seems to have had leaf-shaped segments, or fronds, that collectively formed lobes. The firm, leathery lobes grew in three directions from a stem by which the organism attached itself to the sea floor. The fronds are believed to have collected microscopic organisms floating by in the ocean water.

The majority of the specimens of Pteridinium have been found in Russia and are part of a group of Precambrian animals referred to collectively as the Ediacarian fauna. The so-called "Efird fossil" found near Bear Creek, N.C., is thought to be of very late Precambrian age, perhaps younger than 620 million years. Since no Ediacarian fossils are presently known from other areas of the Appalachians, the animal's presence in the Carolina Slate Belt reinforces evidence that the Avalon Terrane was located closer to the ancient Euro-African continent than to the ancient North American continent. The fossils, together with extensive trace-fossil[4] evidence from the same area, provide proof that a variety of soft-bodied life forms flourished on the sea floor around the volcanic islands of the Carolina Slate Belt. [81–84]

About 600 million years ago, eruptions seem to have stopped along the length of the island arc. Geologists are not certain why the volcanoes, which had been erupting for 140 million years, suddenly became quiet. While the erosional surface that marks the break in volcanic eruptions is well exposed along the Virginia border it has not been seen farther south. Some geologists believe the evidence is buried beneath the Asheboro area while others have suggested that the interruption of eruptions was a local phenomenon. [86–88] In any event, the eruptions resumed after a brief period of dormancy.

About 575 million years ago, there were active volcanic vents near Roxboro in Person County and just south of Chapel Hill in Chatham County. [90,91] Thick layers of material were deposited by these younger volcanoes. Much of the deposited ash and lava is thought to have been eroded and carried away during later times. If that is the case, then most of the evidence we see today reflects only the early eruptions along the island arc.

Changes Farther West

While the rocks of the Carolina Slate Belt were being formed in an oceanic island setting, changes were also occurring on the eastern margin of the North American continent. There, far to the west of the island volcanoes, the land was sinking. About 630 million years ago, along the North Carolina–Tennessee bor-

---

4. Trace fossils include evidence other than the preserved remains of an animal. Tracks, trails, burrows, and tubes left behind by worms and other burrowing animals are common examples of trace fossils.

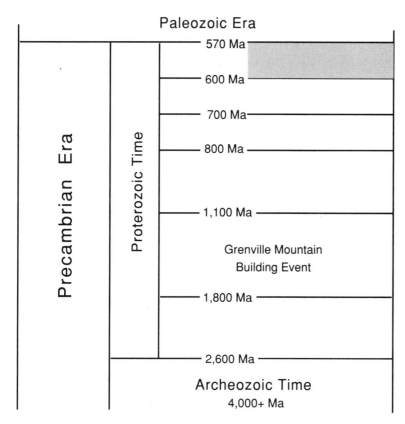

Figure 5–6:   Geologic time column showing the Late Precambrian era in relation to the Paleozoic era (Ma = Million years ago).

der, a long period of erosion was coming to an end. The mountains raised by the Grenville Orogeny had been reduced to sea level. The shoreline was moving west as the edge of the continental crust subsided. Streams flowed eastward over a subdued terrain into the advancing sea. [92,93]

At first the streams deposited sheets of pebbly conglomerate as they entered the ocean waters. Within the lower layers of sediment several sheets of basalt mark floods of lava. The lavas apparently spread out like pancake syrup from newly opened fractures. [54,56] Later, a large, fan-shaped delta developed along the shore. The streams slowed and the conglomerates of the Unicoi Formation were replaced by muddy layers of the Hampton Shale and coarse sandstones of the Erwin Formation. The conglomerates, sandstones, and shales form the lower portion of a larger sequence of formations known as the Chilhowee Group (see figure 6–3, page 51).

The deposition of the fossil-free lower portions of the Chilhowee Group mark the end of Precambrian time in North Carolina. Around the world, the appearance of abundant fossil evidence marks the end of the Proterozoic era and the beginning of the Paleozoic era. [8–10] Many later deposits would reveal fossil evidence resulting from major changes in the biological community. The developments in life forms not only changed our view of later events but would also change the face of our planet.

6

THE PALEOZOIC ERA BEGINS

Changes in Life

The years that preceded the beginning of the Paleozoic era include more than 87 percent of the earth's history, spanning more than 4,000 million years. The beginning of the Paleozoic, which geologists refer to as the Cambrian-Precambrian boundary, occurred approximately 570 million years before the present. Several important trends were developing through the Precambrian era. First, as time progressed, geologic events moved toward the Carolinas. Once activity reached the Carolinas, increasing numbers of events were recorded in the rock record. This is, in part, because the details preserved in the rock record have become more complete. These same trends continue as time proceeds toward the present.

Because of a substantial increase in the amount of evidence provided by the fossil record, geologists have been able to subdivide the Paleozoic era into periods. Periods are still rather large segments of time. The first period in the Paleozoic era is called the Cambrian.[1] The Cambrian period lasted for about 65 million years. Its beginning was marked in the geologic record by the sudden appearance of animals with shells. When the Cambrian period began, living organisms had existed on the earth for at least 2,750 million years. During that time, life had developed from very primitive single-celled organisms into complex plant

---

1. The Cambrian period is named after Cambria. Cambria was the Roman name for the portion of the United Kingdom known as Wales, where rocks of this age were first described.

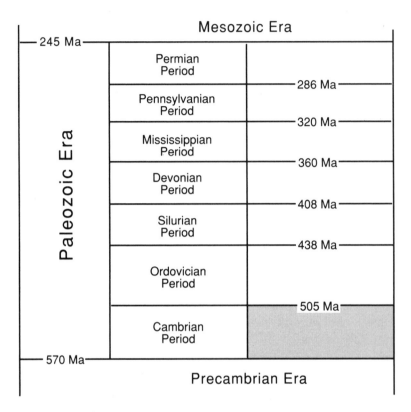

Figure 6–1:   Geologic time column showing the Paleozoic era in relation to the Precambrian and Mesozoic eras (Ma = Million years ago).

and animal forms. Yet, in spite of their complexity, plants and animals had not moved from the sea to the land. In addition, because they lacked skeletons or other hard parts, they left few fossil records reflecting their presence or activities.

Fossils with shells first appeared at the beginning of Cambrian time. Scientists have suggested a number of possible explanations for the rapid development of shells. Some paleontologists believe that an astronomical event caused the ozone layer surrounding the earth to disperse. As the layer thinned, more ultraviolet light passed through to the earth's surface. It is thought that many animals developed shells to protect themselves from the ultraviolet rays. Others believe that shells were developed as protection against predators.

Still other paleontologists have suggested changes in the acidity of the oceans or a shift in the overall temperature of the planet. Such changes would have allowed the development of shells by decreasing the amount of lime that could dissolve in sea water, thus leaving excess lime from which shells could be constructed. A fourth group has proposed that limy shells are the result of an excretory process used by animals to eliminate lime that would have otherwise been toxic. [8–10,94]

Whatever the cause, the development of shells caused the fossil record to explode at the beginning of Cambrian time. The appearance of fossils in rock layers around the world preserved a relatively complete fossil record for the first time. The fossils made it possible to understand and study the life forms which lived on the ocean floor and in its waters some 570 million years ago.

In addition to the explosion in the fossil record, at least two unique events preserved more fragile animals. During Cambrian time, large colonies of algae called **stromatolites** flourished throughout the world. Near Saratoga, New York, their fossils have yielded evidence of a sudden change in the environment. Those changes deprived the animals of oxygen, causing them to die in large numbers while at the same time preventing their decay and thus preserving their remains (plate 6).

Another rare case of preservation occurred in British Columbia. There the mud flows covered soft-bodied animals living on the sea floor. Today, the animals' remains are preserved in the Burgess Shale (figure 6–2). Burial by very fine mud preserved the minute details of a large group of animals. What makes this case so unusual is that, like the algae, the animals lacked shells and their remains would not have been preserved under normal conditions. The detailed body features of these animals provide evidence of how complex the various forms of life had become. [95,96]

By far the most common animals in the fossil record of the Cambrian period were **trilobites**, followed closely in numbers by **brachiopods**. Trilobites were invertebrates whose bodies were made of jointed segments covered with hard exoskeletons much like those of modern crabs. The animals crawled on the ocean floor and apparently ate a variety of smaller organisms. During Paleozoic time, a variety of trilobites thrived in oceans all over the world before becoming extinct at the end of the era.

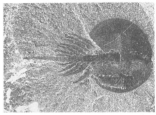
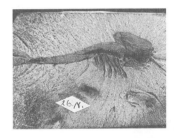

Figure 6–2: The incredible detail preserved in the fossils of the Burgess Shale shows the complexity of the invertebrate animals that lived in late Precambrian and early Cambrian time. (Courtesy of American Museum of Natural History, Smithsonian Institution.) [96]

Brachiopods have also been part of the fossil record since the beginning of the Paleozoic era. Brachiopods are filter feeders that live in shallow-water environments. The animals live within a two-part shell and move by means of a single foot. Brachiopods populated the seas in extraordinary numbers during Paleozoic time. Only about 220 species live in our seas today.

Large numbers of corals, filamentous algae, and jellyfish also lived in the seas (plate 7). [8–10] In spite of its increasing complexity, life was still concentrated in the seas. There is no evidence that any life forms had even ventured onto land. Without plant cover, the forces of erosion had a free hand on the land surface—a situation that would continue for millions of years to come.

Early Cambrian Time

As Cambrian time began in the Carolinas, the shallow seas that had developed toward the close of Precambrian time continued receiving sediment. Motion, along faults that had developed millions of years earlier, caused the eastern margin of the continent to subside.[2] In response, the sea covered the eastern edge of the continent, and the shoreline slowly shifted westward across the eastern portions of today's states of Kentucky and Tennessee. [54] Along the developing continental shelf and slope, depositional processes were building a thick sequence of sedimentary layers.

The earliest rocks deposited on the gently sloping ocean floor were conglomerates and sands that make up the Unicoi Formation. In many areas, such as the deposits near Grandfather Mountain in Avery County, the rock record suggests that the sediments were first deposited as a series of **alluvial fans**. The fans formed when streams flowed into tectonic basins and across the flood plains of a coastal plain.

As the basins filled, the slopes lessened and the coarse-grained sediments were replaced by finer sands and muds. The finer sediment, known as the Hampton Shale, covered the faulted

---

2. See page 24.

surface, creating a gently sloping continental shelf and burying the older Precambrian rocks of the Ocoee Series. The muddy layers were deposited on and off the front of a coastal delta.

The Hampton Shale is overlaid by another series of sandy beds known as the Erwin Quartzite. The unit formed as a complex of beach and longshore bar deposits which blanketed the muds as the sea level rose and fell, causing the shoreline to move back and forth across the land surface.

This series of formations is collectively known as the Chilhowee Group (figure 6-3). While the formations change slightly and bear different names, the sequence of sediments can be traced along the Blue Ridge from central Alabama through Georgia and the Carolinas and up through Tennessee, Virginia, West Virginia, and Pennsylvania. [92]

In the lower middle portion of the Chilhowee layers, fossil animals with shells appear for the first time. The animals were simple creatures that crawled on the ocean floor. Their remains were preserved when avalanches of mud called **turbidity currents** buried and preserved their remains. [93]

In the upper layers of the Chilhowee rocks, numerous and recognizable fossils appear. Imprints of worm tubes (Scolithus) have been found in the base of an ancient sandstone. [97] In slightly younger rocks near the top of the Chilhowee group, other fossils have been found. The trilobite fragments and brachiopods are evidence of a major turning point in earth history. [98]

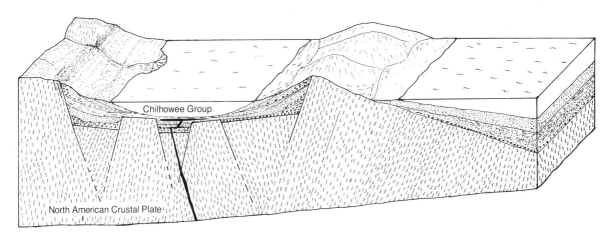

Figure 6-3: On the edge of the continental landmass, fracturing and subsidence (sinking) of the crust created a tectonic basin. Streams flowing into the basin deposited a thick sequence of sands and muds which, along with several sheet-like sills of basalt, formed the deposits known collectively as the Chilhowee Group.

In the upper portions of the Mount Rogers Volcanics[3] this time is also marked by the appearance of fossils. A fossil brachiopod was found about 500 meters (1,640 feet) below the uppermost beds which mark the last eruption. The fossil's presence indicates that the upper portions of these volcanic layers were deposited in the earliest part of Paleozoic time. [93]

In addition to the fossils, the Mount Rogers rocks tell still another story. In the upper beds, wine-colored layers of glacial sediment called **till** are interbedded in the rocks. The till marks the passing of ancient glaciers and indicates a change to a much colder climate. Very fine and uniformly bedded layers of clay are also interlayered in the till. These layers, called **varves**, were formed where finely ground rock flour, produced by the glaciers, was deposited in glacial lakes. Within the varved clays, occasional chunks of rock have disrupted the layers. Their presence suggests that rocks and other debris were carried by small icebergs from the toe of an alpine glacier out onto the lake. When the ice melted, the rocks sank to the lake floor, disturbing the fine layers of silt and clay. The rock fragments were soon buried, however, by successive layers of mud and silt. [54,99]

Deposition on a Continental Shelf

Across the eastern continental margin, early Cambrian time witnessed slow but continued subsidence of the continental crust. This slow subsidence caused the ocean to deepen between the edge of the continent and the Piedmont Terrane. As the water depth increased, a thick sequence of **dolomitic**[4] limestones was deposited over the sandy layers of the Chilhowee Group. The limestones provide evidence of a long period of warm seas and quiet, relatively shallow waters. Some geologists have suggested that the environment was much like that of today's Grand Banks in the Bahamas. Within the lime-rich layers of the Shady Dolomite, numerous mud cracks, ripple marks, and raindrop impres-

---

3. See page 32.
4. Dolomitic limestone is a carbonate sedimentary rock composed primarily of magnesium carbonate $CaMg(CO_3)_2$.

sions reveal the existence of mud flats and a reef-like environment (figure 6–4). [3,47,101,102]

Tens, and perhaps hundreds, of kilometers farther east, streams flowed westward from the low land surfaces of the Piedmont Terrane. Like those flowing from the continent, the streams deposited their loads of mud and sand on the ocean floor. Later, the sedimentary layers were metamorphosed, forming the schists and gneisses that make up the rocks of today's Inner Piedmont and Chuaga belts (figure 6–5). [103,104]

Farther east, on the steeper continental slope, layers of mud and sand were deposited in deeper water. Today, the layers of the Alligator Back Formation are exposed in Wilkes and Surry counties. The layers of mud and sand have been metamorphosed to mica schists and gneisses. The schist is well exposed along Interstate 77 where it climbs the Blue Ridge escarpment from Surry County northward into Virginia. [54]

Tectonic motion within the crust periodically caused the land to the west to rise and fall. During each period of gentle uplift, streams washed fine sands and muds into the ocean. There the sediment settled in thin layers covering the developing limestones. Today, the Rome Formation contains those interbedded layers of sandstone, shale, and limestone. The mixture of sediments reflects the changing nature of deposition during this period.

By about 500 million years ago, ocean waters stretched from somewhere in middle Tennessee eastward to the islands of the

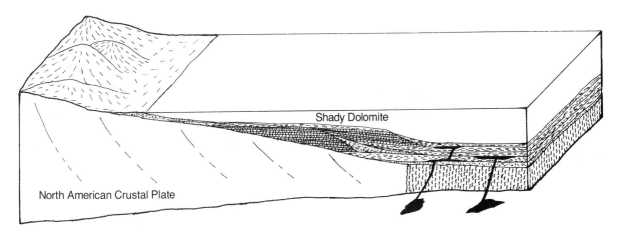

Figure 6–4: The formation known as the Shady Dolomite records deposits formed in a warm, shallow continental shelf environment. Today, the deposits are part of the Inner Piedmont and Chauga belts in the western Piedmont.

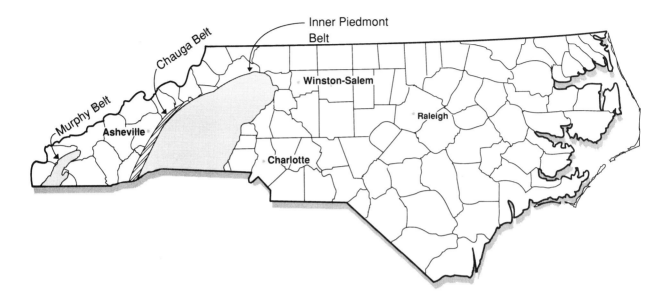

Figure 6–5:   The sedimentary layers that were deposited in the shallow sea between the Piedmont Terrane and the margin of the North American continent form the Murphy, Chauga, and Inner Piedmont belts. [2]

Piedmont Terrane and on to the volcanoes of the Avalon Terrane and the Theic-Rheic Ocean. The eastern edge of the continental crust was slowly sinking under the increasing weight of sediment, creating a shallow trough. As the trough deepened, beds of limestone were deposited in the warm, relatively shallow waters. Later the limestones were metamorphosed, forming a series of gray and pure white marbles. Today, the marble forms the land surface near Murphy in Cherokee County. The nearly pure, flawless, white marble is quarried and shipped throughout the United States for use in the construction of buildings and monuments (plate 8a & b). [102]

A Second Arc of Island Volcanoes

By the middle of Cambrian time, the shoreline of the developing continent was located near the thirtieth parallel (30°S). The climate was warm and temperate. [22] The slowly closing crustal plates were moving the Piedmont Terrane toward the continental land mass. As the two land masses slowly came together during the latter part of the period, the first evidence of a new mountain-building event began appearing in the rocks.

About 540 million years ago, the crust fractured along the western side of the Piedmont Terrane. The oceanic crustal plate, caught between the continent and the Piedmont Terrane, was pulled downward forming a subduction zone which plunged eastward under the Piedmont Terrane (figure 6–6)[5]. Sediments carried downward on the subducting plate melted, forming bodies of magma which melted some of the surrounding rocks of the Piedmont Terrane. Where the magmas reached the surface they erupted, forming volcanoes that erupted a mixture of ash deposits and lava flows. Streams eroding the volcanic deposits carried the resulting sediment into the shallow sea. Eruptions beneath the ocean surface caused submarine landslides while deposits of **barite**[6] formed where hot springs bubbled up through the ocean floor. The tuffs, lava flows, submarine landslides, and barite deposits formed a complex region known as the Kings Mountain Belt.

Today, the Kings Mountain Belt lies just west of Charlotte. The rocks lie under the land surface in Iredell, Catawba, Lincoln, and Gaston counties and in large areas of South Carolina. The belt is well known for its variety of mineral resources including

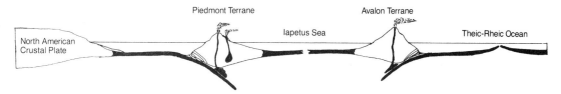

Figure 6–6:   About 540 million years ago a second subduction zone developed in North Carolina. The oceanic crust on the western side to the Piedmont Terrane plunged eastward beneath the landmass producing a new belt of volcanoes that we know as the Kings Mountain Belt.

---

5. See page 35.

6. Barite, $BaSO_4$, (Barium Sulfate) is a semi-hard (2.5–3.5), heavy, semi-transparent mineral that varies in color from colorless to red, yellow, or green. Barite is deposited in low-temperature hydrothermal veins, in limestone and dolomite deposits as a replcement mineral, and in hot spring deposits.

iron ore, lithium-bearing spodumene, lead, gold, tin, and lime in the form of marble (figure 6–7). [100–113]

Late Cambrian Time

Volcanic activity during Cambrian time was not limited to the western Piedmont and Blue Ridge. Farther east in the Avalon Terrane, the mass of volcanic rocks known as the Carolina Slate Belt had been accumulating for almost 200 million years. While some island volcanoes became dormant or extinct, new ones developed in other areas. Eruptions continued, blowing immense clouds of ash and dust into the air. Winds carried the debris westward where the ash and dust settled to the ocean surface and eventually to the sea floor. The sinking volcanic grains formed new layers of sediment. [67–69]

In the warm, shallow seas, trilobites and brachiopods grew in large numbers while **graptolites**[7] floated overhead. Graptolites

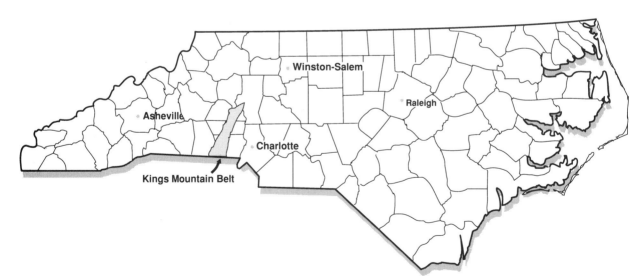

Figure 6–7:   The Kings Mountain Belt extends from Catawba County through Lincoln and Gaston counties into South Carolina. [2]

---

7. Pronounced: GRAP toe lite.

are found today as carbon-trace fossils in fine-grained sedimentary rocks. The animals, whose name means "written stones," once lived in seas around the world. Some forms lived on the ocean floor with slender branches extended in the currents above while others floated like modern-day "jellyfish" trailing slender branches below them. The branches were used to filter food, in the form of microorganisms, from ocean water.

Crinoids, a new animal form, also developed and flourished on the muddy bottom. The animals looked much like a strange form of the flowers we call tulips. Crinoids obtained their food by filtering microorganisms from the water using frond-like structures that branched from a tulip-shaped head called a calix. The calix was held above the sea floor by a long stem whose other end was attached to the bottom.

Geologists believe that trilobites, graptolites, crinoids, and other animals existed in the Carolinas, but the evidence for their existence is very sparse. The only verified discovery of such fossils lies outside the state near Batesburg in South Carolina. There, along South Carolina Highway 26, fragments of *Paradoxides*, *Peronopsis*, and what is thought to be *Tomagnostus* have been identified in a mudstone that was once a quiet ocean floor (plates 9a, b, & c). [66]

Deep beneath the ocean floor, on the western side of the Avalon Terrane, magma bodies were formed as a result of the subducting oceanic plate that produced the volcanoes of the Carolina Slate Belt farther east.

Fluid magmas invaded fractures in the surrounding rocks where they formed several series of sheet-like dikes and sills. Later, these same rocks would undergo several episodes of intrusion, folding, and metamorphism before being uplifted and exposed by erosion. Today, these igneous, volcanic, and sedimentary rock units form the Charlotte and Milton belts in the central Piedmont (figure 6–8). [104,114,115]

The waters of late Cambrian time appear to have been rather shallow, but they were also widespread. As the Cambrian period came to a close the sea covered all of what is now the Appalachian Plateau Province and Ridge and Valley Province. The ocean spread from Missouri and Wisconsin, across Kentucky, Tennessee, West Virginia, and much of western Virginia, to the volcanoes of the Carolina Slate Belt. Only the eastern most margin of the North American crustal plate—the volcanoes and narrow

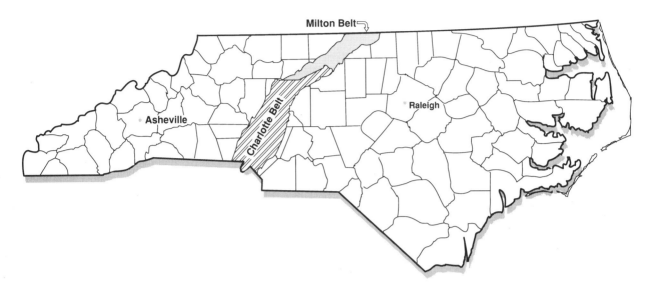

Figure 6–8:   The rock units which form the Charlotte and Milton belts in the central Piedmont were once part of the subduction zone that created the Carolina Slate Belt. [2]

landmass of the Piedmont Terrane and the island volcanoes of the Carolina Slate Belt—were exposed above the ocean's surface. Winds blowing westward from the exposed land surface at the edge of the continent carried fine particles of sand out over the waters where they were deposited, forming sandy layers within limestones. Today, these interlayered beds of sand and limestone make up part of the Copper Ridge and Conococheague formations in the Knox Group. The deposits all lie in other states to the north and west of the Blue Ridge. These units represent widespread deposition in those relatively shallow ocean waters—the same kind of deposition that would continue throughout much of the Paleozoic era. [116,117]

Part 3

Raising a Mountain System

As the gigantic North American and Euro-African crustal plates closed on each other they began crushing the rocks trapped between them. About 400 million years ago, forces created by the pressure of the closing plates caused folding and metamorphism that changed the character of rocks beneath the ancient sea floor and caused the land to begin rising from the sea. In some areas, large masses of rock melted and moved upward, invading the rocks of today's Piedmont. The plastic nature of the deeply buried rocks resulted in the formation of large folds in the western Piedmont and Blue Ridge. One such fold forms the Sauratown Mountains.

The slowly closing plates also pushed the land upward across the entire state. The rising surface was promptly attacked by erosion. Streams carried the products of weathering north and west into a shallow sea. There they deposited layer upon layer of mud and sand creating a great delta that would later make up the rocks of the modern-day Ridge and Valley and Plateau provinces of the Appalachians.

Finally, as the two continental plates smashed together, the land was raised to great heights. The resulting mountain peaks may have been as high as the modern Alps or Andes. The tallest peaks probably formed in the area of today's eastern Piedmont and Coastal Plain while the easternmost portion of the mountain system extended into the African Sahara. The sediments of the growing delta slid slowly northwestward away from North Carolina as the great mountain mass rose. The sliding layers buckled and folded, forming tremendous thrust sheets and long open folds. Uplift and erosion more than 100 million years later removed the softer rocks forming the Ridge and Valley Province located west of the Carolinas. This final uplift brought the building of the Appalachians to an end. Erosional processes then began the long task of destruction that eventually produced our modern landscape.

7

THE APPALACHIAN REVOLUTION BEGINS

The Cambrian period drew to a close, the Ordovician period began, and once again change came to the Appalachians. Geologists describe such a surge of igneous and metamorphic activity combined with folding, faulting, and uplift as an orogeny, or mountain-building event.

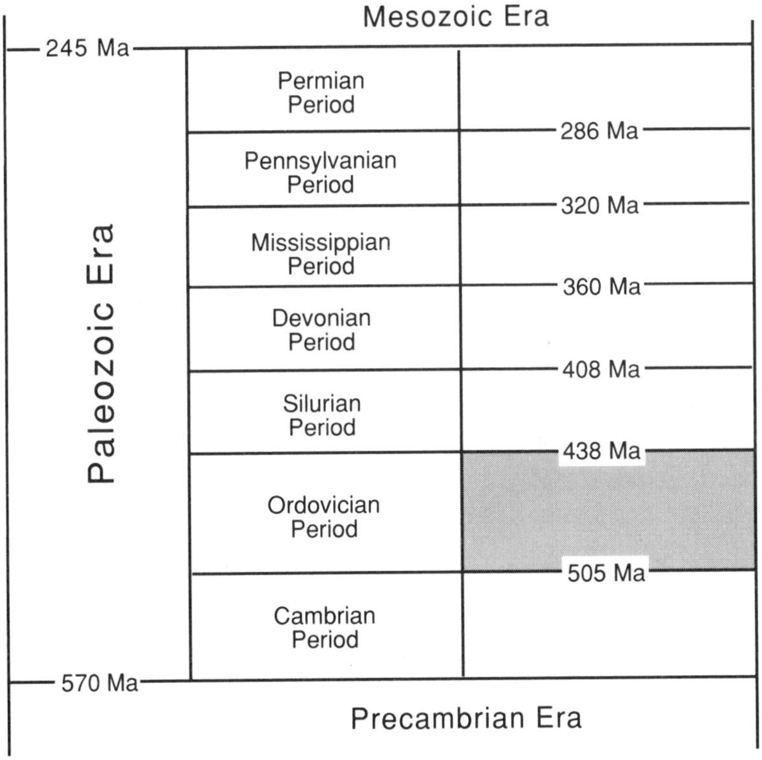

		Mesozoic Era	
245 Ma	Permian Period		
		286 Ma	
	Pennsylvanian Period		
		320 Ma	
Paleozoic Era	Mississippian Period		
		360 Ma	
	Devonian Period		
		408 Ma	
	Silurian Period		
		438 Ma	
	Ordovician Period		
		505 Ma	
	Cambrian Period		
570 Ma		Precambrian Era	

Figure 7–1: Geologic time column showing the Ordovician period in relation to the Paleozoic era (Ma = Million years ago).

The first surge of mountain building in what would become the Appalachians is referred to as the Taconic Orogeny.[1] The two crustal plates that had been moving toward each other finally began colliding with a hinge-like motion. The first contact took place near the northern portions of the plates. There, the oceanic crustal plate plunged eastward beneath the Piedmont Terrane. As a result, the first signs of this orogeny occurred in the area we now call Scotland and England.

The rock and sediment carried down on the subducting plate melted, forming large masses of magma. The molten rock migrated upward through the crust, finally erupting at the surface to form groups of volcanoes. Eruptions occurred throughout much of modern-day Maine, New Brunswick, and southern Quebec, covering the region with lava flows and volcanic debris. [8–10,117]

As millions of years passed, the plates continued colliding. The hinge-like nature of their movement caused the intensity of the eruptions to increase in the north while activity began to take place farther south.

In the southeastern United States, the first signs of tectonic activity appeared during the early part of the Ordovician period. The volcanoes that had been building the offshore island arc known as the Avalon Terrane (Carolina Slate Belt) stopped erupting. Evidence also suggests that the site of the eruptions along the island arc had shifted westward during the preceding millions of years. As a result, when the eruptions stopped, the island chain may have been located somewhat closer to the North American continent than in earlier times. [35,87–90]

Far beneath the surface, rocks formed during Precambrian and early Paleozoic time began to change. Geologic evidence indicates that these rocks must have been buried at least 15,000 meters (49,200 feet or 9.3 miles) beneath the surface in order for the heat and pressure to produce the metamorphic effects that can be seen on the surface today.

As the heat and pressure increased, the sediments of the Raleigh Belt slowly folded into gentle up-and-down folds called **an-**

---

1. The Taconic Orogeny was named for the Taconic Mountains in southeastern New York State. The rocks of the Taconic Range are the result of metamorphism and deformation that occurred during this portion of Paleozoic time.

ticlines and **synclines**. At the same time, the overlying layers of less consolidated volcanic debris were compressed, forming tighter folds. Layers of oceanic sediment and volcanic ash buried deeper in the ancient island arc overlying the Raleigh Belt rocks did not melt but began to change in character. Mineral grains were welded together and chemical changes formed new minerals while the water-laid layers of volcanic ash were compacted into shales.

Tens of millions of years later, during early Devonian time, more extensive metamorphism changed the sediments into slates, phyllites, schists, and quartzites. Today geologists call the folded and metamorphosed region of rocks which stretches from Virginia to South Carolina the Carolina Slate Belt (figure 7–2). [43,87]

The forces that bent and warped the rocks of the Carolina Slate Belt varied widely in intensity. Near Hillsborough in Orange County, layers of metamorphosed volcanic slate crinkled, forming very steep folds (plate 10). In other areas, such as Albemarle in Stanly County and near Monroe in Union County, the folds were gentler and more widely spaced. [87,117]

Farther west, subduction of the oceanic crust adjacent to the North American continent continued as the ocean closed. The interaction of the Piedmont Terrane and the continental crustal plate continued, producing new deposits of volcanic debris on land and in the sea.

Over the next few million years, sediments were deposited across western Virginia, Kentucky, and Tennessee. In contrast, during the preceding period of deposition, sediment had been developed on the Grenville landmass and transported in an easterly direction. The sediments deposited in this shallow sea came from the tectonic uplift of land to the east.

In Virginia, the first Ordovician sediments were deposited in a marine environment. Later, changing conditions are marked by increasing fossil evidence suggesting a change to warm reeflike conditions. One unit, the Sevier Shale, has been studied extensively. The resulting evidence reveals something of typical conditions in these shallow seas. The sea floor sloped very gently toward the west. Changes in sea level alternately flooded and drained the surface in a cycle that lasted from 140,000–200,000 years. The changing sea level caused the shoreline to shift east or west at a rate between one and five kilometers (0.6–3.1 miles)

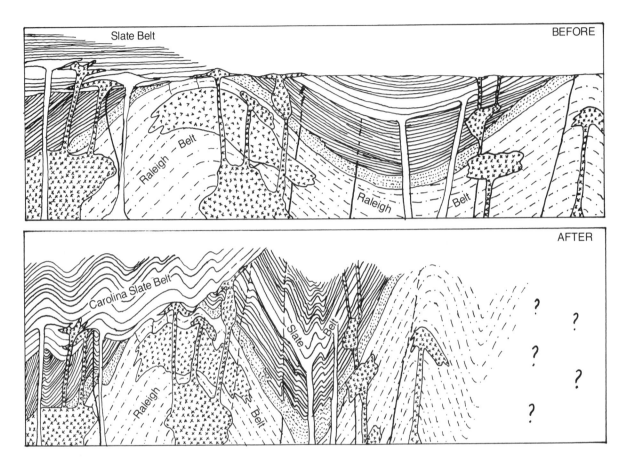

Figure 7–2:   Responding to increasing heat and pressure, gentle open folds developed in the rocks of the Raleigh Belt. Much steeper folds with parallel sides developed in the less consolidated sediments of the overlying Carolina Slate Belt. [87]

every thousand years. As one cycle followed another, the sea floor slowly subsided under the weight of accumulating sediment.[2]

The cyclic flooding and exposure of the sea floor produced alternating layers of sediment. Sand layers mark the passage of beaches, with crossbeds produced by the high energy of breaking waves. Finer muddy layers formed as silt settled to a bottom undisturbed by wave action. Mud cracks developed when the muddy sea floor was exposed and dried out. Limestone reef structures grew when the gently sloping coastal area was flooded to a depth of several tens of meters. Layers of mud and wave-

---

2. 1–4 centimeters (0.4–1.6 inches) per thousand years.

transported sand were mixed by storms and the burrowing action of numerous marine organisms. All these different kinds of depositional features are preserved in the layers of the Sevier Shale. [118]

Within the shale, beds of a clay called **bentonite**, which formed from the decomposition of volcanic ash, marked volcanic eruptions in nearby areas. Centers of volcanic activity in the Piedmont Terrane seem to be the most likely source for these ash deposits. [11]

Many animals must have lived in North Carolina during the Ordovician period, but no fossils have been found to verify their presence. However, in the shallow sea west of the developing mountains, the fossil record reflects a change from warm semitropical conditions to a somewhat cooler climate. Important changes were occurring in the living community. While all life was still restricted to the sea, plants and animals continued to increase in variety.

The trilobites continued to expand in numbers of species, and by early Ordovician time they seem to have reached a peak in both variety and numbers. From this point in time, the trilobites declined in importance in the fossil record until they finally became extinct near the end of the Paleozoic era.

The brachiopods had also expanded in variety and numbers. During the Ordovician period they were the dominant bottom-dwelling animal form. Corals and pelecypods—including clams, mussels, and oysters—appeared along with echinoderms such as crinoids, starfish, and sea urchins. All three groups flourished, and by mid-Ordovician time many species that lived on the ocean bottom bore striking resemblance to those living in our modern ocean environment. Other animals, including a group of floating animals called graptolites, had become widespread. Today, all that remains of this unique animal are fossils in the form of carbon traces. The carbon-trace fossils appear on the surfaces of shales and sandstones that were being deposited in the shallow waters.

The largest of the bottom dwellers was a highly developed group of **cephalopods**[3] including ammonites and nautiloids. By

---

3. Cephalopods have definite heads and cone-shaped shells. The shells of some forms were straight (nautiloids) while others were curved into circular forms (ammonites). Their relatives, including octopuses, squids, and cuttlefish still swim in modern seas.

the middle of Ordovician time nautiloids were abundant, and a straight-shelled variety (endoceroids) produced shells up to 5 meters (16 feet) long and 25 centimeters (10 inches) in diameter.

Farther west, in what is now Wyoming and Montana, the fossils of primitive fish with armored external skeletons indicate that more complex organisms were developing (plate 11). [8–10]

Action Within the Changing Crust

During middle and late Ordovician time, the oceanic plate just east of the continent continued moving down under the Piedmont Terrane. The first signs of an impending collision were intensifying levels of heat and pressure that caused changes deep in the crust. Iron minerals in some of the sediment layers within the Kings Mountain Belt were concentrated and converted into commercially valuable deposits of **magnetite** and **hematite**.[4] These deposits were first mined prior to the Revolutionary War. Mining activity continued until the late 1800s, when improved transportation made ores from other parts of the country less expensive and local mining became unprofitable. [109,111]

About 22 or 23 kilometers (13.7–14.3 miles) below the surface, bodies of molten rock developed. The new magma bodies began migrating toward the surface by melting the overlying rocks. Those surrounding rocks which did not melt were heated to the point where new minerals developed and the rock units flowed in a plastic manner. The process converted the sedimentary rocks into new metamorphic and igneous forms. [114] One example of such a highly metamorphosed rock unit is the Henderson Gneiss. The rocks which make up this unit were first formed when sediments were melted, forming granites. The granites were later metamorphosed, forming the gneiss which is now exposed by erosion. Today, the Henderson Gneiss is exposed southward from Caldwell County, through Burke, McDowell, Henderson, and Transylvania counties and into South Carolina.

---

4. Magnetite and hematite are both oxides of iron. Both are common products of metamorphic reactions involving hot water solutions.

Further east, the sediments of the Ashe and Alligator Back formations[5] were heated to temperatures of 600–650° C (1,024–1,112° F) and subjected to extreme pressures. Elements within the sediments responded to the new conditions by moving about within the rock mass and combining to form new minerals. Today, the resulting schists and gneisses contain minerals such as **biotite mica**, **garnet**, **kyanite**, and **staurolite**[6] which formed during this metamorphic episode. [119]

By about 440 million years ago, the unnamed ocean between the Piedmont Terrane and the North American crustal plate had been consumed as the oceanic plate was pulled downward beneath the landmass of the Piedmont Terrane. As the terrane collided with the continent, the momentum of the collision pushed the Piedmont landmass up onto the crustal plate, welding the Piedmont Terrane to the North American crustal plate (figure 7–3). [6]

Large-scale faults and folds developed as slices of the crust were thrust westward. Several large thrust surfaces developed between the moving blocks. The net motion along hundreds of faults helped absorb the momentum of collision. The Greenbrier and Hayesville **thrust faults**[7] carried large slabs of rock northwestward into Virginia and West Virginia. The largest and most important thrust surface in North Carolina was the Brevard fault zone. The Brevard fault is named for a small mountain town in Transylvania County. Today, the fault zone can be traced for several hundred miles from Georgia into Virginia. In North Carolina, it generally follows a north to northeast curving path along, and just to the east of, the Appalachian Escarpment.[8]

---

5. See pages 30 and 53.

6. Biotite mica, garnet, kyanite, and staurolite are all silicate minerals. Each mineral forms from clay minerals when physical conditions within the earth reach certain ranges of pressure and temperature. Geologists who study metamorphic rocks use the various mineral assemblages as indicators of the pressure and temperature conditions to which a given rock or rock unit was subjected during its formation.

7. A thrust fault occurs when one rock unit is pushed over another. The fault is defined as the surface between the two blocks and, in the case of a thrust fault, is nearly horizontal.

8. The Appalachian Escarpment is a steeply sloping region which forms the easternmost boundary of the Blue Ridge Province. Headward stream erosion carved the escarpment while reducing the elevation of the Piedmont land surface.

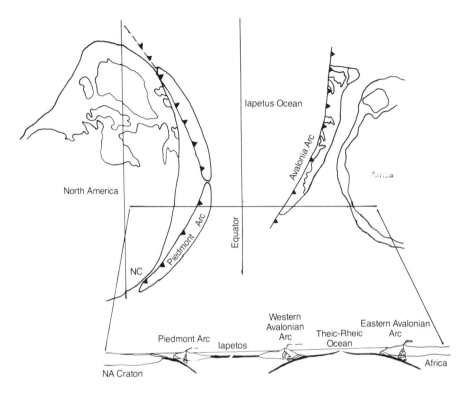

Figure 7–3:   During Ordovician time, a subduction zone carried significant amounts of sediment down underneath the Piedmont Terrane. The melting sediments produced a series of magma bodies that metamorphosed older rocks. About 440 million years ago, the subducting oceanic plate was destroyed as the Piedmont Terrane collided with the North American crustal plate. [6]

Some 200 million years later, toward the end of the Paleozoic era, the Brevard fault zone would be destined to form one of the very large sliding surfaces involved in the final uplift of the Appalachians (figure 7–4). [6,7,38–39,120]

One excellent example of complex history preserved by this combination of folding, faulting, and erosion is the Sauratown Mountains in Stokes and Surry counties. There, the Ashe Formation had been incorporated in the deeper portions of the growing landmass.[9] The deeply buried mud and sandstones were folded, thrust-faulted, and metamorphosed along with other rock units within the Piedmont and Blue Ridge (figure 7–5). [45–51]

---

9. See page 30.

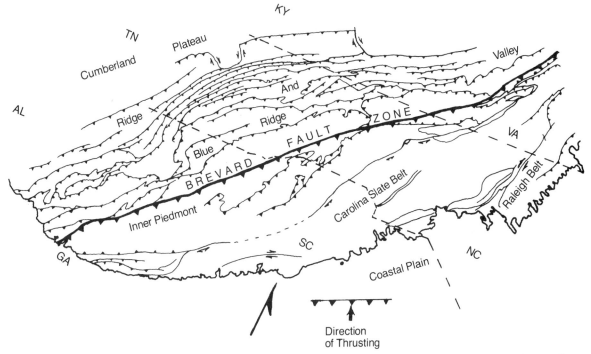

Figure 7–4: The Brevard fault zone is one of the largest and longest faults which trend northeast-southwest along the Appalachians. Evidence suggests the fault represents a major break in the earth's crust. A number of geologists believe there was significant movement along the Brevard zone at several different times during the Paleozoic era.

The erosion that exposed the Piedmont failed to destroy completely the welded quartzites protecting the underlying softer rocks in the Sauratown Mountains. Today you may visit Pilot Mountain and Hanging Rock state parks. There you can observe evidence revealing this large anticline composed of quartzite and schist lying on its side and only partly destroyed by erosion (figure 7–6). [45–52]

The net result of the collision was an uplifting of the land surface. The uplift was rapid in geologic terms, averaging about 2.4 centimeters per century (1 inch per hundred years). Evidence suggests that the rate of uplift varied from a minimum of 0 centimeters per century to a maximum of 8 centimeters per century (3.1 inches per one hundred years). [121]

The largest uplift occurred north of the Carolinas. In some areas, such as the Taconic Mountains of New Jersey, the land may have risen several thousand feet above sea level. In western North Carolina, the uplift seems to have resulted in a somewhat lower land surface (figure 7–7). Still, erosion of the rising land surface

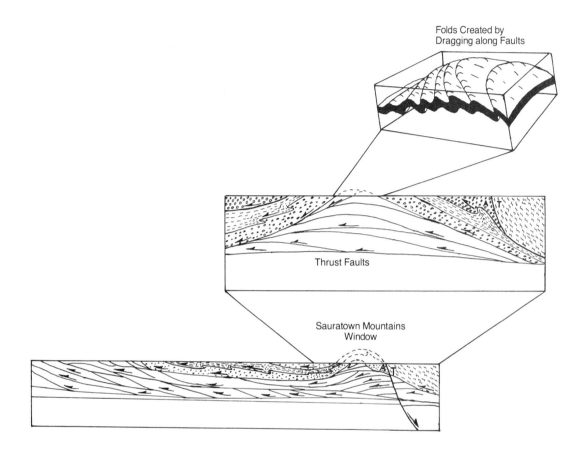

Figure 7-5: The impending collision of the Piedmont Terrane with the North American continent produced a series of folds and overthrust faults deep within the crust.

in North Carolina and Virginia produced large quantities of sand and mud. Streams carried the debris westward where it was deposited in a shallow sea. Today those **clastic**[10] deposits form the Oswego Sandstone and the Martinsburg Shale. The layers reach thicknesses of several thousand feet, suggesting that a significant landmass was being destroyed not far east of the basin. [7,121,122]

There is no way to determine precisely how high the land rose as a result of the collision. The available evidence suggests that the surface was no more than a few thousand feet above sea level. Geologists do know that erosion carved valleys in the new surface

10. Clastic sediments are composed primarily of broken rock fragments.

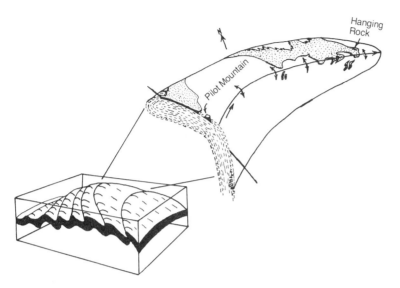

Figure 7-6: The Sauratown Mountains Anticlinorium is a fold that developed deep within the crust. Pilot Mountain, Sauratown Mountain, Hanging Rock, and Cooke's Wall are all remnants of the fold that have been exposed by erosion and now rise above the Piedmont land surface.

with reliefs of as much as 130 meters (426 feet). The erosion is preserved as a break in the rock record which includes caverns and sinkholes. These were developed where acidic water dissolved limestone in layers of the Knox Dolomite across parts of Kentucky, Tennessee, and Virginia. [7,122]

Silurian Time Begins

Through the early portion of the Silurian period, the climate was warm. Streams removed material from the landmass which was being raised by events along the continental margin in the Blue Ridge Province. The running water carried its load of sand, silt, and mud westward to the sea. The accumulating material filled the shallow ocean and slowly caused the shoreline to migrate northwestward. In what is now Virginia and Tennessee,

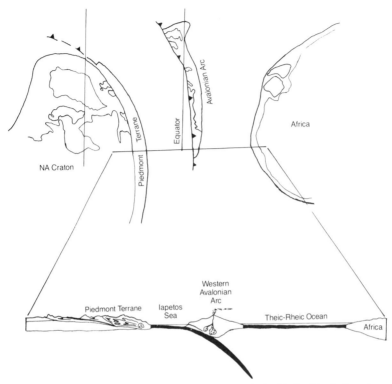

Figure 7–7:   In late Ordovician time the Piedmont Terrane collided with the North American continent. The resulting folding and faulting raised the eastern edge of the continental landmass.

red-colored layers of shale reflect a change from marine to non-marine conditions. [7,116,122]

As sediment poured into the basin it deepened rapidly. Geologists have named the growing wedge of material the Queenston Delta (figure 7–9). The delta stretched from New York in the northeast into Tennessee and Alabama on the southwest. [116] In Virginia, beach deposits formed as waves reworked the delta's edge during early Silurian time. Those sands were later cemented, forming an erosion-resistant rock known as the Clinch Sandstone. Today the Clinch forms mountain ridge lines throughout much of the Ridge and Valley Province of Virginia. [122]

Trying to reconstruct the beach environment of the Silurian period really stretches one's imagination. The beaches, which are preserved in the layers of the Clinch Sandstone, formed in Ashe and Allegheny counties in northwestern North Carolina.

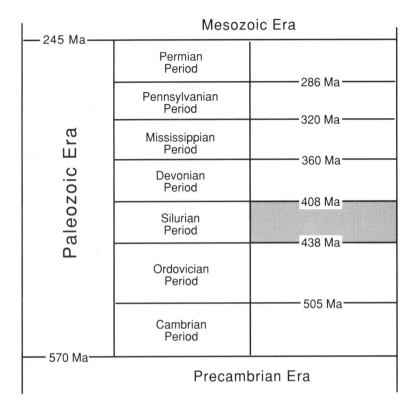

Figure 7–8: Geologic time column showing the Silurian period in relation to the Paleozoic era (Ma = Million years ago).

Walking along that ancient shoreline would have revealed barren, but gently rolling, hills rising away toward the southeast. Toward the northwest, open water stretched to the horizon. The shore looked much like that of our coastline, with sandy beaches and shallow bays whose muddy bottoms covered large areas. [116]

The Queenston Delta continued growing for more than 100 million years. Later events caused the easternmost beds of the delta to be moved northwestward from North Carolina to their present position in Virginia (figure 7–10). [6,123,124]

Offshore in Silurian waters, hundreds of crinoids lived on the sandy bottom. Horn and honeycomb corals were also common. By the middle of the Silurian period, these same corals were building reefs in the warm seas. The reefs stretched from Tennessee across Kentucky and into Indiana. [116] A trilobite might have wandered by, but their numbers were decreasing, along with those of the graptolites and jawless fish that floated and swam overhead. Within the brackish waters of the Queenston Delta, numerous worms and shrimp lived on the muddy bottom. The larger scorpions (*eusarcus*) and sea scorpions (*ptertogus*) were less numerous but dominated the scene because of their size (plate 12). [8–10]

Toward the end of the Silurian period, the climate became more arid. The water covering the Queenston Delta took on a character similar to the Dead Sea. Layers of salt, clay-rich sands, and dark gray limestones mark this change in climate. These layers suggest that a barrier island system formed in which typical tidal marshes and swamps alternated with low sandy islands. Farther north, in the area that now forms the states of Pennsylvania, Ohio, New York, and Michigan, deposits of salt and hydrated calcium sulfate (gypsum) accumulated because of the evaporation of sea water in the arid climate.

In recent years the salt has been mined by injecting water through wells drilled into the salt-bearing layers. The water is then pumped back to the surface carrying the salt in solution. After the water is evaporated, the salt is sold for a variety of commercial applications (plate 13).

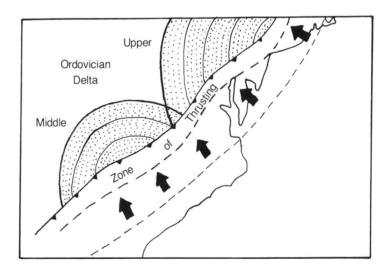

Figure 7–9:   The Queenston Delta developed northeast of the rising Appalachian land surface. The Appalachians were rising in response to the collision of the Piedmont Terrane with the North American crustal plate.

Today the sedimentary rocks that underlie the Ridge and Valley and the Appalachian Plateau provinces reflect this period of deposition. Within the quartzites, shales, and limestones, the story of the delta is recorded by fossils, crossbedded channel deposits, mud cracks, and raindrop impressions. Each of the layers reflects the conditions that existed on the delta when the sediments were deposited. The delta's story is truly written in the rocks.

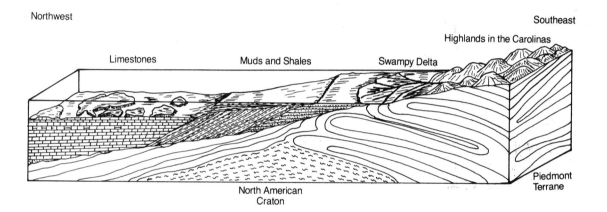

Figure 7-10: The Queenston Delta was a large wedge of mud and sand that was deposited by streams flowing northwestward from the highlands raised by the Taconic Orogeny.

8

METAMORPHISM AND INTRUSION

During the Taconic Orogeny the Inner Piedmont, Chuaga, and Kings Mountain belts, along with the Charlotte and Milton belts were caught up in the collision of the Piedmont Terrane with the North American continent.[1] Large sedimentary units were folded and metamorphosed as the terrane smashed up against the mass of the continent. As the heat and pressure increased, shale units were transformed to schists and gneisses while sandstones were welded into massive quartzites and limestones recrystallized into marbles.

The deeply buried layers flowed like soft putty, forming large, upwarped folds called anticlines and similar downwarped folds called synclines. Large faults also cut through the crust. Motion along these faults shortened the land surface as one layer was thrust over another. During the millions of years that followed the building of the Appalachians, weathering and erosion removed thousands of meters of overlying rock. As a result, the once deeply buried rocks are exposed at the surface of the Piedmont and Blue Ridge provinces. Where the ancient rocks were folded into synclines, younger layers of metamorphosed sedimentary material were carried downward, protecting them from erosion. The layers that were folded upward into anticlines lifted older rock units, allowing erosion to expose them as it carved the modern surface. The complex folding that took place far beneath the earth's surface was followed by millions of years of erosion. The processes exposed a long and complex history which would have otherwise been buried beneath the surface or destroyed (figure 8–1). [7,33]

Deep in the complex of colliding rock units, areas of intense heat developed. In some of those areas, the rock units melted,

---

1. See pages 53, 55, and 57.

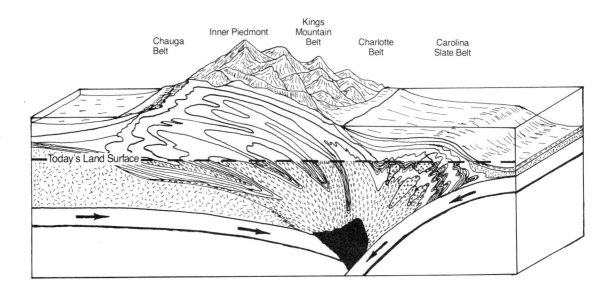

Figure 8–1:   Folding, followed by erosion, has exposed many rock units that would otherwise lie buried beneath the modern land surface or would have been destroyed by the erosion that created today's landscape. (Note: The horizontal line marks the present land surface.) [4]

forming large bodies of magma. The developing magmas melted overlying rocks and metamorphosed others nearby. South of Asheville, in Jackson and Transylvania counties, the Whiteside Granite was formed as one of those magma bodies cooled and crystallized. Erosion has exposed the Whiteside Granite in a series of large domes, such as Looking Glass Rock (9386 ± 37 Ma), that stand above the eroded land surface near Brevard (plate 14). [125]

Farther north, in Wilkes County, a similar mass of magma formed at about the same time. Today, that granite, exposed by erosion, is protected for the public in Stone Mountain State Park. Another "hot spot" occurred in what is now Surry County. The Mount Airy Granite today provides a source of large, uniform, and fracture-free blocks. The quarried slabs are shipped throughout the country for use as building stone (plate 15). [45,46,125–128]

Several hundred kilometers east of the continental margin, the Avalon Terrane continued moving westward. The movement was caused by the subduction of an oceanic crustal slab that was plunging eastward beneath the growing mass of volcanic and sedimentary rocks.

Within the Avalon Terrane, super-heated water moved along fractures in the folding and shifting rocks. The water, sweated out of rocks around the developing magma bodies, moved upward, carrying large amounts of quartz along with gold, silver, copper, tungsten, and a variety of other metals.

Four hundred million years later, men would discover and mine these minerals at many sites across the Carolina Slate Belt. Tungsten extracted from the mineral **heubnerite**[2] formed the base of a large mining operation in Vance County, north of Oxford and Henderson (plate 16). Other smaller prospects and mines extracted copper from **malachite** and **bornite**[3] near Roxboro in Person County. But the most important and long-lasting mineral discoveries occurred farther to the south and west, in areas near Asheboro and Albemarle. Those discoveries changed the economy of North Carolina and set off the first gold rush in the United States. [126,129]

John Reed was a German-born farmer who carved a small farm from the wilderness and settled in Cabarrus County. One Sunday morning in the summer of 1799, his twelve-year-old son, Conrad, decided to skip church and go fishing. While walking along the banks of Little Meadow Creek he discovered a strange rock. The rock was very heavy for its size and is said to have weighed about 7.7 kilograms (17 pounds) (plate 17).

Conrad took the pretty yellow rock to his father. John Reed couldn't identify the dull, metallic-looking rock, but he decided to keep it. So, for the next three years, the strange rock served the Reed family as a door stop. Finally, out of curiosity, Reed took the stone to a jeweler in Fayetteville who paid him three dollars and fifty cents for the gold nugget. It is estimated that 8 kilograms of gold was worth about $3,600 at that time. Reed soon

---

2. Heubnerite (iron manganese tungstate) is a reddish to blackish-brown mineral that is the primary ore of tungsten. The mineral is deposited by high-temperature hydrothermal veins associated with magma bodies.

3. Malachite (hydrous copper carbonate) and bornite (copper iron sulfide) are both ores of copper metal. Bornite is deposited by high-temperature hydrothermal solutions that are "sweated" out of magmas. The mineral commonly occurs as a dark granular mass that tarnishes, producing a iridescent blue and purple surface. Malachite is produced by the reaction of copper sulfide with carbonates in the surrounding rocks. The result is a brilliant green mineral that is valued as a decorative stone and an ore of copper.

Figure 8–2: Mines like this one near Gold Hill in Davidson County were commonplace during the 1800s throughout the Carolina Slate Belt (courtesy: North Carolina Department of Cultural Resources).

learned the true value of gold and began a mining operation near the stream.

In 1803, a second large nugget weighing 12.7 kilograms (28 pounds) was discovered near Little Meadow Creek. As word of Reed's discovery spread, exploration and mining began in earnest (plate 18). Large quantities of gold and other ores were taken from the rocks of the Carolina Slate Belt over the next several decades. Numerous mines were developed as new prospects were discovered at Gold Hill (figure 8–2), Silver Hill, and a variety of other sites throughout the region. Production peaked in the early 1800s, and until the discovery of gold at Sutter's Mill in California in 1849, North Carolina was the largest producer of gold in the United States. Even today, many amateur prospectors find small quantities of gold by panning in the streams of the slate belt during weekend outings. Unfortunately, the concentration of gold in the ore-bearing quartz veins is too small to support the large-scale operations necessary to make modern mining and refining profitable. [131–133]

Today, gold *is* being mined in several locations in South Carolina along the eastern edge of the Carolina Slate Belt (plate 19). The gold in these deposits was originally deposited by high-temperature hydrothermal solutions that boiled off magmas deep within the rocks of the Carolina Slate Belt. Because gold is chemically non-reactive, the element remained when erosion exposed the veins and weathering reduced the surrounding rock to soil. Streams eroding the land surface then carried the gold eastward and deposited it along with enormous volumes of sand at the western edge of the Atlantic Coastal Plain. Today, careful mining of the sand deposits in South Carolina is producing between 25,000 and 40,000 ounces (710–1,136 kilograms) of gold per year. [134]

Devonian Time Begins

As the Devonian period began 408 million years ago, the effects of the collision between the Piedmont Terrane and the North American crustal plate continued making themselves felt across the Carolinas.

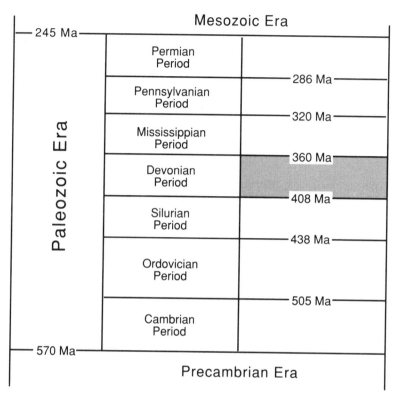

Figure 8–3: Geologic time column showing the Devonian period in relation to the Paleozoic era (Ma = Million years ago). (Courtesy of Ridgeway Mining Company.)

Super-heated water, saturated with silica and other minerals, escaped from magmas buried deep in the crust. The water traveled upward away from the magmas, through fractures in the crust. Because the crust had been heated by regional metamorphism, the rocks surrounding the fractures were warm and, as a result, the hot water cooled very slowly. As the dissolved minerals crystallized on the walls of the fractures, the slow cooling rate allowed the growth of unusually large crystals. The resulting fracture fillings contain large mineral crystals and are called **pegmatite dikes**.[4]

Pegmatite dikes of Devonian age occur in four different areas of the Piedmont and Blue Ridge. One large group, or swarm, of dikes invaded the rocks in Lincoln, Cleveland, and Gaston counties. The most important dikes in this swarm contained large amounts of the element lithium, contained in the mineral **spodumene**.[5] The deposit is the largest lithium reserve in North America. It is being worked at the Foote Mine near the town of Kings Mountain and at the Lithium Corporation Mine near Bessemer City. The lithium is refined and sold for a variety of uses ranging from medicine to industrial alloys (plate 20).

In Alexander County, a small group of pegmatite dikes contain the world's only known deposit of a lithium-bearing mineral called **hiddenite**. Specimens are very rare and considered by mineralogists to be valuable collectors items. [112,113,137]

In the western Blue Ridge, a third swarm of pegmatite dikes invaded Swain County, near Bryson City, and Macon and Jackson counties near the town of Franklin. During the past century these pegmatites have become famous as a source of a very pure form of **corundum**. In its purest form, corundum (Al_2O_3) is called **ruby** when it is red in color. All other colors of corundum are called **sapphire**. The corundum minerals are thought to have been derived from ultramafic[6] rocks near the mantle by the superheated waters which formed the pegmatites. Later the gemstones were weathered from the dikes and concentrated in stream gravels. A number of the small, commercial gravel deposits are open to the public. There, for a fee, you may prospect and perhaps find a gem-quality specimen to take home.

A fourth swarm of pegmatite dikes intruded along fractures in Mitchell County near the towns of Bakersville and Spruce Pine. Large books of **muscovite** mica and giant crystals of quartz and feldspar[7] are common in these dikes. Less common

---

4. Pegmatite dikes are produced when mineral bearing hot water solutions invade fractures in the rock surrounding a magma body. Because the hot water solutions are buried deep in the crust, long cooling periods allow minerals deposited from the water to form large grains or crystals. Pegmatite dikes are often zoned and contained rare, gem quality, minerals including ruby, sapphire, and emerald.

5. Spodumene (lithium aluminum silicate) forms gigantic crystals that range in color from whitish yellow to gray, pink, and light green. An unique emerald-green form is known as hiddenite. Spodumene is formed in pegmatites and often occurs with quartz, feldspars, beryl, lepidolite, and tourmaline.

6. Ultramafic is a general name for an igneous rock formed deep in the crust and composed of dark-colored ferro-magnesian (mafic) minerals including olivine, pyroxene, and minor amounts of amphibole.

but more famous pockets in the dikes have produced large, gem-quality **garnet**, **aquamarine**, and **emerald** crystals. Many specimens recovered from the Franklin and Spruce Pine areas are displayed in museums such as the American Museum of Natural History in Washington, D.C. (plates 21a & b). [136–138] It is also interesting to note that the mirror which forms the heart of the 200–inch (5 meter) telescope on Mount Palomar was made from very pure quartz mined from the center of one of the pegmatites in this area.

Large bodies of dark-colored iron and magnesium-rich rocks called **gabbro** intruded the Inner Piedmont, Charlotte, and Milton belts. Field evidence suggests that several large molten masses intruded the overlying rocks. In the process, the original large magma bodies separated, producing a number of smaller, related masses.

One intrusion occurred near the town of Concord. There the gabbro is surrounded by a ring-shaped dike of **syenite**.[8] Geologists believe that the circular fractures filled by the syenite were produced by upward pressure from the magma body. The evidence suggests that the syenite separated or boiled off the gabbroic magma. The molten syenite moved up along the circular fractures and cooled, forming the present ring-shaped dike (figure 8–4). [139–141]

The origin of these ferromagnesian-rich bodies is still a matter of debate. The most likely source of the rocks which melted to form the mafic intrusions would seem to be the layers of basalt and **dunite**[9] near the contact of the ancient oceanic crustal plates

---

7. Quartz, feldspar, mica, and garnet along with aquamarine and emerald (both forms of beryl) are all silicate minerals. Each is composed of some variation of elements in combination with silicon and oxygen (SiO_4).

8. Syenite is a plutonic rock usually containing orthoclase, microcline, or perthite along with a small amount of plagioclase, hornblende, and quartz.

9. Dunite is an ultramafic intrusive igneous rock composed of the magnesium iron silicate mineral called olivine. The rock generally appears to be made of sand-sized grains that are translucent and light green in color.

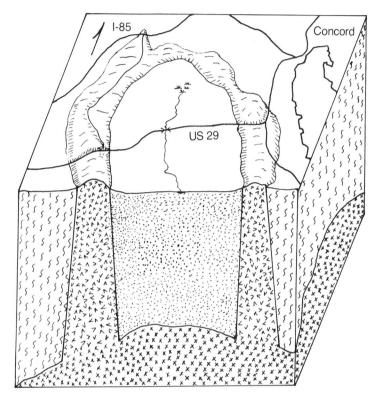

Figure 8—4:   This map shows the circular nature of the syenite dike that surrounds a gabbro intrusion near Concord in Cabarrus County. [138]

and the upper portion of the mantle on which they floated. Such a source would indicate that the collision of the Piedmont Terrane with North America ripped the crust apart down to its very contact with the mantle. [6,139] Very small bodies of ultramafic rocks in the Blue Ridge and Piedmont also suggest that uprooting of the lower crust probably did take place during the Taconic Orogeny in the Carolinas. [140—142]

9

The Climate Changes

Sedimentary rocks deposited in the Queenston Delta during Silurian time record shallow waters in which life was abundant. Black, fossil-rich muds and clay-rich sands gave way to barrier island deposits near the close of the Silurian period. Later, in the Devonian period, the climate became warmer and moderately humid. [8,84,143]

Prevailing winds carried the products of occasional volcanic eruptions northwest, covering the land and sea with thin layers of ash and dust. One such layer, the Tioga Bentonite, records such an eruption which took place about 375 million years ago, spreading debris across the entire United States. Recently gathered evidence suggests that the eruptions were centered near Fredericksburg, Virginia. [144,145]

Devonian time was a period of diversification in the plant and animal communities. In the warm seas, corals had become the dominant form of life. At least 700 different species of brachiopods lived on the ocean floor along with lily-like crinoids which were scattered everywhere.

Plants had made their first feeble efforts at living on the land surface during the Silurian period. During the early portion of the Devonian period they made the move permanent and by mid-Devonian time there were hundreds of species thriving everywhere that land rose above the sea (figure 9–1). [85,146–157]

Insects appeared during the middle of the Devonian period and were common by the end of Pennsylvanian time. Their fossil remains include cockroaches up to 10 centimeters (4 inches) long and dragonflies with a wingspread of 74 centimeters (29 inches). Scorpions, spiders, and centipedes also contributed large numbers to the total of more than 400 species that were flying and crawling about (figure 9–2). [84,158]

Among the vertebrates, fish continued to expand and diversify. One group, the lungfish, developed the ability to breathe air

Figure 9–1:   The long-barren land surface was covered with green as plants moved out of the seas during Silurian time.

at the surface. Some lungfish still survive today in African waters. By late Devonian time, the first primitive amphibians had developed from this group. [8–10]

During the last 25 million years of Devonian time, the intense metamorphism and plastic deformation taking place far beneath the surface tapered off. As a result, intrusions of magma occurred less frequently, and the folding that had characterized the Taconic Orogeny during the preceding 75 million years also came to an end. [145]

Plate 1:   The possible remains of ancient marine organisms are preserved as lens-shaped pods of the carbon mineral graphite. The gray area in the bank above is a typical exposure of such a lens-shaped body.

Plate 2:   Near Asheboro fine grains of volcanic ash fell into the sea and settled to the ocean floor. Later, the thin layers were metamorphosed, forming slate that can be split into large uniform slabs. Today the slate is quarried at Jacobs Creek and used for a variety of purposes including flagstone. [75]

Plate 3a & b: These fine, needle-like crystals of pyrophyllite are the result of metamorphism that changed the crystal structure of geyserite formed by hydrothermal alteration of volcanic ash deposits.

Plate 4: These trails were left by worms crawling in mud on the sloping ocean floor near an island volcano about 620 million years ago.

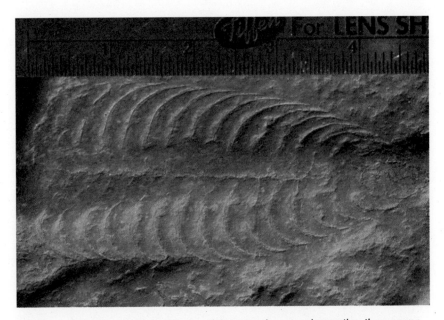

Plate 5: Pteridinium was the first proof that complex organisms other than worms lived on the sea floor of the Precambrian volcanic island arc. (Courtesy of Steve Teeter.) [82,83]

Plate 6: The detailed structure preserved in this fossil algae colony provides evidence of the complex nature of Precambrian single-celled organisms. (Courtesy of American Museum of Natural History, Smithsonian Institution.)

Plate 7: Trilobites, jellyfish, brachiopods, and other invertebrate forms of life dominated the ocean floor during Cambrian time (Courtesy of American Museum of Natural History, Smithsonian Institution.)

Plates 8a & b: Undisturbed conditions in the warm shallow sea near Murphy in Cherokee County resulted in deposits of very uniform limestone. Later metamorphism produced the pure white marble that is quarried in the area today.

Plates 9a, b, & c: Incomplete specimens of several trilobites have been recovered near Batesville in Lexington County, South Carolina. (Courtesy of Dr. Donald Secor, Dept. of Geology, University of South Carolina.) [66]

Plate 10: In Orange County near the town of Hillsborough, layers of metamorphosed volcanic sediment were compressed and broken, forming steeply dipping "crinkled" folds. The steeply dipping layers in this quarry form one side of such a fold.

Plate 11: A typical sandy sea floor as it might have appeared about the middle of the Ordovician period somewhere in the state of Illinois. Trilobites, cephalopods, gastropods, and brachiopods moved over a surface dotted with colonial and solitary corals. (Courtesy of American Museum of Natural History, Smithsonian Institution.)

Plate 12: Flower-like crinoids, trilobites, cephalopods, and brachiopods competed for space with coral on the Silurian sea floor.

Plate 13: This "walking beam" pump has been restored near the town of Saltville in Smythe County, Virginia. The pump was used to lift salt water from the base of the McCrady Formation. (Courtesy of Virginia Division of Geology, Charlottesville.)

Plate 14: Looking Glass Rock in Transylvania County stands above today's countryside. Four hundred million years ago, the Whiteside Granite cooled some 22 kilometers (13.7 miles) below the ancient land surface. Erosion during the Mesozoic and Cenozoic eras removed thousands of meters of overlying rock exposing the granite on today's land surface.

Plate 15: Uniformly grained slabs of granite that formed about 400 million years ago are quarried near Mount Airy and shipped across the United States for use as building stone. (Courtesy of Pat McArthur.)

Plate 16: The Hamme mine, located near the North Carolina/Virginia border in Vance County, was the largest producer of tungsten in the United States before it closed for economic reasons in 1963.

Plate 17: Conrad Reed and his sister discovered the first gold nugget in this creek in Cabarrus County.

Plate 18: John Reed built a sizable gold mining and refining operation at the site of his children's discovery. Today, the site has been restored as a state historic site and is open to the public. (Courtesy of North Carolina Department of Cultural Resources.)

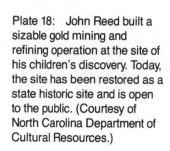

Plate 19:   Gold is being extracted from this sand deposit on the edge of the
Coastal Plain near Ridgeway, South Carolina. [134]

Plate 20:   The wide, light-colored pegmatite dike on the floor of the Foote Mine
near Kings Mountain is made of nearly pure spodumene. The mineral is mined
and used to produce the element lithium.

Plate 21a & b: Miners cut down the center of this pegmatite dike near Spruce Pine in search of a pocket containing gem quality minerals. Today, gems recovered in the district, such as the aquamarine, amythest, and emeralds, are used for jewelry or are displayed in museums.

Plate 22:   Plant and animal life flourished in the swampy deltas of the Mississippian period. (Courtesy of American Museum of Natural History, Smithsonian Institution.)

Plate 23:   Forty Acre Rock is a very small erosional exposure of a much larger igneous intrusion called the Pageland Granite. (Courtesy of Tom Bell.)

Plates 24a & b: Visitors to Linville Gorge along the Blue Ridge Parkway can see the fault where it forms a terrace between the upper and lower portions of Linville Falls. At other overlooks, visitors can view Table Rock. The tilted rock slab is part of the Grandfather Mountain thrust sheet. The entire mass of Grandfather Mountain lies in the overthrust sheet which protected the underlying rock units from erosion. [178]

Plate 25:   These tilted and faulted layers were deposited on beaches in North Carolina. Today they form a road cut along Interstate 77 just north of the town of Wytheville in Virginia. [123]

Plate 26:   Erosion of the folded and faulted rock units has produced long ridges of resistant sandstone separated by valleys eroded from limestones and shales.

Plate 27:   Today, streams which once meandered over the flat surface of the Appalachian Plateau have cut downward while maintaining their channels. The result is a region cut by steep-sided valleys that makes travel extremely difficult.

Plate 28:   The final product of the long sequence of events ending in the Alleghenian Orogeny was a major range of mountains with the rocks of the modern North Carolina land surface buried deep in their roots.

Carboniferous Time

The beginning of the Mississippian period, 360 million years ago, is also known as the beginning of Carboniferous time. The term **carboniferous** was coined by British geologists in 1822 and refers to coal-bearing strata in England, where the word referred to carbonaceous rocks. Later, the term was extended to include similar rock units in Europe.

In the United States, geologists mapped units that allowed them to divide Carboniferous time into two distinct periods. The Mississippian period was defined in 1870 based on fossil assemblages in that state. The Pennsylvanian period was defined

Figure 9–2: Insects also made their appearance during Devonian time. Most were small, but a few grew to sizes larger than the largest insects living today. [158]

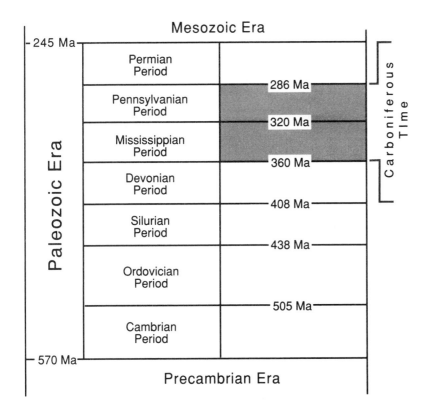

Figure 9–3: Geologic time column showing the Mississippian and Pennsylvanian periods in relation to the Paleozoic era. The two periods are also referred to as Carboniferous time (Ma = Million years ago).

twenty-one years later, in 1891. The two units are equivalent to the carboniferous rocks in England and Europe, with the result that the terms are often used interchangeably. Because there are no fossils in North Carolina to define rock units as being Mississippian or Pennsylvanian in age, the events of that time will generally be discussed here as belonging to the larger block known as Carboniferous time. [84]

About 360 million years ago, the Avalon Terrane collided with the easternmost portion of the North American crustal plate. The line along which the collision occurred lies somewhere between the western border of the Carolina Slate Belt and the Blue Ridge. Geologists have been unable to find field evidence that would allow them to define the actual contact. [6]

In North Carolina, the collision of the Avalon Terrane with the North American crustal block marked the beginning of a second orogeny or mountain-building event referred to as the Acadian Orogeny (figure 9–4). Acadian is a French term that referred to the maritime region of southern Canada and northern New England. In that region, a number of different terranes collided with the North American crustal block. The collisions resulted in regional metamorphism and igneous intrusions throughout the New England states and southern Canada. [6,40,125,126]

During Carboniferous time, North Carolina continued serving as a major source area for sediment deposited to the north and west. As the oceanic plate beneath the Theic-Rheic Ocean plunged slowly under the Avalon Terrane the energy produced by the subduction was added to that produced by the collision between the Avalon Terrane and North America (figure 9–5).

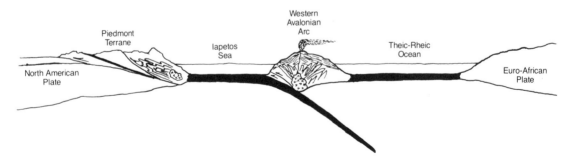

Figure 9–4:   During the Acadian Orogeny, the Avalon Terrane collided with the North American crustal block. [6]

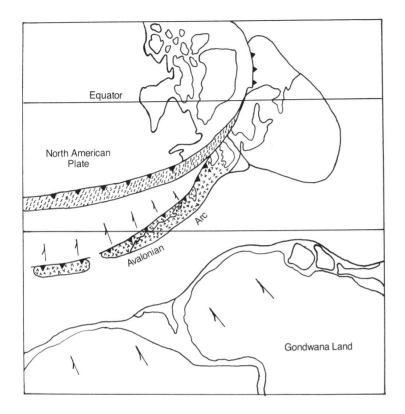

Figure 9–5: As the Avalon Terrane closed with the North American crustal block, the Euro-African continent also closed with the North American plate, slowly destroying the Theic-Rheic Ocean. [84]

The colliding landmasses shifted along a system of faults that stretched from Nova Scotia south into Georgia and Alabama. In Wake County, evidence suggests that rock units located east of the Nutbush Creek and Hollister faults were moving southward. Evidence of the same kind in other areas shows that similar movement was also occurring along other faults throughout the Piedmont and Blue Ridge. Shifting along these faults moved rock units toward the south and southwest. As a result, the rocks east of each fault originally formed north and east of their present location. This displacement adds to the complexity of precisely determining their original location (figure 9–6). [40,159–160]

Figure 9–6: The forces which thrust rock units over one another along major faults throughout the Blue Ridge and Piedmont also shifted the rocks toward the south and southwest. As a result, the rock units presently located in central and eastern North Carolina probably formed north and east of their present locations, in what is now Virginia. The situation is similar in many ways to the San Andreas fault system in California where a series of faults are offsetting rock units between two crustal plates.

Only one major igneous intrusion occurred in North Carolina during this time. In Anson County, the Lilesville pluton is exposed at the surface. This mass of granite formed deep in the crust and solidified about 324 million years ago. [125,126]

Life of Carboniferous Time

There is no fossil record in North Carolina for Carboniferous time; therefore, we must turn to other areas to find evidence of the kinds of plants and animals that may have inhabited the Piedmont and Blue Ridge. Such a record is preserved to the west in the sedimentary rocks of the Ridge and Valley Province and the Appalachian Plateau Province.

In western Tennessee and Kentucky the land surface was tilted slightly and raised above the sea. Following a period of erosion, the land was flooded once again and another large delta developed, fed by streams flowing westward from higher land areas in North Carolina. The rushing streams slowed as they entered the sea and deposited a wedge of sediment that thickened rapidly toward the west. The Virginia-Carolina Delta also changed from continental to marine in character as the distance from North Carolina increased.

Geologists have developed a picture of the growing delta's history by studying the sedimentary layers deposited in Virginia, Kentucky, and Tennessee. Across those states, more than 60 million years of the delta's history is preserved in the Ridge and Valley Province and the Appalachian Plateau Province.

The bottom layer of the delta was a conglomerate deposited by rapidly flowing waters. Coarse sands, interbedded with layers of mud, were deposited over the conglomerate by streams flowing into the sea. As the delta expanded, the streams flowed more slowly and deposited finer sands and muds as they meandered across the marshy tidal delta.

While the delta was active, swampy conditions with a humid climate and rare freezing temperatures resulted in lush plant life. Rapid changes in conditions occurred as streams carried debris from the rising mountains to the east. The changes which resulted from the shifting of streams on the delta are reflected in the rocks. Sandstones, shales, and limestones interbedded with the coal reflect conditions created by closed bays and tidal lagoons. In the closed swamps, accumulating layers of decaying plant material produced numerous layers of coal throughout Pennsylvanian time. [8–10,122,152–154]

Near the town of Saltville, in Smythe County, Virginia, a brief period of very dry climate is reflected in the rocks. Several relatively small deposits of salt and **gypsum**[1] formed when water-

---

1. Gypsum (hydrated calcium sulfate) is produced when calcium sulfate combines with water during the evaporation of marine basins in hot, arid climates.

filled basins on the delta evaporated. The evaporites are part of a unit called the Maccrady Formation which is made up of continental shales and sands deposited on the delta.

The deposit of evaporites has served as valuable mineral resource since colonial times. Salt was drawn from brine wells in the Saltville area and sold for various commercial uses. The wells varied in depth from about 275 meters (900 feet) to 365 meters (1,200 feet) The wells varied in design because the salt-bearing unit (the Maccrady Formation) was flooded with ground water on the southeast side but dry on the northwest side of the ancient "flat." Pumps like the "walking beam" (plate 22) were used to pump the salt laden ground water to the surface while on the dry side the salt was mined by injecting water through wells drilled into the salt-bearing layers. The water, carrying the salt in solution, was then pumped back to the surface. While salt from the Maccrady Formation presently has little commercial value, the gypsum deposits are still being mined and processed into industrial raw materials. [11,155]

The fossil record preserved in the beds of the Virginia-Carolina Delta reflects flourishing life on land and in the sea. During Mississippian time (350–320 million years ago), microscopic **foraminifera**[2] became so abundant the numerous limestones in Indiana are formed entirely of their remains. Tiny colonies of animals called **bryozoa** built lacy, moss-like limestone structures. Their fossils were exceedingly fragile but so numerous that their fragments often cover entire bedding plane surfaces. Throughout Carboniferous time, the brachiopods continued to be the most successful shellfish, but protected communities of pelecypods and gastropods also thrived. [8–10,84,146]

Crinoids waved in the current above the ocean floor. In places the animals grew in such numbers that entire layers are made of their broken bits and fragments. [8–10,84]

Coelacanths[3] swam in the streams of the Carboniferous along with numerous other lung-finned and lobe-finned fish that had developed during Devonian time. The amphibians expanded

2. Foraminifera are tiny, mostly marine animals that form microscopic to near-microscopic shell-like chambers called tests of calcite. The tests of foraminifera form enormous deposits of marine sediments throughout the world.

3. Pronounced see' la kanth.

Figure 9–7:   Hylonomus is the earliest known, true land-dwelling reptile. Fossil remains were recovered from a late Pennsylvanian or early Permian coal bed in Nova Scotia.

in numbers but remained rather small in size. Most were less than 20 centimeters (8 inches) long, with the largest just slightly less than 2 meters (6.5 feet) in length. Toward the end of mid-Pennsylvanian time, the first reptiles appeared. Their fossils are preserved in Ohio and Nova Scotia. The size and features of the reptiles suggest that they may have developed long before the first of their fossils were preserved (figure 9–7). [8–10,84]

During Carboniferous time, plants were the most abundant organisms. In the warm and humid climate, scale trees (*lepidodendrons*) grew to heights of 35 meters (115 feet), forming dense forests. At the same time, forerunners of the conifers formed an umbrella of foliage as their tall, slender trunks were topped by a crown of large, simple leaves. A large variety of ferns at ground level added to the lushness of the growth. As generations of plants lived and died, their remains were buried in the swamps. There, decay and burial combined to convert their carbon-rich bulk into coal seams that continue to be a major economic resource across the Ridge and Valley Province and the Plateau Province of the Appalachians (figure 9–8). [156,157]

Figure 9–8:   Large trees which flourished in the swampy deltas of Pennsylvanian time are preserved in shales and coal beds throughout Tennessee, Kentucky, and West Virginia.

10
One Final Uplift

About 320 million years ago, the Mississippian period ended and the Pennsylvanian period began. The 320-million-year boundary also marks the end of the Acadian Orogeny and the beginning of the final surge of Appalachian mountain building. This final episode of folding, thrust faulting, metamorphism, and uplift is referred to by geologists as the Alleghenian Orogeny. The term Alleghenian refers to the rocks of the Ridge and Valley Province and adjacent Allegheny Plateau. Rock units in those provinces of the southern Appalachians were deformed in Pennsylvania, Virginia, West Virginia, Kentucky, and Tennessee. The orogeny is now known to have been much wider in scope, causing changes throughout all of the southern Appalachians.

The Alleghenian Orogeny marks the collision of the North American and Euro-African continents. The first sign of the collision was the uplift of the crust caught between the two gigantic colliding plates. Deep in the crust, the energy of compression, along with the final remnants of subduction of the Theic-Rheic Ocean, heated the rocks and produced a number of magma bodies. Because the pressure and heat did not increase uniformly, the magmas developed in a variety of places at different times.

Units deep in the eastern portion of the Carolina Slate Belt were among the first to melt. About 314 million years ago masses of molten rock began forming in Nash County near Castalia. At about the same time, other granitic magmas developed near Sims (278 Ma) and Elm City in Wilson County, and not far from Lillington (297 Ma) in Harnett County. During the same general period of time other magmas intruded the Raleigh Belt rocks near Rolesville in Wake County, near the Virginia border at Wise in Warren County, and near Lemon Springs in Lee County. [125,126,162]

Farther south and west, a large granite mass intruded rocks of the western Carolina Slate Belt near Pageland in South Carolina about 296 million years ago. Today, this granite has been exposed by erosion and forms large, soil-free areas in Lancaster County. The most impressive of these is a broad, barren, sloping exposure known locally as Forty Acre Rock (plate 23). [162]

The bedrock surface of the Rolesville, Pageland, and other granites in the Piedmont is often very close to the land surface. The thin veneer of soil presents problems for contractors and engineers engaged in building highways and other projects. Across much of northern Wake County, the Rolesville Granite crops out on every hill and along every stream course. The resulting land surface is so unique that Mitchell's Mill Pond State Park has been established to preserve the fragile landscape.

Toward the end of Pennsylvanian time, the ancient North American and Euro-African crustal plates were slowly grinding to a halt following their collision. On the surface, the great landmasses were finally joined in one enormous landmass geologists named **Pangaea**.

While the two continents were joined, the energy produced by the motion of the plates had not been consumed. As the Alleghenian Orogeny began, the two crustal plates pressed together. The rocks beneath the Blue Ridge, Piedmont, and Coastal Plain were caught between them and pushed upward (figure 10–1). [4–6]

The uplift was widespread, stretching from the New England states south as far as Georgia and Alabama. The greatest uplift apparently occurred in the area that now forms the Atlantic Coastal Plain and continental shelf. The uplift resulted in relatively rapid cooling of the crust. As a result, the most recent of

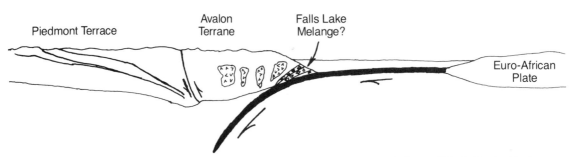

Figure 10–1:   As Carboniferous time came to an end, the Euro-African crustal plate collided with the North American plate. The (T) and (A) in the diagram indicate that the rock units are moving toward (T) or away (A) from the observer along a strike-slip fault. [6]

the igneous intrusions solidified during the last years of the Pennsylvanian period and the early years of Permian time.

On the eastern side of the Avalon Terrane in northern Wake County, blocks up to several square kilometers in area were thrust upward. The blocks were most likely torn away along the boundary between the lower crust and upper mantle. This jumble of blocks is known as the Falls Lake **Mélange** (figure 10–2).[1] [40,163]

Field evidence from other places around the world indicates that a mélange forms within a subduction zone when blocks of crust are shuffled and reworked between the two moving crustal plates. Blocks of oceanic crust caught up in a mélange may be carried down into the crust, metamorphosed, and then returned to the earth's surface.

The exact series of events which led to the creation of the Falls Lake Mélange is not well understood. Some geologists believe the feature developed during the Taconic Orogeny.[2] Others have suggested that it was produced during this final mountain-building event, the Alleghenian Orogeny.

Life of Permian Time

The Permian period includes the last years of the Paleozoic era. Throughout the Permian period (286–245 million years ago), life forms continued to increase in number and variety. In the oceans, many of the invertebrates developed into extremely specialized forms and then became extinct. While some animal groups disappeared completely, the simpler and more broadly adapted forms survived. Among the invertebrates the more important extinctions included the trilobites, eurypterids, blastoids, and rugose corals.

The climate on land became cooler at the beginning of Permian time. Later, a warming trend near the end of the period re-

---

1. Mélange is a French term meaning a mixture or hodgepodge. When used in geological terms it refers to a mappable body of rock which is composed of a mixture of blocks of rock that are different sizes and come from a variety of source units.

2. See page 62.

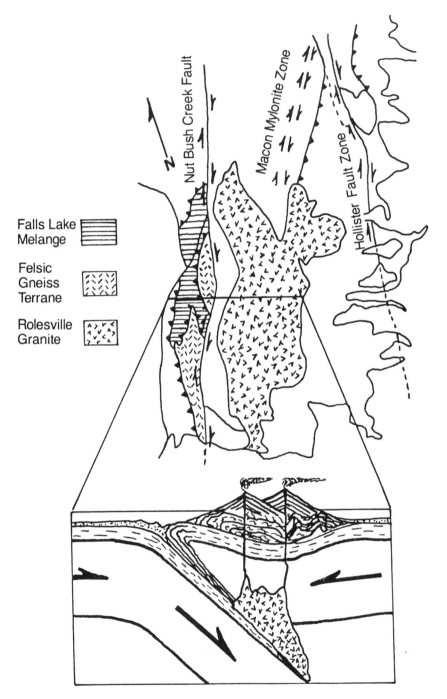

Figure 10-2: The Falls Lake Mélange is located in northern Wake County. It is thought to represent a jumbled group of rocks that were formed between two crustal plates in a subduction zone. [163]

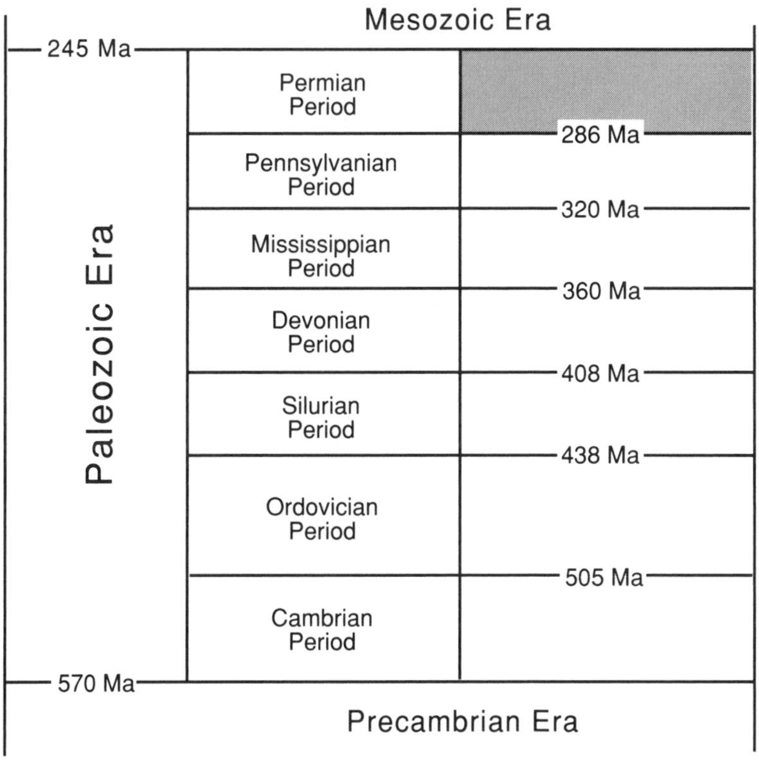

Figure 10-3: Geologic time column showing the Permian period in relation to the Paleozoic era (Ma = Million years ago).

sulted in conditions that are much like our present climate. Plants responded to the climatic changes along with all other forms of life. Scale trees that had flourished in near-tropical conditions declined almost to the point of extinction. Meanwhile, the true conifers, which were better suited to cooler climates, emerged as the dominant woody plants. [8–10,84]

The insects underwent a rapid expansion in variety and number. Their physical size generally decreased, however, probably in response to the cooler climate. [158]

The amphibians continued a steady expansion but also remained small, while the reptiles began an expansion that would lead to their dominance in later periods. By this time, many of the reptiles had mastered living on the land, and the group had begun to develop along two general lines. The most common group evolved long bodies and short legs. One example of this group, called the pelycosaur, had large fins which may have played a role in controlling the animal's body temperature.

Another group is of special interest in spite of the fact that its fossils come from Russia and South Africa. The therapsid reptilian order shows changes in the structure of the jaws and teeth that later appear in early mammals. These meat-eating reptiles carried their bodies off the ground and chewed their food using canines, incisors, and molars. [8–10,84]

Around the world, the end of the Paleozoic era was a time in which about 75 percent of the amphibians and more than 80 percent of the existing reptile families became extinct. Many families of plants and invertebrates also died out. Some paleontologists have speculated that a combination of overspecialization and climatic change, coupled with or brought about by massive mountain building around the world, caused significant environmental changes. These changes may have caused the extinctions, but at present, there is little evidence to support one definite cause.

The Appalachians Rise

As Permian time began, the events caused by the collision of the Euro-African continent with North America produced a series of extensive thrust faults. Geologists do not agree concerning the exact mechanism which produced the faults or precisely when they developed. Most believe that some faults were new while others had developed during earlier mountain-building events and were reactivated by the continental collision (figure 10–4). [164–166]

There is little question that rock layers in the Piedmont and Blue Ridge moved along the Brevard, Greenbrier, and numerous other faults. Farther east the faults may have been new responses to the final collision of the Euro-African continent with North America. Extensive seismic profiling of the crust in the late

3. A strike-slip fault is a near-vertical break in the crust along which motion is occurring. In the case of a strike slip-fault, the blocks of rock on either side of the fault move parallel to the fault surface.

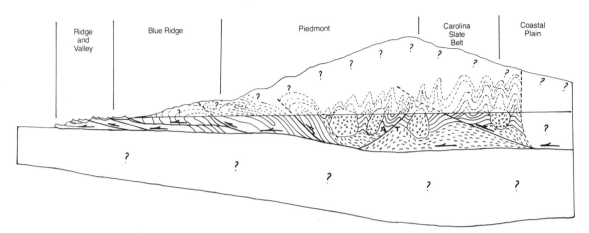

Figure 10–4:   As the Euro-African crustal plate ground to a halt against the North American continent, the enormous pressure created a gigantic horizontal fault deep in the crust. The overlying rocks of the décollement, including those of the Coastal Plain, Piedmont, and Blue Ridge, moved northwestward, sliding on the fault surface. The (T) and (A) in the diagram indicate that the rock units are moving toward (T) or away (A) from the observer along a strike-slip fault.[3] [6]

1970s revealed the existence of a widespread break in the crustal rocks. The nearly horizontal fault is located between 10 and 15 kilometers (6.2–9.3 miles) beneath the modern land surface. The fault is referred to as a décollement[4] because the sheet of overlying rocks has been separated from the crust beneath and thrust along the fault surface.[5] The décollement was very widespread, covering the area beneath the Chauga Belt, Inner Piedmont, Charlotte Belt, and Carolina Slate Belt. The décollement also extended eastward beneath the Coastal Plain. Geophysical studies east of Lumberton in Robeson County revealed a granite intrusion. The granite body is cut horizontally by the décollement at a depth of 18 kilometers (11.2 miles) beneath the modern land surface. [167–176]

The energy of collision pushed the rocks above the décollement as much as 175 kilometers (109 miles) toward the northwest. Motion along older faults, such as the Brevard fault zone,

---

4. The term décollement is French, meaning "unsticking or detachment."

5. The term décollement is applied to rock strata detached from related rock units. In this case, the overlying rock layers were detached from a widespread horizontal detachment or sole fault which is referred to as the décollement fault.

diverted energy upward, pushing the rocks up and over the younger rocks in the Blue Ridge (figure 10–5). [177]

The pressure of collision seems to have been concentrated deep in the crustal rocks of the Raleigh Belt. Evidence there suggests that the metamorphism caused by the final collision reached its peak about 300 million years ago. [117,164–166]

The rocks of the Kings Mountain, Charlotte, Milton, and Inner Piedmont belts were thrust upward from locations south and east to their present locations. At the same time, the rock units continued shifting southwestward along the faults.[6] The shifting moved rocks on the east side of the Blue Ridge, Brevard, Gold Hill, Hollister, and Nutbush Creek fault zones. [169,172]

The faulting moved large masses of early Precambrian rock northwestward, covering younger rock units. Evidence in the

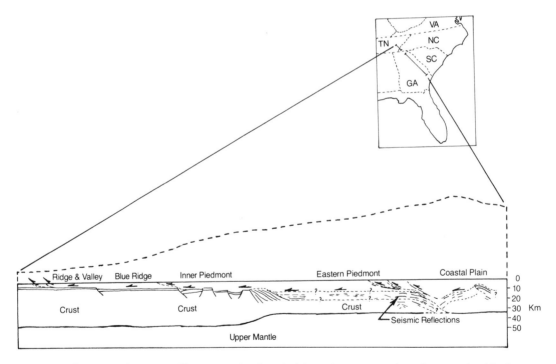

Figure 10–5:   Seismic reflection profiles across the Appalachians demonstrate the existence of a décollement stretching from New England to Georgia and Alabama. The fault surface lies beneath the Coastal Plain, Piedmont, and Blue Ridge provinces. Smaller sliver, or splay, faults carried blocks upward as the entire upper surface of the Appalachians moved northwestward. [169–172]

6. See page 90.

northwestern portion of the state indicates that the rocks of the Sauratown folds are visible today because they were covered by a thrust sheet which protected them from erosion.

The Sauratown anticlinorium is a relatively small feature that provides an excellent example of this overthrusting phenomenon. The anticlinorium lies in a much larger structure known as the Smith River **Allochthon**[7](figure 10–6). The unit consists of a series of large slices of rock which have been thrust over one another. The process pushed older rocks up and over younger rocks. Where erosion later exposed the younger rocks, the overthrusts formed a structure which geologists call a **window**. Geologic windows allow us to view rock units which would otherwise have been destroyed by erosion. [47,49]

Farther west, the Grandfather Mountain Window was created when early Precambrian rocks were pushed over younger late Precambrian rocks of the Blue Ridge complex. The cap of older rock has since been partially eroded away, exposing the younger rocks which have been destroyed in other areas (figure 10–7 and plates 24a & b). [178]

Visitors to the gorge of the Linville River may see one of the major faults which formed this window. The fault is exposed in the west side of the gorge just above the lower falls. There, coarse-grained early Precambrian gneissic rocks lie on top of younger Precambrian quartzites of the Chilhowee Group. Today, some

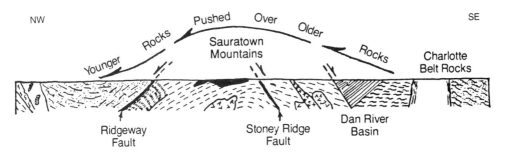

Figure 10–6:   The folded rocks of the Sauratown Mountains are a small portion of a larger block called the Smith River Allochthon. The younger rocks of the Smith River Allochthon were shoved over the older rocks of the Sauratown Mountains. Erosion has since destroyed the overlying younger rocks, exposing the older rocks at the present land surface. [49]

---

7. The term "allochthonous" (uh LOCK thuh nuhs) is applied to rocks that were formed in one place and later moved to another. The movement usually involves thrusting along a low-angle fault surface.

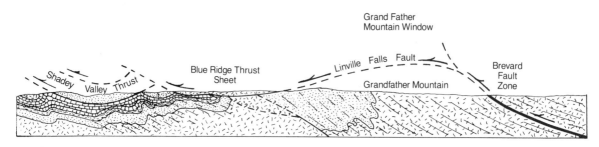

Figure 10–7: The Grandfather Mountain Window was created when rock units were thrust over one another. (Also see plates 24a & b).

units, such as the Grandfather Mountain Formation, can only be seen inside this structurally formed window where they were first protected from, and later exposed by, erosion. [59,178,179]

Farther south, in Madison County, a similar situation resulted when early Precambrian rocks moved along the Mine Ridge fault. The thrusting covered younger rocks ranging in age from late Precambrian to middle Cambrian. Later, as the Appalachians were worn down by erosion, the overlying rocks were destroyed. Today, this opening to the past, called the Hot Springs Window, may be visited in Great Smoky Mountains National Park (figure 10–8). [97,180]

The enormous energy involved in this thrusting event throughout the Appalachians is well illustrated in the Ridge and Valley Province. Today, the Ridge and Valley Province stretches across Tennessee, Kentucky, Virginia, and West Virginia, barely

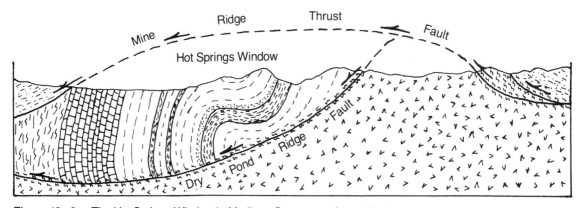

Figure 10–8: The Hot Springs Window in Madison County was formed by the same basic mechanism which formed the Sauratown Mountains and Grandfather Mountain windows. [97]

missing North Carolina's western boundary. The province, whose rocks were deposited in the ancient Queenston and Virginia-Carolina deltas, moved northwestward and were folded and faulted by the forces involved in mountain building (figure 10–9).

Evidence suggests that the once-horizontal layers were dipping gently toward the northwest as a result of the uplift of the rocks of the Blue Ridge and Piedmont provinces further south and east. The pressure exerted on the rocks by the thrusting from the southeast was likely coupled with gravity which helped move the layers of sediment that had been deposited over the preceding millions of years. Then, finally, the rocks of today's Ridge and Valley Province moved slowly northwestward off the rising landmass. [123,181–184]

The major break occurred within a widespread layer of shale that had been deposited during Cambrian time. The shale of the

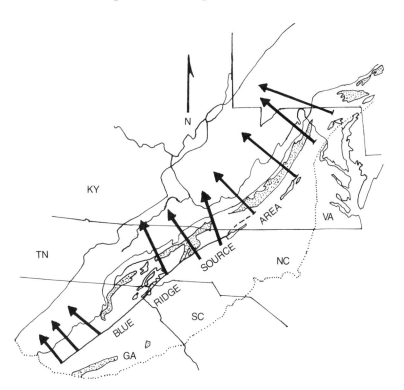

Figure 10–9: The pressure of thrusting is well demonstrated in the Ridge and Valley Province where extensive thrust faulting and folding shortened the land surface by many kilometers.

Rome Formation sheared easily, allowing the décollement formed by overlying, younger rocks to move northwest with little difficulty. Some geologists believe that water in the rock layers provided a buoying force that relieved the friction between the layers, allowing the sliding to take place on a slope that dipped only one or two degrees (figure 10–10). [181]

Where the buoying force of the water was released by the sliding rocks, sedimentary layers broke and turned upward along faults. The faults were curved much like the runners on a sled, causing the front edge of each bed to move out of the plane in which the rock layers were sliding. As the front of each succeeding slab shifted, the beds stacked up in repeating layers like slices of bread. The stacking also removed one section after another, allowing the entire mass to move down the very gentle slope. [182–185]

Mapping of the rock units suggests that the sedimentary mass in the Blue Ridge probably moved about 107 kilometers (66 miles), but individual blocks or layers often moved relatively short distances. Sedimentary layers that had been deposited as beach sands in Ashe and Allegheny counties millions of years earlier now moved into Virginia. As they moved, the sequence of sedimentary layers broke into blocks and was folded into anticlines and synclines. Today, the folded and faulted strata can be seen near Wytheville, Virginia. The movement and deformation bear witness to the powerful forces released by the collision of the two continental plates (plate 25). [183–185]

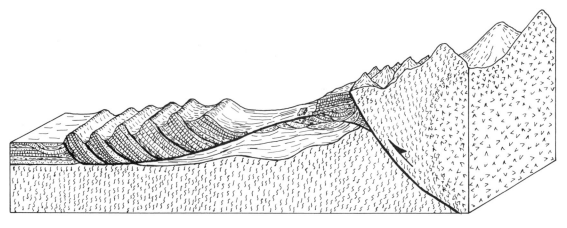

Figure 10–10:   Weakness of the Rome Shale coupled with the buoyant force of water allowed the forces produced by the collision to the southeast to push thick layers of sediment down a gentle slope toward the northwest.

One of the largest fault blocks, the Pine Mountain thrust sheet, stretches some 200 kilometers (124 miles) from Pine Mountain in Tennessee to its northeastern end at Breaks Interstate Park in Kentucky. The sheet of rock includes layers deposited beginning in the Devonian period and ending in the Pennsylvanian period, a time span of approximately 100 million years. The entire mass moved northeast an average of nearly 9 kilometers (5.6 miles) (figure 10–11). [182,186–188]

Across the entire Appalachian mountain chain the sliding of the present-day Ridge and Valley rocks relocated major rock units. The sliding seems to have occurred slowly, and life may have continued without interruption as the rock layers slowly moved down slope toward the northwest. In the millions of years to come, they would be reshaped by the agents of erosion. The more resistant quartzites, raised by folding and thrust faulting, would form long, high ridge lines while fault traces and limestone

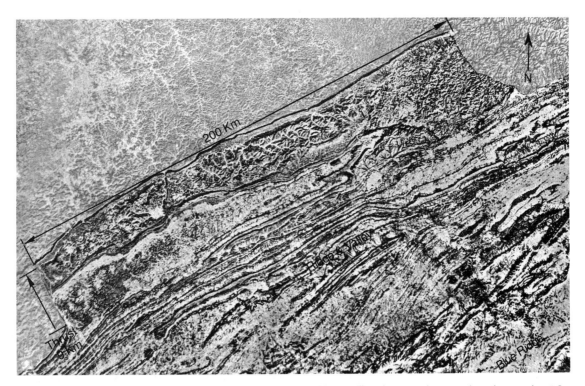

Figure 10–11:   The Pine Mountain thrust block, marked in this satellite photograph, moved northwest about 9 kilometers (5.7 miles) over the rocks of the Appalachian Plateau. (Courtesy of United States Geological Survey.)

units formed valleys. The resulting land surface is one of long ridges and valleys for which the region is named (plate 26).

The rocks of the Appalachian Plateau[8] were also eroded by streams which cut steep-sided meandering valleys in the ancient flat surface. The resulting region is characterized today by horizontal layers of rock that have been dissected by erosion. The resulting land surface is incredibly rugged, making travel and economic development very difficult (plate 27).

A Major Mountain System is Complete

The end of this episode of faulting and folding marked the close of the raising of the Appalachians. The complex series of mountain-building events, which had begun in early Ordovician time, lasted more than 260 million years, finally ending late in the Permian period. During that immense span of years, rock units were folded and metamorphosed by at least three different surges of mountain building. Rock units buried under tens of kilometers of overlying material were invaded by magmas and changed into new forms by incredible heat and pressure. Some geologists have calculated that the distance across the Appalachians was shortened at least 260 kilometers (161 miles) by the folding and faulting that took place as the two ancient continents collided. [169]

The Euro-African continent welded to North America, forming an enormous crustal landmass called Pangaea. The North American boundary between the two crustal masses is buried beneath the sediments of the Atlantic continental shelf. The African boundary is located just off the western coast of the African continent. Careful study of the magnetic properties of the deeply buried rocks has allowed geologists to locate the boundaries. Re-

---

8. A plateau is a large, comparatively flat area that is significantly elevated above sea level. In the case of the Appalachian Plateau, the land surface is bordered by the Ridge and Valley Province on the southeast and the Mississippi River Valley on the northwest. The plateau has been dissected by streams which carved the land surface into an irregular pattern of flat highland surfaces separated by steep-sided valleys.

construction of the continents' position in the ancient Pangaean landmass confirmed the position of the two crustal blocks some 250 million years ago (figure 10–12).

The completed mountain range was 1,000 kilometers (620 miles) long, stretching from Canada, Great Britain, Greenland, and Scandinavia south to Louisiana. The tallest peaks were located above our Atlantic Coastal Plain and continental shelf. From a center near the suture line, the rocks stretched east to today's African Sahara and west toward the edge of the present Mississippi River Valley. The mountains towered as high as today's tallest mountains and the peaks were undoubtedly covered with glacial ice and snow (plate 28).

The roots of the magnificent mountains we call the Appalachians are beneath our feet today. Rocks that formed as island volcanoes, hundreds of kilometers beyond an ancient coast line, are intermingled with sediments deposited on continental

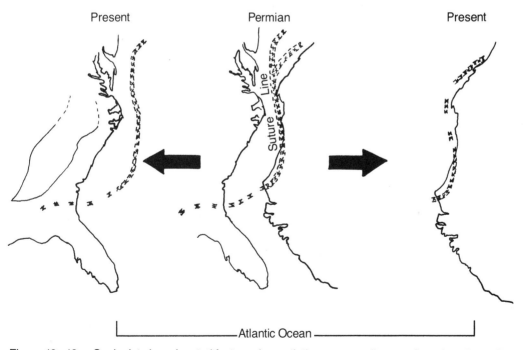

Figure 10–12: Geologists have located features beneath the ocean sediments along the edges of North America and Africa that are thought to represent an ancient suture line between the two crustal plates. The center map shows the two continental crustal plates as they would have appeared following their collision during Permian time. The diagrams to the right and left show the present continental margins with the ancient crustal boundaries placed on the basis of the geophysical evidence.

shelves. Contorted, folded, and metamorphosed layers reflect past events that raised some rocks far above the present land surface while others were carried deep into the crust. Rocks were also changed by heat and pressure as large magma bodies formed deep in the earth. The rocks reveal a crust shortened by hundreds of kilometers as ancient terranes collided with the continent and transformed into lofty mountains in response to the enormous energy of the continental collision.

During the 230 million years before the appearance of man, as much as 13,000 meters (43,000 feet or 8.1 miles) of rock were eroded, exposing the modern surface on which we walk. Today, those once-immense and magnificent peaks are represented only by the rounded mountains and rolling hills of the Blue Ridge and Piedmont. Yet, in many ways, the rocks that form today's land surface are even more impressive than towering mountain peaks because their tortured shapes and changed forms contain the history of the building of this ancient mountain system.

Part 4

A New Ocean Opens

As the Mesozoic Era began, the Appalachians stood higher than the level of today's land surface. While the shape of that ancient surface will never be known, the highest mountain peaks probably stood in the area of today's eastern Piedmont and Coastal Plain with rugged highlands sloping away to both the east and west. Streams carved the mountains, carrying the debris east onto the African continent and west to the ancient Mississippi River. As the mountains were being destroyed, activity in the mantle began moving the crustal plates apart. The crust fractured along north-south lines as the continental crustal plates separated along the site of the present-day Mid-Atlantic Ridge. Blocks caught between moving faults formed a series of basins along the newly created eastern coast of the United States. Streams flowing into the forming basins created swamps in which a diverse group of animals and plants thrived. As millions of years passed, the two landmasses moved apart, opening the Atlantic Ocean. The North American continent moved northwestward and its trailing edge sank beneath the sea. The first sediments were deposited on the eroded land surface that would form the base of the Coastal Plain.

11
A NEW ERA BEGINS

Geologists divide the Mesozoic era into three sections: the Triassic, Jurassic, and Cretaceous periods. The Triassic[1] period began about 245 million years ago. At that time, most of today's crustal plates were gathered into one supercontinent known as

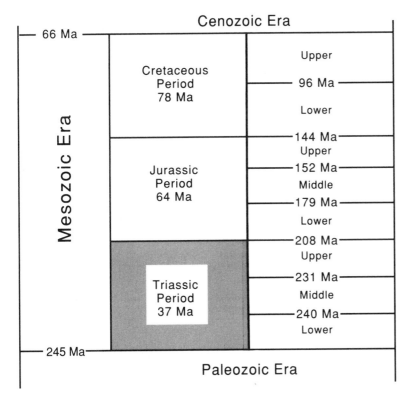

Figure 11–1:   Geologic time column showing the Triassic period in relation to the Mesozoic era (Ma = Million years ago).

---

1. The name Triassic comes from the fact that rocks of this age were divided into three distinct groups when they were first studied in Germany.

Pangaea. The Appalachian mountains were located along the boundary between the North American and African plates (figure 11–2). The mountain mass which had been raised by the collision of the two plates stretched from New England to Alabama. It seems likely that rugged peaks rose to heights of as much as ten kilometers (30,000 feet). The tallest of those peaks were probably in the area of today's eastern Piedmont and Coastal Plain with lower mountains and hills sloping away toward both the east and west. [189,190]

The Triassic period lasted approximately 37 million years. During that time, erosion continued to carve the newly raised

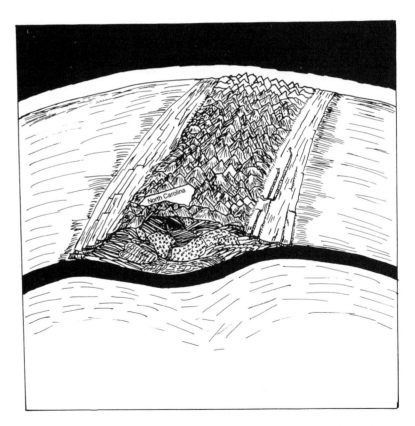

Figure 11–2:   This hypothetical view portrays the Appalachian Mountains near the beginning of Triassic time. The continental plate to the east is the northwestern portion of the African plate and the plate to the west is the North American continent. Some geologists have suggested that the peaks of the newly raised Appalachians were as high as today's young mountains, reaching elevations nearly ten kilometers (30,000 feet) above sea level.

mountains across the entire state. Weathering processes changed rocks to soil across the entire state. Glaciers may have helped carve the highest peaks, while the rushing waters of mountain streams carried away the debris. Rivers flowing east carried mud and sand onto the African continent while others, flowing west, deposited their loads in the ancient Mississippi River Valley.

As millions of years passed, erosion slowly destroyed the rugged mountains. Field evidence suggests that by late Triassic time (about 230 million years ago) the mountains had been eroded to a surface of gently rolling hills. The surface formed by the tops of the hills sloped east and west from today's eastern Piedmont and Coastal Plain. There is some evidence that the highest hills may have stood only about 300 meters (1,000 feet) above sea level. [189]

The erosional destruction of the Appalachians produced tremendous amounts of material which was removed from the area by streams. As a result, there is no fossil record in North Carolina for early or middle Triassic time. Many plants and animals lived on the ancient land surface, but their remains were destroyed along with the mountains.

Geologists use fossils from rocks laid down in other parts of the United States to indicate what life might have been like in the Carolinas during early and middle Triassic time. Those fossils suggest that a wide variety of plant and animal forms must have lived on the land.

Great Fractures Form in the Crust

After some fifteen to twenty million years of erosion, events far beneath the surface once again began changing the shape of the land. About 230 million years ago, movement of material in the mantle began to produce forces which would finally tear the North American and Euro-African crustal plates apart.

As the stress increased, the crust began to fracture. A large network of cracks developed throughout Europe, Africa, and eastern North America. The pattern suggests that the stress was centered along a line between the two continents. Today, that line is represented by the Mid-Atlantic Ridge, located near the center of the modern Atlantic Ocean floor (figure 11–3).[2] There, new crust formed as magma welled up through the crust from the mantle. [190–193]

Crustal Blocks—Tectonic Basins

In North Carolina, the fractures formed two separate sets. One set runs northeast-southwest, while the other runs nearly north-south. Most of the fractures remain today just as they formed many millions of years ago. They may be seen across the

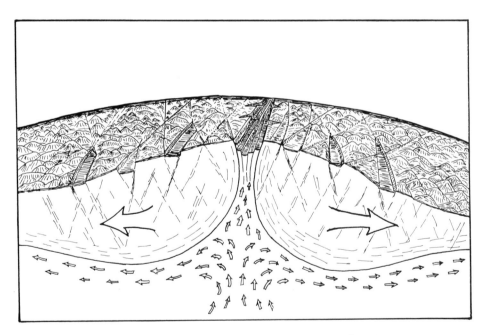

Figure 11–3:   As conditions far beneath the earth's surface changed, new forces in the mantle began pulling the overlying crustal plates apart. A system of fractures developed in response to the increasing stress. The principal break formed along a zone that later formed the margins of the North American and Euro-African crustal plates. Water filled the central rift, creating the Atlantic Ocean.

---

2. See page 109 (figure 10–12).

Piedmont and Blue Ridge provinces as cracks in the older Paleozoic rocks. Forces within the crust caused movement along some
of the fractures, producing faults that reflected motion within
the continental crustal plates. Where land shifted along such
faults, enormous blocks of crust dropped slowly below the level of
the surrounding land surface. [193] The subsiding blocks
formed long, northeast-southwest trending basins that are inset
into the Appalachian Piedmont from Nova Scotia to South Carolina (figure 11–4). While the most obvious outcropping basins

Figure 11–4:   This map shows the location and size of the known Triassic
basins along the eastern coast of the United States. The straight lines mark the
trend of the cracks or fractures that developed because of the stress which
eventually pulled the supercontinent of Pangaea apart. [191]

occur in the Piedmont, others are known to exist beneath the younger sediments of the Coastal Plain and continental shelf. Most of the Triassic basins which are buried beneath the Coastal Plain are indicated by their magnetic signatures on large-scale maps. The existence of a few of the buried basins has been proven by drilling wells and taking samples of the rocks at depth. [192-195]

In North Carolina, the Deep River and Dan River basins were formed by the largest down-dropped blocks. The Deep River Basin has been divided into sections known as the Durham, Sanford, and Wadesboro basins. Individual basin names are often used by geologists working in a particular area.

Geophysical mapping shows that the bottoms of the basins are broken into a series of faulted blocks. The blocks sank at different rates, causing the basins to have irregular floors. In North Carolina basins, the deepest blocks are as much as 3,000 meters (10,000 feet) below today's land surface. [191,196-199]

The edges of the basins are usually marked by major faults. In many cases the break is really a series of small faults called a **shear zone**. Rocks within such shear zones are often broken and crushed by the motion of the rocks on either side of the zone. Across shear zones, rock structure usually changes rapidly. One such shear zone marks the eastern edge of the Durham portion of the Deep River Basin in Wake County. Where the zone crosses U.S. Highway 70 west of Raleigh, a walk of less than 100 meters (300 feet) carries the observer from early Paleozoic metamorphic rocks of the Raleigh Belt across the shear zone and onto the sedimentary rocks of the Durham Triassic basin.

The rocks nearest the edges of the basins are usually conglomerates. The conglomerates mark places where streams poured down the **fault scarp**[3] and out across the down-faulted basin floor (plate 29). Water rushing down the steep slopes carried material of all sizes. As the rushing waters slowed at the base of the slopes they deposited boulders, cobbles, gravel, and sand. Later, mineral-bearing ground water cemented the deposits into solid masses of conglomerate. In many localities along the edges of the North Carolina Triassic basins, such "border con-

---

3. A scarp is a very steep slope formed by some geologic process. In this case, the steep slope was formed by the movement of rocks along a fault plane.

glomerates" include boulders up to half a meter (20 inches) in diameter. Yet, a short distance from the border of the ancient basin one finds sandstones and shales that record deposits of streams flowing slowly across the basin floor.

Within the basins, the streams formed fan-shaped deposits of sand and mud. On the fan surfaces, stream channels moved back and forth, depositing sequences of sand, silt, and fine gravel. Today, similar series of repeated bedding are exposed at several locations in the Deep River and Dan River basins (plate 30). [191,200–207] Near the centers of the basins, water flowing in from surrounding highland areas collected in shallow lakes and swamps. Some areas were alternately buried by growing deposits of silt and mud and reflooded as the basin floor sank.

Paleoclimatic evidence suggests that during this time the Carolinas were located about ten degrees north of the equator. As a result, the climate during the late Triassic time was generally warm. The temperature probably averaged about 27° Celsius (80° Fahrenheit) with few cool days.

The amount of moisture appears to have varied in cycles that lasted about 20,000 years. During dryer episodes, evaporation removed water from some of the shallow areas more rapidly than it was replaced by rainfall or stream flow. In such areas, the lakes and ponds shrank or dried up completely during the drier periods. The evaporation caused the deposition of thin beds of **chert**[4] and limestone interbedded with mudstones. Outcrops of these rocks in the Research Triangle Park and near Bethesda in Durham County mark the sites of some of those shallow **playa lakes**. In the limestone layers, fossils of tiny bivalve crustaceans (called ostracods) along with the burrows of other small animals provide evidence of life in those alkaline waters. [191,208–213]

While playa lakes alternately filled and dried up in some areas of the basins, larger streams and very slow-flowing springs called seeps, which formed along faults in the basin floors in other areas, provided a steadier water supply. The lakes which formed in those areas did not dry up completely during the more arid portions of the climatic cycle. Swamps formed near the edges of

---

4. Chert is a hard, dense, sedimentary rock formed by the evaporation of water containing silica. Chert is usually a mixture of very fine grains of quartz (chalcedony) and the noncrystalline form of quartz and water called opal.

such lakes and a wide variety of plants flourished in the warm climate. As generations grew and died, layers of decaying plant material were deposited on the muddy bottoms. Where floods carried large quantities of mud into a lake, leaves and stems are preserved in layers of black to maroon shale. Such layers are common throughout the Deep River and Dan River basins. Where less sediment was available, layers of plant debris formed peat beds that were later buried and changed to coal.

A number of thin layers of coal occur near Sanford in Lee and Chatham counties. The beds were mined during the Civil War for use by blockade-runners based at Wilmington. Coal was mined sporadically until 1950, although the operations were generally not profitable. Today, little remains of the effort except for abandoned shafts and a small monument placed in memory of miners killed by explosions and other accidents. [214–215]

In recent years, geologists have uncovered many new fossils from the North Carolina basins which provide a picture of the plant and animal community of late Triassic time. Fossils are not generally abundant or obvious in the basin sediments. However, those that have been collected indicate that large numbers of plants and animals probably lived in the lakes, swamps, and wooded land areas of the basins.

The warm climate helped to support the plant community which flourished in the basins. Mats of algae grew rapidly in the shallow water and may have covered the surface in stagnant areas. In more swampy locations, rushes and ferns grew in abundance. On higher ground, club mosses, similar to today's running cedar, competed with strange-looking plants called cycads for the sunlight filtering through the leaves of conifers and early fruit-bearing plants (figure 11–5). Some of the trees must have reached heights of nearly 30 meters (96 feet). Petrified trunks more than a meter (3.3 feet) in diameter have been found in Durham County, and logs averaging 30 centimeters (1 foot) in diameter are common in all the basins. [216–220]

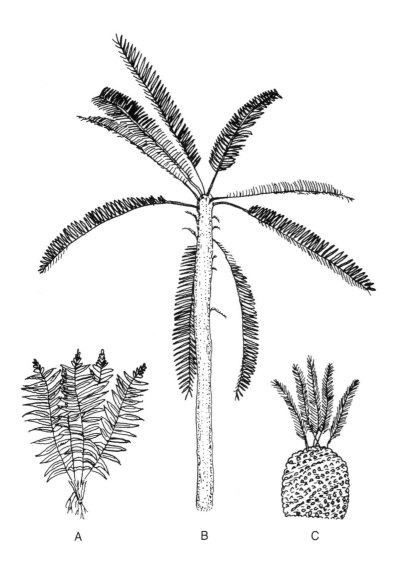

Figure 11–5: Three of the most common plants in the Triassic flora
(A) A typical low-growing fern; (B) tree fern—one of the taller Triassic plants;
(C) a cycad—one of the most unusual of the Triassic plants.

Life in the Basins

Quarrying at various locations within the basins has exposed shales which tell a remarkable story. The fossils preserved in those ancient muds reflect the wide variety of invertebrates that once lived on, in, or near the water. Impressions of tiny clams, crayfish, millipedes, cockroaches, and water bugs are preserved in shales near Durham and Eden (figure 11-6). In the rocks near Eden, carbon traces reveal the presence of many insects, including several kinds of flies that once lived near the stagnant waters. The layers of mud also contain fossils of wood-boring and sap beetles, suggesting that a varied and abundant group of insects existed in the wooded areas. [200,209,213,220]

Other fossils from the sites near Durham and Eden include at least five different major groups of fishes. Many of the fossils occur near Eden, and among those the most common are the **holosteans**, or intermediate ray-finned fish. Both intermediate and primitive ray-finned forms have been identified, but perhaps the best known of the fossil fishes is the coelacanth (plate 31).

Coelacanths were believed to be extinct until 1938 when natives fishing off the coast of Africa brought living specimens to the surface in their nets. Remains of that ancient subgroup of lobe-finned fish have been found near Eden and in coal beds near the small town of Cumnock outside Sanford in Lee County. [209,213,221-223]

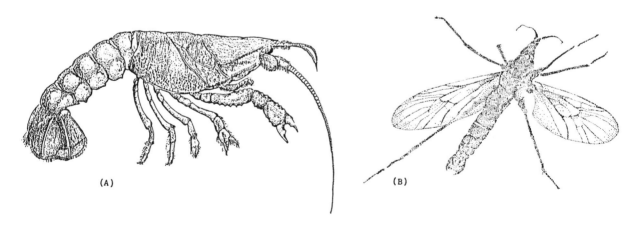

(A)

(B)

Figure 11-6:   Two of the many smaller inhabitants of the North Carolina Triassic basins. (A) A typical crayfish from the Deep River basin and (B) a crane-fly from the Cow Branch formation near Eden. (Courtesy of Dr. Paul E. Olson.)[209].

Dinosaurs in the Carolinas

The variety of plants and animals living during Triassic time is remarkable, but the period is best known for its reptiles. Reptiles developed from amphibians late in the Paleozoic era. Many had adaptations that allowed them to venture far from water. As a result, reptiles were able to move into areas where the climate was too dry for any of the animal forms of earlier periods.

In the Triassic rocks of the Carolinas, hard-part fossils and track impressions provide evidence of a number of different early relatives of the dinosaurs. More than a hundred skeletons of a long-necked reptile, *Tanytrachelos* (figure 11−7), with several lizard-like features have been found in the Dan River basin. *Tanytrachelos* was a small aquatic animal with a streamlined head and body. Several specimens have been found which preserve traces of the animal's outline and skin. From them we know that *Tanytrachelos* had smooth skin on its legs while its body surface was granular in texture. The legs and feet were apparently adapted for swimming and the animal is thought to have spent most, if not all, of its life in the shallow basin lakes. [209,213,224]

Throughout all of the Triassic basins, tracks and fossils of the phytosaurs, or "false" crocodiles, such as *Rutidon*, have been

Figure 11−7:   Tanytrachelos, a swimming dinosaur relative that is known to have lived in the Dan River Triassic basin. [224]

found. This crocodile-like reptile grew to lengths of at least three meters (10 feet) and had nostrils near its eyes (plate 32). [225]

The tracks of several other reptiles and amphibians have been found along with fossil fragments. They suggest that a variety of animals competed for food and territory. Two small mammal-like forms (*Dromatherium* and *Microconodon*) [226] are known only from jaw fragments.

One fossil found in North Carolina basins reveals the presence of a group of flat-bodied amphibians (*Dictyocephalus*). These animals were roughly 1.2 meters (4 feet) long, rather large and seem to have resembled the modern salamander known as the hellbender (plates 33a & b). [227228]

Other lizard-like reptiles (Rhynchosauria) [33] grew to lengths of about half a meter (1.6 feet) and served as food for the larger animals. There were also armored reptiles (*Typothorax*) of about the same size that grew to lenghths of about 1.2 meters (4 feet). [229] Heavier reptiles, such as the dicynodont (*Placerias*), also roamed the basins (plate 34). Early dinosaurs included both the predatory, reptile-hipped, or saurischian type (*Coelophysis*) and turkey-sized plant-eaters of the bird-hipped or ornithischian type.

By far the biggest predators of this time were the rauisuchid thecodonts (figure 11−8). Fossils of their large, knife-like teeth suggest that these large carnivores were the most fearsome of all the animals found in the Triassic basins. Fossils from other areas suggest that they grew to about 3 meters (10 feet) in length.

Many other reptiles are known to have lived in the North Car-

Figure 11−8:   The rauisuchid thecodonts were large carnivorous reptiles that probably dominated the animal community in the Carolina Triassic basins. Photograph courtesy of the Pennsylvania Museum of Natural History.

olina basins and other basins along the east coast. Unfortunately, conditions in the basins did not promote the preservation of hard-part fossils, so many animals are known only because their footprints were preserved in the soft muds of the swamps and playa lakes (figure 11–9). [228]

Plants and animals similar to those in the basins probably also lived on the adjacent highland regions. Unfortunately, erosion destroyed the record that might once have existed on the uplands of the Piedmont and Blue Ridge. As a result, all we know of life in North Carolina during Triassic time must be based on what we can observe in the rocks of the basins or can infer from fossils of the same age found in Texas, New Mexico, and Arizona (plate 35).

The erosion of the ancient upland surface surrounding the Triassic basins produced gently rolling hills. The general land surface sloped downhill toward the west from higher elevations east of the Piedmont. On that ancient surface, erosion was carving the rolling hills and valleys that now lie buried beneath the modern Coastal Plain. Streams flowed west from the Carolinas and Virginia across what is now Tennessee and Kentucky to the ancient Mississippi River valley where they dumped the debris produced by the destruction of the Appalachian Mountains.

Many changes lay ahead as the Triassic period came to a close. Those changes would reshape the land surface in North Carolina during the next 208 million years and gradually produce today's familiar landscape.

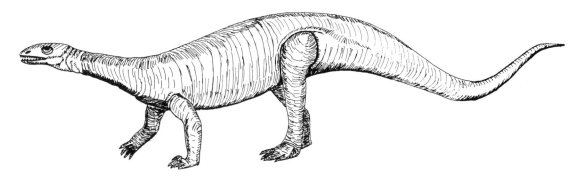

Figure 11–9: A few scattered footprints are the only evidence of the existence of a bird-hipped reptile known as Anchisaurus that lived in the Dan River basin. The animal, which grew to a length of about 2.1 meters (7 feet), was identified based on fossil remains preserved in other areas of the United States.

12

A NEW OCEAN OPENS

About 208 million years ago, as the Triassic period ended and the Jurassic period began, great changes came to the Carolinas. The forces within the crust, which had created the great fractures earlier in Triassic time, continued to increase. Physical

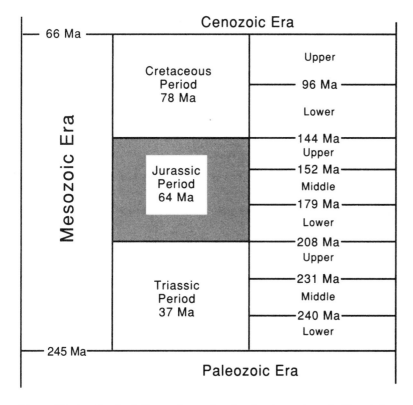

Figure 12–1: Geologic time column showing the Jurassic period in relation to the Mesozoic era. (Ma = Million years)

and chemical evidence suggests that one or more "**hot spots**"[1] may have existed in the mantle far beneath the surface of the Carolinas. [231]

Molten Rock Invades the Crust

On land, the great series of cracks, or joints, which had formed during Triassic time filled with basalt as magma welled up from far beneath the surface. Mapping of the **intrusions** shows that they occurred along the length of the eastern United States. Similar intrusions have been mapped in Europe and Africa. The large pattern revealed by the intrusions supports the hypothesis that the cracks formed as stress built up in the rocks of the larger continent, Pangaea, just before Africa separated from North America. [191,192,231]

Most of the magmas flowed into nearly vertical cracks, forming long thin sheets of rock called dikes. The dikes cut across the metamorphic and igneous rocks of the Piedmont as well as the Triassic sediments in the basins (plate 36).

Within the basins, the magmas also flowed between sedimentary layers forming flat sheets of rock known as sills. In the northern portion of the Deep River Basin, in Durham County near the town of Butner, several sills reach 90 or 91 meters (300 feet) in thickness. The average dike or sill found in other portions of the basins and the Piedmont is only about one or two meters (3–7 feet) thick (plate 37). [232–234]

The age of the dikes and sills poses a problem for geologists. Radiometric dates have placed the time of intrusion over a period spanning some of both the Triassic and Jurassic periods. Unfortunately, efforts to narrow the dates to a more specific time have been unsuccessful. So, for the present, geologists can only say that the best evidence suggests the intrusions probably took place early in Jurassic time. [4]

---

1. Hot spots are thought to represent plumes of hot rock rising within the mantle. Magma bodies and bulges seem to form in crustal rocks over such hot spots.

In the Blue Ridge, Piedmont, and Coastal Plain provinces the 64 million-year span of Jurassic time saw erosion complete the destruction of the uplifted Appalachian mountain mass. The nearly flat surface that remained may be seen today in the Piedmont just west of the western edge of the Coastal Plain. Sediments were deposited there in later years, covering that portion of the Piedmont, and have been removed by erosion only in the last few thousand years.

The Atlantic Ocean Opens

In the area east of today's Atlantic Coastal Plain and continental shelf, the heat and upward pressure produced by the "hot spot" caused the crust to bulge. Near the center of the bulge the crust finally tore apart, forming the North American and Euro-African crustal plates from the supercontinent geologists know as Pangaea.

As the two continents separated, the North American crustal plate began moving slowly toward the northwest. The trailing edge of the North American crustal plate sank slowly beneath the sea, while the modern Atlantic Ocean began forming in the ever-widening gap between Africa and North America (figure 12–2). Ever since, new oceanic crust has been forming as basaltic magmas moved up from the depths along the rift between the two plates.

On the floor of the modern Atlantic Ocean, activity in the rift continues to generate new crust. Drilling carried out by the Glomar Challenger in 1968 proved that the rocks of the ocean floor are older near the continental margins and younger near the Mid-Atlantic Ridge. In addition, ancient bands of magnetized rock in the ocean floor indicate that the continents have been moving away from one another since the great rift formed almost 200 million years ago. [190,235–238]

By the close of the Jurassic, the eastern edge of the continent had subsided and was below sea level. As a result, the sea invaded the land, creating a shoreline located near the present Outer Banks. Invertebrate fossils recovered from exploratory oil wells drilled near Hatteras are the only evidence of life in the Car-

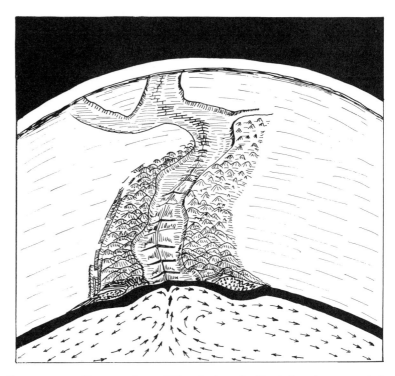

Figure 12–2:   Near the close of Triassic time, the North American crustal plate and the African crustal plates began moving in opposite directions away from a rift zone. On both plates, the trailing edges of the continents were slowly subsiding while the Atlantic Ocean filled the widening gap between the continents.

olinas from this period. Today, the ancient Jurassic muds and sands are buried more than 2,800 meters (9,200 feet) below the surface in the area of the Outer Banks. [3,239–242]

Although erosional forces working in the Carolinas during Jurassic time destroyed any rocks that may have contained evidence of plant and animal life, there is reason to believe that land organisms similar to those living in other areas of the country also flourished in the Carolinas. Fossils from Wyoming and Colorado suggest that the trends begun during Triassic time were continuing.

The forests were populated by pines and conifers, mixed with tree ferns and ginkos. The ground surface beneath the trees was covered by ferns and cycads because the grasses so prevalent today had not yet developed. More than 1,000 species of insects, including many of the modern forms, flew and crawled over the land. In Europe, the first bird-like reptiles appeared in a form that only slightly resembled birds of today. In North Carolina, the Jurassic is simply a nearly blank space in the geologic record. One can only use fossils known elsewhere in the world to make an educated guess about the life forms that might have inhabited the region. [3,239,240]

Part 5

New Land in the East

The Cretaceous was the last period of the Mesozoic era. During the seventy-seven and a half million years of Cretaceous time, the eastern margin of the United States slowly sank and tilted eastward. The North American crustal plate continued moving northwestward, while the Atlantic Ocean basin grew as the gap between North America and Africa widened. Farther south, the African and South American crustal plates were still joined, forming one large land mass. Later in Cretaceous time they separated also, creating the southern Atlantic Ocean.

The majority of Cretaceous time in the Carolinas was characterized by erosion as streams wore down the Appalachian mountain surface. During the last half of the period, the easternmost portion of North Carolina sank slowly below sea level and the ocean invaded what is now the Coastal Plain. At the same time, the rocks of the Blue Ridge and Piedmont rose slightly, causing greater erosion across the central and western portions of the state. Growing deltas built a wedge of mud and sand in the shallow sea. Dinosaurs roamed across the gently rolling Coastal Plain, eating the flourishing plant life and each other! Where conditions were favorable, their remains were buried and preserved, providing a fossil record of their presence.

During Cretaceous time, erosion and uplift generally kept pace with each other. Erosion slowly changed the form of the Piedmont and Blue Ridge. As the sea alternately flooded and retreated from the land, the growing Coastal Plain developed. The result was a gently rolling landscape of low relief across the entire Piedmont. On the Coastal Plain, deposits of limestone, phosphate rich sands and muds, and fossil-laden sands reflect variations in climate and a record of evolving life forms.

13

CRETACEOUS TIME

As the Cretaceous period began, forces within the mantle continued moving the North American crustal plate away from the Mid-Atlantic Ridge. The movement was accompanied by the formation of new oceanic crust produced when basaltic magma moved up from the mantle along the rift zone at the center of the Mid-Atlantic Ridge.

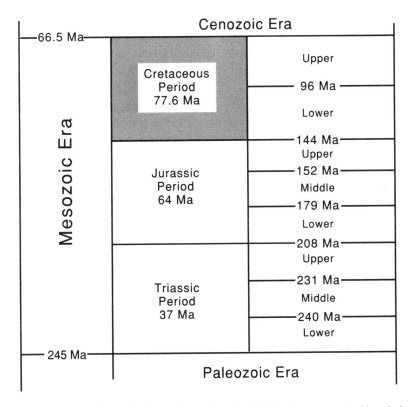

Figure 13–1:   Geologic time column showing the Cretaceous period in relation to the Mesozoic era (Ma = Million years).

Through almost fifty million years that made up the early and middle portions of Cretaceous time, erosion was the dominant process shaping the land. As weathering broke down the rocks, streams carried the debris east and west from the Appalachian landmass. The removal of rock produced **isostatic**[1] changes in the mantle that raised the underlying rock layers. As a result, the Blue Ridge and Piedmont provinces were not worn down to sea level, but were slowly reduced to a surface of very gently rolling hills called a **peneplain**.

As the continent moved northwestward, the trailing edge of the crustal plate slowly sank. East of the Piedmont, the easternmost portion of the Coastal Plain sank below sea level. The ocean responded by invading the land, shifting the shoreline westward across the surface of eroded igneous and metamorphic rocks. Streams, flowing eastward, were carrying debris from the Piedmont and Blue Ridge to the ocean's edge. There the streams deposited the material, building a wedge of sand and mud over the ancient eroded surface. [2,3,239−245]

The peneplain surface that developed during early and middle Cretaceous time stretched across today's Blue Ridge, Piedmont, and Coastal Plain provinces. Material worn away during those years was deposited east of our modern shoreline where it now forms the lowest portions of the continental shelf. Fossils and samples from these sediments have been obtained from deep wells. The samples contain fossils that reflect a mixture of marine and brackish water communities. The sedimentary record suggests that shallow estuaries and delta environments developed where rivers deposited their loads of sediment in the ocean waters.

---

1. Isostatic changes occur because the crust floats on more dense mantle rock. When rock is removed from an area, pressure from the mantle pushes the lightened crust upward. In the same way, deposition of sediment in an area increases its mass, causing it to sink.

Construction of the Coastal Plain Begins

The earliest deposits exposed on the Coastal Plain also reflect a mixture of shallow estuaries and deltas. On the western edge of the province, in Moore County, interbedded layers of "clayey" sand and sandy clays were deposited in a shallow marine environment (figure 13–2). Other outcrops of this unit, called the Cape Fear Formation, occur in counties along the western edge of the Coastal Plain (see Appendix B). The deposits lack evidence of animal life, but fossil pollen in the sediments reflect plant life typical of about one hundred million years ago. [248] Farther east the layers are much thicker, but they in turn are buried beneath hundreds, or even thousands, of feet of overlying younger sediment. [2,3,239,240,250–252]

As time passed, the crust beneath the developing Coastal Plain continued to subside, causing the shoreline to migrate farther west. Streams and rivers flowing into the rising sea built new deltas over the older sands and muds of the Cape Fear Formation. The new deposits, called the Middendorf Formation, were formed by meandering streams which deposited layers of mud and sand as they swept back and forth across a low-lying delta plain (see Appendix B). Clumps of clay which were rolled along the channel bottoms are preserved in the layers, along with crossbedding created by the currents. [2,245,251,252]

In South Carolina and Georgia, lens-shaped bodies of a commercial grade clay called kaolin are found in the Middendorf For-

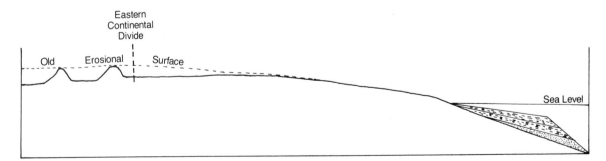

Figure 13–2:   One hundred million years ago the western edge of the Atlantic Ocean was located just east of the present western edge of the Coastal Plain. The deposits of the Cape Fear Formation were laid down by streams which built a thick wedge of interlayered muds and sands on the eroded surface of the ancient Appalachians. [239]

mation. Kaolin is composed of a group of clay minerals that produce a white porcelain china when heated to high temperatures. Josiah Wedgewood sent Thomas Griffiths to South Carolina in 1767 in search of clay for his company's china. He apparently ignored clay deposits in the Coastal Plain and instead collected a "tun of fine clay" from a site called Ayoree in what is now Macon County North Carolina. That clay was most likely produced by weathering of feldspar-rich gneiss. There is no evidence that Wedgewood ever expressed further interest in the clays of the Carolinas as a raw material for his fine china. Today, the kaolin, mined in South Carolina and Georgia, is used as a raw material in the manufacture of paper, rubber, refractories, ceramics, and paint. [253,254]

The original western extent of the Middendorf deposits will never be known because erosion has destroyed much of the original deposit. The present-day western boundary of the Middendorf Formation stretches from South Carolina to exposures around the town of Fuquay-Varina in southwestern Wake County. The ancient delta deposits also cover much of Moore, Harnett, and Johnston counties. Farther east, the unit is covered by younger deposits. The buried layers form a wedge of sediment that ranges in thickness from 90 to 120 meters (300–400 feet) beneath the eastern Coastal Plain. The beds were formed from the enormous quantity of eroded material that was carried east from the Piedmont and Blue Ridge during this time. [239]

The climate was warm and a variety of trees grew in the swamps of the Middendorf deltas. In Harnett and Cumberland counties, fossils—formed when fragments of wood were replaced with silica—preserve the characteristic structure of one tree fern which grew in the area. The fern-like trees, called *Tempskya*, grew to heights of three to five meters (10–17 feet). The plant took the form of hundreds of stems that were bound up into one "trunk" by a network of roots and rootlets (figure 13–3). [255–259]

The trailing edge of the westward-moving North American crustal plate sank unevenly throughout Cretaceous time. Near the North Carolina–South Carolina border a large ridge of basement rock slopes gently southeastward from a point northwest of Fayetteville, in Cumberland County, to a point well beyond the present coast line. The arch slopes unevenly to the northeast and southwest, reaching a depth of 1,500 meters (4,900 feet) near

Figure 13–3: The Cretaceous tree fern Tempskya was formed from a large number of individual stems bound together by a matrix of roots. In contrast to modern trees and tree ferns, these plants had large numbers of small fronds on the upper portions of the "trunk." [255]

Cape Lookout in North Carolina, and 760 meters (2,500 feet) near Cape Romain in South Carolina. There has been much speculation concerning the origin of the so-called Cape Fear Arch. The best evidence suggests that the arch was formed over a long period as minor uplifts along the center line of the present arch interrupted the general sinking motion of the crust underlying the Coastal Plain (figure 13–4). [3,239,242]

The Coastal Plain was flooded for many of the millions of years that made up the Cretaceous period, but the actual position of the shoreline and the depth of the sea changed rather rapidly when considered in geologic terms. The changes are reflected in the sediments deposited on the Coastal Plain. An example of one such change occurs in sediments of the Middendorf Formation buried beneath the surface of Martin, Bertie, and Hertford

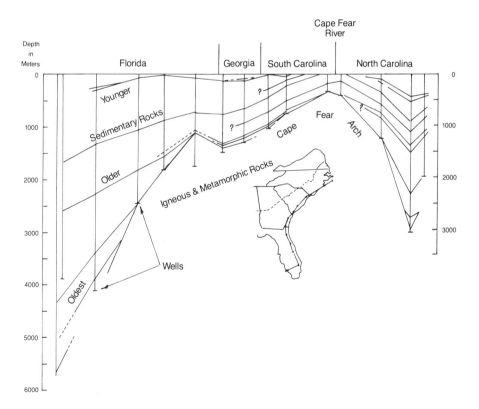

Figure 13–4: This diagram shows a cross section of the Cape Fear Arch as reconstructed from well logs. The numbers above vertical lines in the diagram represent the location of each well. The draping of sediments over the igneous and metamorphic rocks of the crust beneath the arch reflect the slow uplift along the arch. [242]

counties. There, the predominantly marine environment changed to a lagoon filled with fresh to brackish water and populated by invertebrate animals and plants. After a few million years, the environment changed back to the saline character of the open sea. Such changes are typical of the entire sedimentary record on the Coastal Plain.

The upper surface of the Middendorf Formation reveals a period of erosion that was caused either by an uplift of the land surface or a drop in sea level. The sea withdrew completely from the Coastal Plain and erosion at once began to carve the newly exposed surface. The brief period of erosion produced a distinct break in the sedimentary record that marks the erosional episode. [239–244]

Dinosaurs Flourish Near the Early Sounds

During the next seventeen or eighteen million years, the water near shore was very shallow. The dominant environment was one of swamps and wandering shallow streams which flowed eastward toward a constantly shifting shoreline. Fine sand and gray-to-black shales which were deposited during this time contain numerous fragments of lignitized (carbonized) and petrified wood. The layers of light gray sands alternating dark gray-to-black sediment are known as the Black Creek Formation (see Appendix B). The deposits contain a variety of fossils, including abundant foraminifera and a few shark teeth. Detailed studies in the Goldsboro (Wayne County) and Fayetteville (Cumberland County) areas suggest that sedimentary conditions were dominated by shallow estuaries and tidal flats.

The Black Creek Formation is presently thought to be one portion of a large delta that was growing southeastward from the coast in North and South Carolina. Streams carrying loads of sand and mud from their sources in the Piedmont deposited the materials in the waters of the Atlantic.

In North Carolina a delta plain was constructed at, or just above, sea level, in Robeson and Bladen counties. Beneath the ocean surface, finer sediments were deposited along the front edge of the delta in Cumberland, Sampson, and Duplin counties. The very fine silt and mud typical of a continental shelf make up the sediments in Lenoir, Wayne, and Greene counties. Later, erosion destroyed some of the southeastern portions of the delta. Then the remaining fragments were buried by younger sediments. Today, only the sediments of the Black Creek Formation record the existence of a much larger delta that once existed in the region (figure 13–5). [263]

Fossils of plants which produced seed-bearing fruits appear in North Carolina for the first time in this unit. Today, these **angiosperms** are the dominant form of plant life on the earth's surface. Many well-known members of this group—including mag-

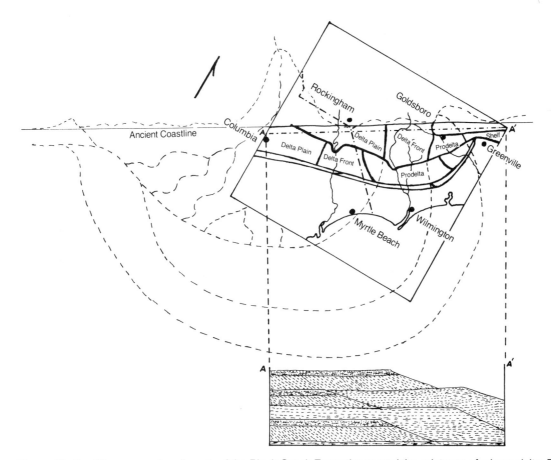

Figure 13–5:   The exposed sediments of the Black Creek Formation record the existence of a large delta. The majority of the delta has since been buried by younger sediments or destroyed by erosion. The relation of the existing exposed Black Creek sediments (units labeled I) to the original delta is shown by the bold dashed lines. Sedimentary units marked II, III, and IV represent older portions of the delta. [263]

nolia, sassafras, maple, and sumac which now live in the Carolinas—first grew here in the swamps of **Black Creek time**[2] approximately 80 to 90 million years ago. The size and number of fragments of lignitized and petrified wood suggest that dense growth occurred in the swamps. Petrified trunks of conifers more than a meter (±4 feet) in diameter may be seen in various sand **borrow-pits**[3] along with smaller logs and stumps of many other species (plate 38). [245,260–266]

Around the world, the Cretaceous period witnessed the development of dinosaurs into the gigantic forms for which they are justly famous. Carnosaurs, ceratopsians, sauropods, tyrannosaurs, and their relatives were dominant land creatures. Ichthyosaurs, plesiosaurs, and mosasaurs dominated life in the seas. The giant reptiles ruled until the end of the period when most of their kind became extinct.

Phoebus Landing is located on the banks of the Cape Fear River, about four miles below Elizabethtown in Bladen County. There, the slowly moving river has uncovered an ancient bed of sandy clay that probably formed in a swampy stream or river during Black Creek time. Many bone fragments have been recovered from the muddy river banks. The bone fragments, and others from similar deposits near Clinton in Sampson County, provide a picture of a diverse animal population.

Small bones and fragments indicate the presence of marine fish and turtles. A number of teeth, collected at various times, suggest that a relatively large number of ghost sharks, which grew to lengths of about four meters (13 feet), swam in the lagoons and tidal rivers. A smaller number of galeoid and hybodont sharks also swam in the brackish waters. There were sawfish and rhinopterid rays, but the most ferocious occupants of the lagoons were members of the marine lizard family called mosasaurs (figure 13–6).

Bone fragments from dinosaurs which lived near the shore have also been found in the sandy clay of the deposit at Phoebus Landing. It seems likely that the bones were trapped when dead carcasses floated downstream and were trapped by a sand bar.

2. The term Black Creek time refers to the part of geologic time during which the Black Creek Formation was deposited.

3. The term borrow-pit is applied to shallow pits where sand or gravel are removed by drag lines, dredges, or front-end loaders.

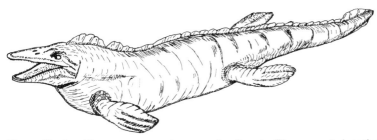

Figure 13–6: Mosasaurs were large marine lizards. They grew to lengths of 9 meters (29.5 feet). Their sharp teeth and strong tails equipped them for eating fish and a variety of other vertebrates.

The fossils suggest that at least four different dinosaurs inhabited the highlands and swampy terrain during Black Creek time. [267]

Hypsibema crassicauda was a duckbilled dinosaur that probably weighed 1,400–1,800 kilograms (3,000 to 4,000 pounds). The bipedal animal is believed to have stood about three meters (10 feet) tall and was nine meters (30 feet) long (figure 13–7). Remains of a smaller, flat-headed duckbill dinosaur have also been found. Both genera are believed to have walked on their hind legs and used their tails for balance. These dinosaurs probably lived in, or very close to, the Black Creek swamps and ate aquatic plants.

Ornithomimus was a hollow-boned coelurosaur that looked very much like a modern-day ostrich. It was slightly less that five meters (16 feet) long and stood a little more than two meters (7 feet) high. The mouth had a flattened hard beak that is believed to have been used to eat insects, fruits, plants, and perhaps smaller reptiles (figure 13–8).

Dryptosaurus was a medium-sized carnivorous dinosaur with a body about 10 meters (33 feet) long. The animal appears to have had a short muscular neck and powerful hind legs which allowed it to leap upon its prey. *Dryptosaurus* balanced on its hind legs and used its claws and sharp teeth to tear flesh from its victims (figure 13–9).

A gigantic crocodile, *Deinosuchus rugosus*, also inhabited the area. Careful study of its fossil remains suggests that *Deinosuchus* grew to lengths of 12 meters (39 feet) and probably included other dinosaurs in its diet.

Figure 13—7:   Hypsibema crassicauda was a huge duckbilled dinosaur that may have weighed 1,800 kilograms and stood three meters high. [268]

The fragments of bone that make up the Black Creek fossils reveal only a small part of what must have been a diverse population, yet the fragmentary picture reveals that the shifting shallow lagoons and tidal flats were home to a considerable variety of animals. There is no reason to believe that they did not also live in other parts of the Carolinas. Unfortunately, the lack of an extensive fossil record makes it impossible to verify their presence. [267—272]

The early years of Black Creek time were characterized by the deposition of dark-colored sands and muds in a deltaic environment. The younger portions of the formation indicate that conditions were changing. As sea level rose, the slightly raised marshes and flats of the delta gave way to partially enclosed shal-

Figure 13-8:   Ornithomimus was an ostrich-like dinosaur that stood about two meters high. [268]

Figure 13-9:   Dryptosaurus was a carnivorous dinosaur of medium size. The animal is thought to have used its strong hind legs to leap upon its prey. [268]

low bays. The change to shallow marine bays introduced more sand where, in earlier years, stagnant waters had allowed the deposition of mud rich in iron sulfide. Constantly shifting sands and water circulating into the new lagoons eliminated the sulfide deposits. As a result, the layers of the upper portions of the Black Creek Formation consist of sandier, lime-rich clays called **marls**. The drab gray marl often contains shells, shell fragments, and shell casts left behind by the animals which lived on the muddy bottom.

The Sea Deepens

During the closing years of Cretaceous time, approximately 80 to 66 million years ago, the lagoonal waters were replaced by a shallow, gently sloping, continental shelf. As sea level continued to rise, the marls of the Black Creek Formation were covered by layers of marine sediment that geologists call the Pee Dee Formation (see Appendix B).

The marine deposits of the Pee Dee Formation consist primarily of dark gray and green sands. Layers of dark-colored marine clay are interbedded with the sands, and most of the layers contain some limestone. In places, individual layers are so lime-rich that they are described as impure limestones and often occur as irregular masses which produce bands of nodules in the bluffs along the lower portions of the Cape Fear River. Fossil shells of marine invertebrates, such as mollusks, occur in layers up to one meter (3 feet) thick. Shark teeth are also scattered through the layers, but bones are rare. [245,273–275]

The most interesting fossils from this formation are a few bone fragments of a short-necked marine reptile called a plesiosaur. While many plesiosaurs had long necks, the fossils found in the banks of the Pee Dee River in Richmond County came from a short-necked species (figure 13–10). All the plesiosaurs had streamlined shapes and strong, paddle-shaped limbs which they used to propel themselves through their ocean environment. [245,276]

Toward the end of Cretaceous time, a series of sand bars formed along the seaward extension of the Cape Fear Arch. Uplift

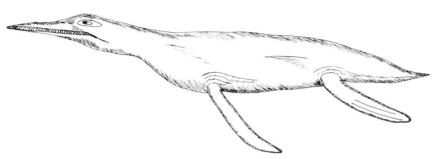

Figure 13–10:   This artist's recreation of Trinacromerum is thought to resemble the type of short-necked Plesiosaur whose remains were found along the Banks of the Pee Dee River in Richmond County. [268]

along the arch caused a submarine ridge to form where the arch stretched under the continental shelf. Currents swirling around the ridge produced an ancient complex of sand bars and shell beds that seem to have formed a cape projecting out into the ancient ocean. These layers are now referred to as the Rocky Point **member**[4] of the Pee Dee Formation. [277]

Events on the Piedmont and Blue Ridge

While deposition was the dominant process in eastern North Carolina during Cretaceous time, erosion dominated the Piedmont and Blue Ridge provinces. Streams removed weathered material and carried it to the developing Coastal Plain. The crust rose slowly in response to the removal of weathered and eroded rock. The rate at which the land rose seems to have matched the rate of erosion. As a result, the upland surface of the Piedmont and Blue Ridge was maintained as a nearly flat or very gently rolling surface known as a peneplain. Evidence suggests that the peneplain sloped toward the east with a generally uniform slope of about 1.5 meters per kilometer (5 feet/mile). [281,282]

4. The Rocky Point Member of the Pee Dee Formation is also referred to as the Scots Bend Member in some literature.

Near the end of Cretaceous time, the sea withdrew from eastern North Carolina and streams carved an erosional surface over the entire Coastal Plain. Throughout the world, this time is marked by significant mass extinctions, the most famous of which were of the dinosaurs. The giant reptiles which had roamed across the Cretaceous Coastal Plain of North Carolina all became extinct. However, they were only a few of thousands of species which disappeared from the face of the earth, making room for other animal forms to expand their domains.

14
THE FINAL ERA OPENS

The **Cenozoic** era covers a span of only sixty-six million years, yet the era contains a geologic record that is far more complete than any other time in earth history. Cenozoic time is usually divided into three major divisions referred to as the **Paleogene**, **Neogene**, and **Quaternary** periods. Because of the completeness of the geologic record in North Carolina, we will further divide Cenozoic time into subdivisions known as epochs.

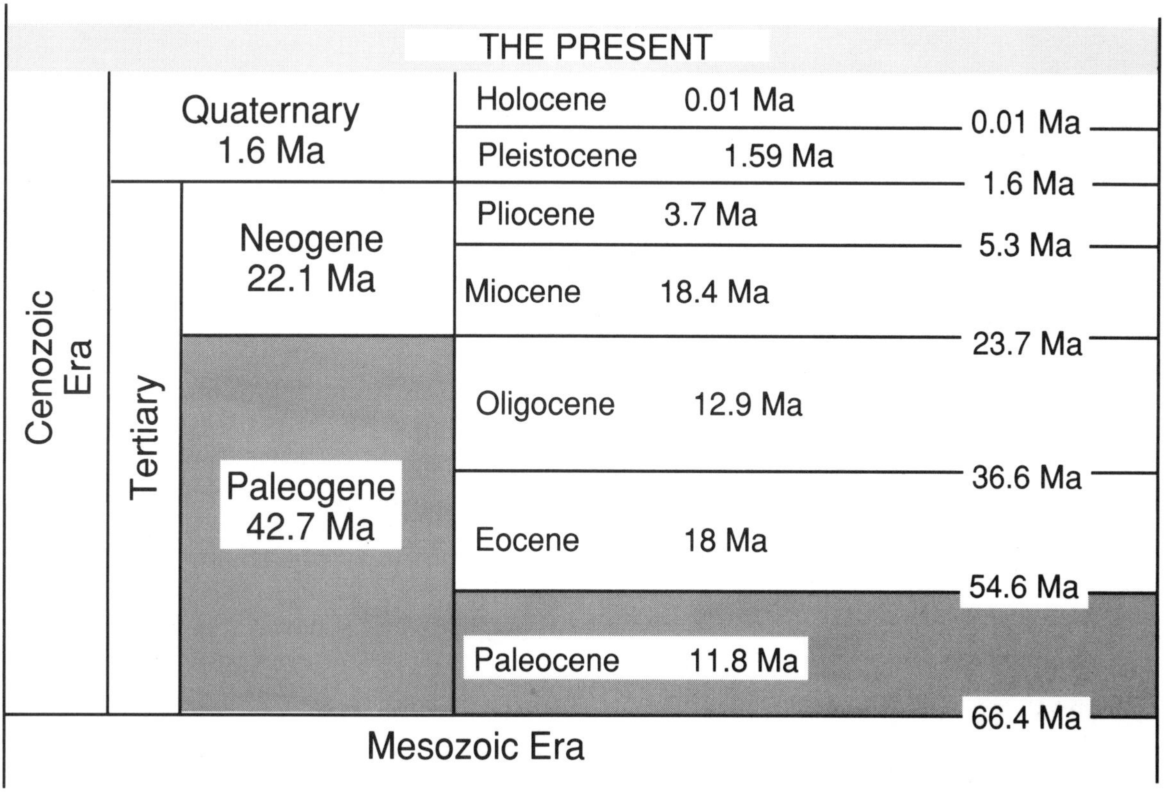

THE PRESENT			
Quaternary 1.6 Ma	Holocene 0.01 Ma		0.01 Ma
	Pleistocene 1.59 Ma		1.6 Ma
Neogene 22.1 Ma	Pliocene 3.7 Ma		5.3 Ma
	Miocene 18.4 Ma		23.7 Ma
Paleogene 42.7 Ma	Oligocene 12.9 Ma		36.6 Ma
	Eocene 18 Ma		54.6 Ma
	Paleocene 11.8 Ma		66.4 Ma

(Cenozoic Era; Tertiary; Mesozoic Era)

Figure 14–1: Geologic time column showing the Paleocene epoch in relation to the Cenozoic era. The term "Tertiary" is shown on this chart because it is used in many older publications and textbooks (Ma = Million years).

The oldest period, the Paleogene, is divided into three epochs known as the Paleocene, Eocene, and Oligocene. The second major division, known as the Neogene period, is divided into the Miocene and Pliocene epochs. The youngest division, the Quaternary period, is divided into the Pleistocene and Holocene epochs. The Holocene epoch is often referred to as recent, or modern, time and those terms will be used here.

Erosion Creates a New Land Surface in the West

Little is known about the events that occurred during the first epoch of the Cenozoic era in North Carolina. From the area of today's mountains to the coast, the land had been leveled by erosion. Wide, meandering rivers were finishing the task of smoothing the land. The streams had been at work since Cretaceous time when they carried vast loads of sand and mud to the growing wedge of sediment offshore. The carving and smoothing resulted in a gently rolling peneplain surface that sloped gently toward the sea. In the ocean, deposition continued, as mud and sand were added to the growing continental shelf.

The continent was still moving northwestward, while the crust responded to changing conditions in the underlying mantle by slowly rising or sinking. During Paleocene time, the southeastern region of the submerged Coastal Plain moved upward, lifting portions of the Cape Fear Arch clear of the sea. Erosion immediately began destroying some of the newly exposed portions of the Pee Dee and Black Creek formations.

In the northern portion of the state's submerged Coastal Plain the land was not pushed upward and, as a result, the shoreline was located farther west. A thin layer of sediment, about 4.6 meters (15 feet) thick was deposited on the shallow bottom of the continental shelf. The first evidence of this deposit was discovered in wells. Later, a surface exposure was found along the banks of Mosley Creek where it forms the boundary between Lenoir and Craven counties northeast of Kinston (see Appendix B).

The unit, now called the Beaufort Formation, is composed of alternating layers of fine mud, sand, and limy sediment which contain numerous fossils. Geologists have used a combination of evidence from **microfossils** and **radiometric** data to date the deposit. The evidence indicates that the layers were deposited about 64.5 million years ago. The fossils and sediments also suggest that deposition took place under rapidly changing conditions on a shallow continental shelf. One interesting feature in these layers is the presence of the mineral **cristobalite**. The mineral, which forms only at very high temperatures, has been interpreted as a "volcanic ash" because it occurs here in very fine grains. The material was probably transported by the wind and suggests that volcanic activity was occurring not too far from North Carolina. [245,278–280]

The crust beneath North Carolina rose slowly in response to erosion of the land surface, and by the end of Paleocene time, the entire Coastal Plain was above sea level. Across the Piedmont, streams which had first created the peneplain during the Mesozoic era responded to the uplift by cutting down into the land surface. Because the downcutting began slowly, the streams continued to flow in the wandering (meandering) channels that had developed earlier on the nearly flat land surface. As time passed, the downward erosion caused the streams to entrench the old meandering channels. Today, many of the stream channels on the eastern edge of the Piedmont reflect that ancient uplift. One of the best examples of such entrenched meandering occurs in northern Wake County. There, the increased rate of erosion caused the Neuse River to cut down along the path of its wandering channel, preserving its ancient course. [281,282]

As the Eocene epoch began almost 58 million years ago, erosion was taking place across all of modern North Carolina. Through the first 10 million years of the epoch, erosion continued and streams produced a distinct erosional surface on the Coastal Plain. Then, about 47 million years ago, earthquakes jolted the Atlantic seaboard. In Highland County, Virginia, near the West Virginia border, magma invaded the limestones which had formed during Ordovician time. The intruding magma created a number of **andesite**[1] dikes and sills. There may have been

---

1. Andesite is a dark-colored, fine-grained extrusive igneous rock that is formed from a magma containing plagioclase feldspar and less than 50 percent biotite. Andesite is commonly associated with tectonic activity that causes magma to form deep within the crust.

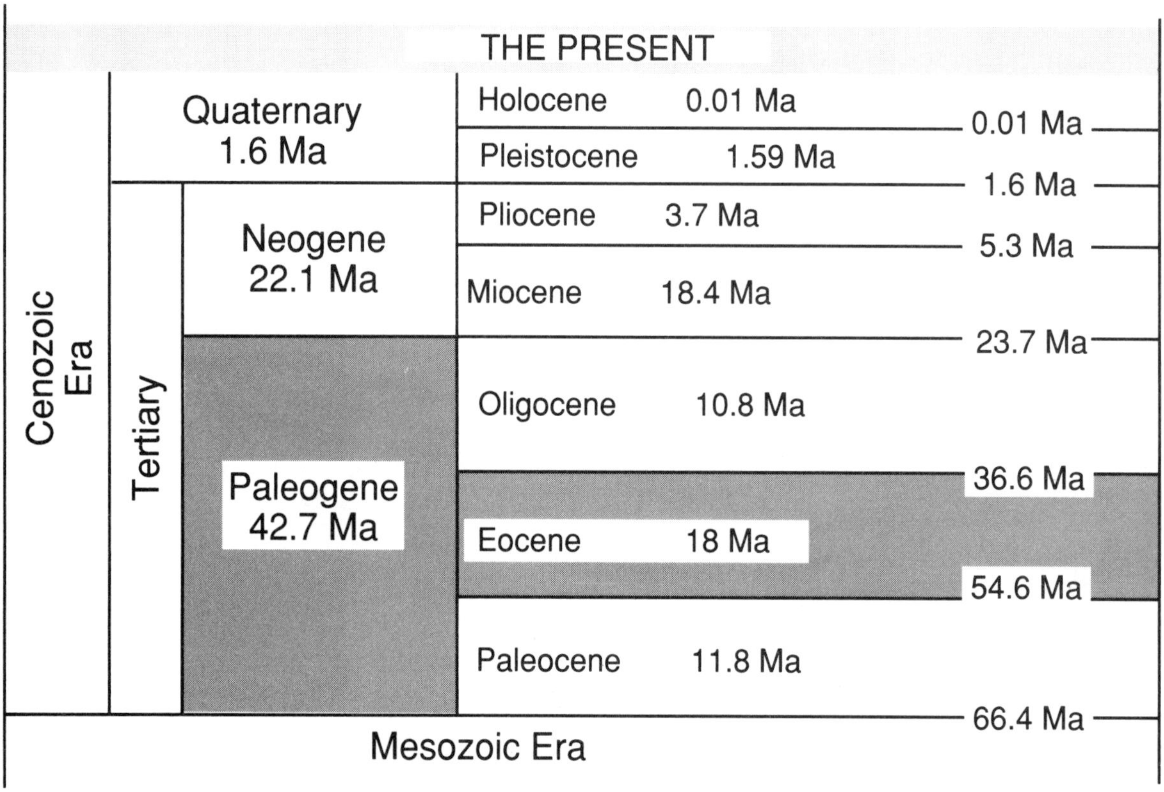

THE PRESENT			
Quaternary 1.6 Ma	Holocene	0.01 Ma	0.01 Ma
	Pleistocene	1.59 Ma	1.6 Ma
Neogene 22.1 Ma	Pliocene	3.7 Ma	5.3 Ma
	Miocene	18.4 Ma	23.7 Ma
Paleogene 42.7 Ma	Oligocene	10.8 Ma	36.6 Ma
	Eocene	18 Ma	54.6 Ma
	Paleocene	11.8 Ma	66.4 Ma

(left side labels: Cenozoic Era, Tertiary)

Mesozoic Era

Figure 14–2: Geologic time column showing the Eocene epoch in relation to the Cenozoic era. The term "Tertiary" is shown on this chart because it is used in many older publications and textbooks (Ma = Million years).

volcanic eruptions, but erosion has destroyed any cones or other evidence that might have existed to prove that the magma erupted above the land surface. [283]

Limestone Deposits on the Ocean Floor

At about the same time as the volcanic eruptions, the crust beneath the Coastal Plain began sinking and the ocean once again moved across the land. Evidence suggests that the water rose higher than in the past, pushing the ocean's edge onto today's Piedmont surface. As the ocean covered the land, a thin layer of phosphate-rich pebbles and other debris was deposited on the eroded surface. Warm, semi-tropical conditions allowed the growth of large amounts of calcareous green algae in the deepening waters. As each succeeding generation died, very fine grains of lime sank slowly to the ocean floor. During the next six million years, a thick layer of lime-rich mud was deposited on the sea floor along with the bones and shells of other animals living in the warm ocean water.

Studies indicate that the sea was probably between 30 and 50 meters (98–164 feet) deep except in the area of the Cape Fear Arch, where the maximum depth was less than five meters (16 feet). Near the present coastline, the water was too deep for wave action to stir the loose bottom sediments. A varied community of bryozoans, pelecypods, and other invertebrates grew rapidly in that area in response to nutrient-rich waters moving onto the continental shelf from the deep ocean. Farther west, in shallower water, wave action stirred the life on the sea floor and burrowing organisms reworked the sediments by tunneling through the debris in search of food.

With the passage of time, the limy mud was consolidated into limestone. Later, ground water moving through the rock leached away most of the original shell material, leaving behind only molds and occasional shells. Today, the rock is easy to recognize because of its characteristic grey-to-brown color and the presence of many fossil molds of mollusks. This limestone, called the Castle Hayne Formation, is quarried in various sites from Wilmington to New Bern and Rose Hill (see Appendix B). After crushing, the limestone is used for road construction and as railroad ballast. Larger blocks are quarried and used in the construction of sea walls and as decorative stone (plate 39).

In those places where shells are abundant, studies of the Castle Hayne Formation have revealed a varied population of marine animal life. The diverse collection includes more than two hundred species of bryozoans, thirty-one different pelecypods, thirty-six gastropods, two cephalopods, five brachiopods, four anthozoans, and one kind of echinoderm. Occasional whale bones and shark teeth are also scattered through the fossil-laden limestone. [245, 284–299]

Near the town of Castle Hayne in New Hanover County, two areas have been recognized in the upper portions of the formation where sponges made layers on the sea floor. Fossils from these so-called "hardgrounds" represent an abundance of sponges, bryozoans, and marine, boring organisms. [294]

One small deposit of volcanic ash called **bentonite** occurs in the Castle Hayne Formation. The ash particles are thought to have been carried by winds and dropped into the ocean. Various geologists have suggested that the ash may have come from the volcanic center in Virginia or from eruptions that were forming the island of Bermuda. [299]

As the years of Eocene time came and went, events once again caused the sea to retreat from the land. About forty-five million years ago, streams began eroding the newly formed limestone. Surface waters rapidly carved the surface, creating channels, while water percolating downward dissolved the limestone, producing small **sinkholes** (figure 14–3).

In geologic terms, the period of erosion was brief, and when the sea rose once again the shoreline moved inland as far as the present-day city of New Bern in Craven County. During the next four million years currents reworked sediment from the land, forming a series of sandy beds now known as the New Bern Mem-

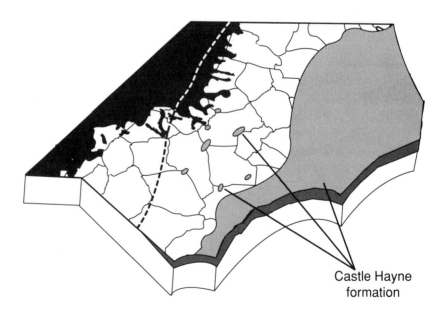

Castle Hayne formation

Figure 14–3: This map shows the estimated western extent of the Castle Hayne sea (westernmost dashed line). The small patches of rock and the massive portion of the formation remaining today are shaded. [239]

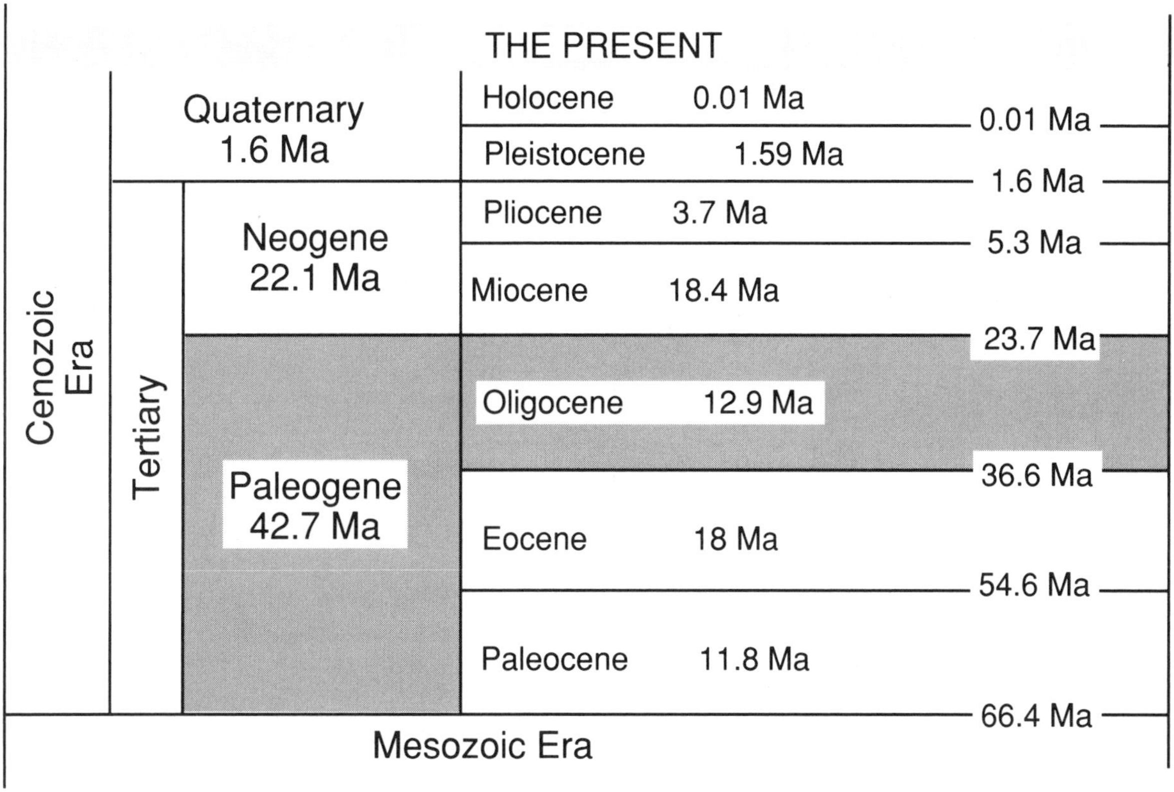

		THE PRESENT		
Cenozoic Era	Quaternary 1.6 Ma	Holocene	0.01 Ma	0.01 Ma
		Pleistocene	1.59 Ma	1.6 Ma
	Neogene 22.1 Ma (Tertiary)	Pliocene	3.7 Ma	5.3 Ma
		Miocene	18.4 Ma	23.7 Ma
	Paleogene 42.7 Ma	Oligocene	12.9 Ma	36.6 Ma
		Eocene	18 Ma	54.6 Ma
		Paleocene	11.8 Ma	66.4 Ma
Mesozoic Era				

Figure 14–4:   Geologic time column showing the Oligocene epoch in relation to the Cenozoic era. The term "Tertiary" is shown on this chart because it is used in many older publications and textbooks (Ma = Million years).

ber of the Castle Hayne Formation. Waves and tides in the surf zone deposited crossbedded layers of sand that indicate the high energy conditions which existed near shore. Farther east, sandy sediment was being deposited on a gently sloping continental shelf. Fossils from these layers reveal that the climate had cooled from the tropical conditions of early-and middle-Eocene time to more temperate conditions similar to our present climate (figure 14–4). [291]

Erosion and Beach Deposits Change the Coastal Plain

About forty million years ago, changing conditions once again caused the sea to retreat from the land, allowing erosion to carve the entire Coastal Plain surface. The erosional event that followed the deposition of the Castle Hayne Formation began in late Eocene time and continued until the middle of the Oligocene epoch, about twelve million years later. The result was a major break in the geologic record of events. Some sedimentary units were deposited far to the east, but they are known only from well cores. None of the deposits can be seen on the modern land surface. [239]

About thirty-one million years ago, the sea advanced once again, pushing the shoreline westward to a point near New Bern in Craven County. As the water slowly deepened, layers of sand and sandy limestone, now called the River Bend Formation, were deposited in the eastern portions of the Coastal Plain (figure 14–5) (see also Appendix B). The formation consists of three distinct units. The oldest reflects a deepening sea with a surf zone moving westward. The second unit was deposited on a shallow,

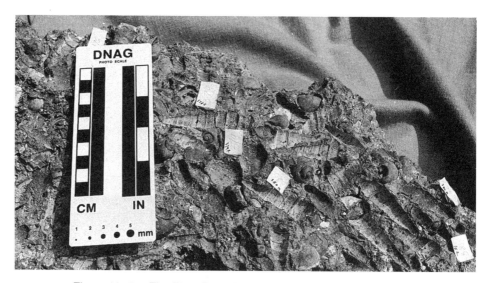

Figure 14–5: The River Bend Formation includes sandy limestones that contain numerous fossil pelecypods.

gently sloping, continental shelf. The sandy limestone layers of the shelf deposits contain fossil pelecypods which indicate that the water ranged from a depth of seven to 40 meters (23–131 feet). The uppermost portion of the formation is also characterized by surf-zone deposits. However, unlike those of the first unit, the crossbedded sands were deposited as the water became shallower and the edge of the sea once again retreated eastward. [245,290,300,301]

The retreating ocean once again changed direction and moved west, covering a relatively small area that now encompasses Onslow, Carteret, and Jones counties. There, deposits of sand and sandy clay containing numerous shells and barnacles reflect a shoreline deposit known as the Belgrade Formation. The deposits are best seen near the towns of Belgrade and Silverdale in Onslow County. During a brief drop in the sea level, streams carved channels into, and in some cases, completely through the Belgrade beds into the older layers of the River Bend Formation. Enormous oysters (up to 0.3 meters or 12 inches long), called *Crassostrea gigantissima*, grew in the channels. In some cases, the oysters were so numerous that they produced bar deposits of shells on the shallow floor of the rising sea (plate 40). [245,301]

Shortly after the beginning of the Miocene epoch, the sea once again withdrew completely from the modern Coastal Plain. During the next one or two million years, erosion was once again the dominant process across all of North Carolina. [301,302]

Part
6

A Familiar
Landscape

By about 1.7 million years ago, streams had carved a familiar landscape across the Piedmont and Blue Ridge provinces of North Carolina. Far north of the Carolinas, continental ice sheets began their cycles of advance and retreat. While glacial ice never reached North Carolina, considerable cooling did occur over the inland counties. The change to a cooler climate had a profound effect on the plant and animal communities. On the Coastal Plain, the sea level rose and fell in response to the growth and retreat of ice sheets around the North and South poles. As the shoreline advanced and retreated, a series of beach **scarps** and terraces formed, stretching from the Piedmont's edge out onto the presently flooded continental shelf. Following the most recent retreat of the ice beginning some 18,000 years ago, the sea level began rising. The advancing ocean began building a sequence of barrier islands along the length of the coast line. Meanwhile, prevailing winds carved and shaped elliptical lakes and swamps known as the Carolina Bays on the sandy surface of the Coastal Plain. Today, the same processes that have worked over millions of years to shape the state are still changing the land. Only man's activity may interrupt the process, and even then the interruption may be only temporary.

15
NEOGENE TIME

The Neogene period is the second major division of the Cenozoic era. The period is subdivided into two epochs known as the
Miocene and Pliocene. The period began about 23 million years
ago and lasted until the beginning of Quaternary time—
1,650,000 years before the present.

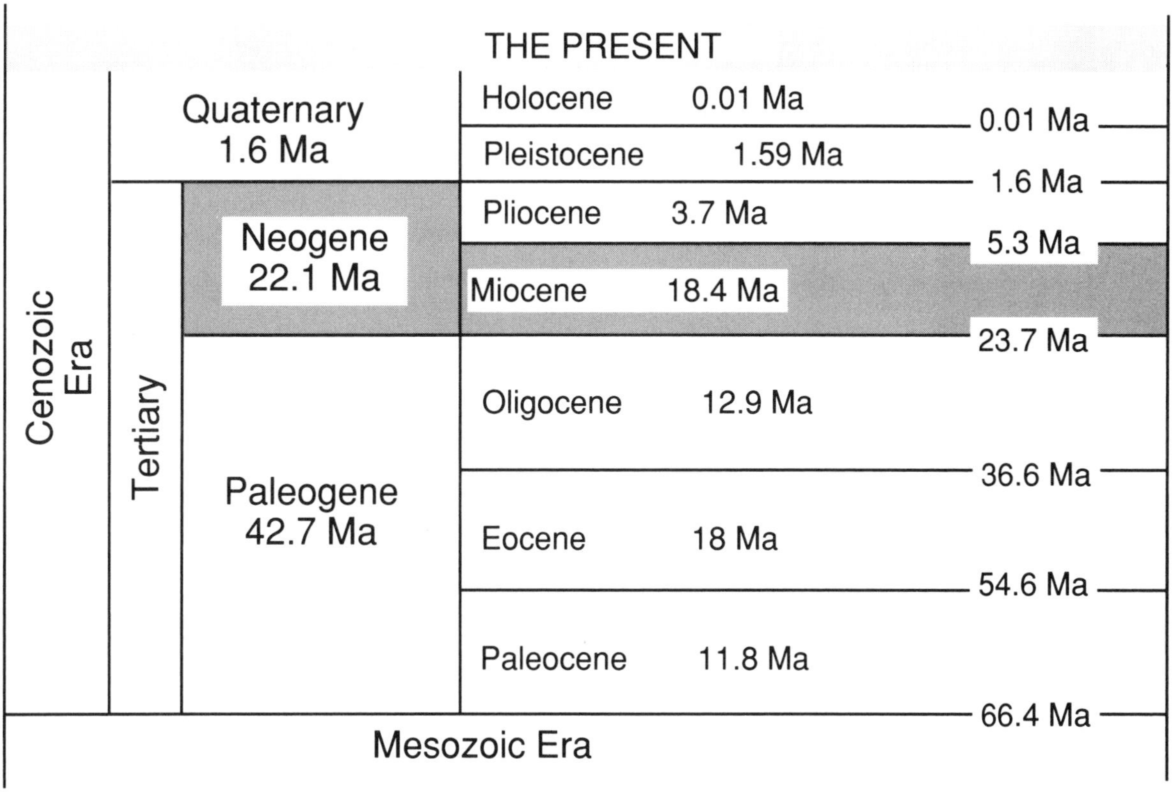

			THE PRESENT	
Cenozoic Era		Quaternary 1.6 Ma	Holocene 0.01 Ma	0.01 Ma
			Pleistocene 1.59 Ma	1.6 Ma
	Tertiary	Neogene 22.1 Ma	Pliocene 3.7 Ma	5.3 Ma
			Miocene 18.4 Ma	23.7 Ma
		Paleogene 42.7 Ma	Oligocene 12.9 Ma	36.6 Ma
			Eocene 18 Ma	54.6 Ma
			Paleocene 11.8 Ma	66.4 Ma
Mesozoic Era				

Figure 15–1:   Geologic time column showing the Miocene epoch in relation to the Cenozoic era
(Ma = Million years).

Erosional Changes in the Blue Ridge and Piedmont

In the Piedmont and Blue Ridge provinces, erosion, which had begun with the raising of the Appalachians, was still reducing the land. During the preceding 200 million years weathering and erosion had combined to destroy the mountains and to **peneplain**[1] the land surface. Uplift of the gently rolling land surface during earlier portions of the Cenozoic era had caused the streams which had been meandering over the nearly flat surface to begin cutting down along their channels. The entrenchment of the streams slowly lowered the land surface until a new surface called the Schooley Peneplain was developed nearer sea level.

The new peneplain sloped slowly upward from the edge of the Coastal Plain to a line near today's town of Ridge Crest in Mc-Dowell County, and then downward into modern Tennessee and Kentucky. Along the line which stretched away to the northeast and southwest, a major erosional divide was developing. Today, the line is know as the Eastern Continental Divide and follows the crest of the eroded Appalachians from Georgia to Maine (figure 15–2). [3]

Streams flowing eastward dropped rapidly toward the sea. Those flowing west from the line had a much greater distance to travel before the water could flow into the Mississippi River and

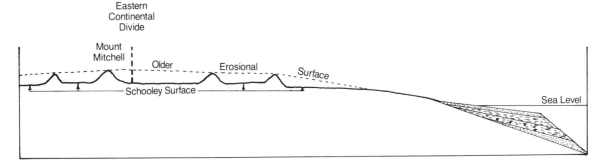

Figure 15–2:   The Schooley Peneplain surface was produced when streams eroded the ancient land surface in the Piedmont and Blue Ridge provinces. The ancient surface is represented in the Blue Ridge by the tops of erosionally resistant remnants such as Mount Mitchell.

---

1. The term peneplain means "almost a plain" and refers to a land surface that has been eroded nearly to sea level. The surface of a peneplain is usually very gently rolling with little relief.

hence to sea level in the Gulf of Mexico. The difference in stream gradients (slope in meters per kilometer) on either side of the line resulted in marked differences in the speed of the flowing water and its resulting erosive power. Because the gradient was greater on the eastern side, erosion proceeded more rapidly. During the next twenty million years, the streams would carve an impressive erosional barrier known as the Appalachian Escarpment (figure 15–3 and plate 41), but at the beginning of Miocene time the Eastern Continental Divide was just beginning to form. The Schooley Peneplain stretched away to the east and west, while masses of rock which were more resistant to erosion stood with their summits above the plain of the Schooley surface (plate 42). Mount Mitchell, Grandfather Mountain, and Mount LeConte are three of the best known among at least a dozen **monadnocks** which still stand on the old Schooley Peneplain surface in the modern Blue Ridge.[2]

Near the eastern edge of the Piedmont, the uplift of the Piedmont and Blue Ridge also resulted in accelerated erosion. The increased erosive capacity of the streams resulted in a band of rapids and steep-sided valleys which now stretches north and south along the length of the boundary between the Piedmont and Coastal Plain. The development of the "Fall Zone" (also called the

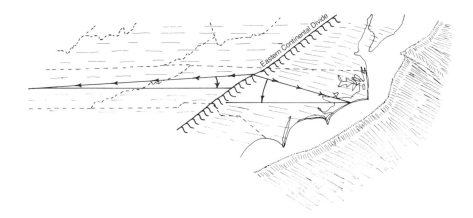

Figure 15–3:   Streams flowing east and west from a line near the present crest of the Blue Ridge produced an erosional divide. Later erosion by the eastward flowing streams produced the modern Appalachian Escarpment. (Courtesy of North Carolina Division of Travel and Tourism.)

2. See Figure 15–2.

Fall Line) began near the beginning of Paleogene time and has continued at varying rates to the present. During the eighteenth, nineteenth, and early twentieth centuries, the Fall Zone was both an impediment to travel and a source of water power. Roanoke Rapids, Franklinton, Wake Forest, Raleigh, Sanford, and Monroe are examples of North Carolina towns which were settled in the Fall Zone to take advantage of the power provided by falling water. The cities of Columbia, South Carolina; Richmond, Virginia; and Washington, D.C., also mark the change in slope and were settled for the same reasons (figure 15–4). [281,282,303,304]

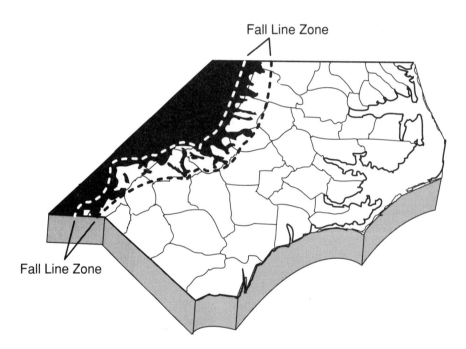

Figure 15–4:   The Fall Zone is sometimes also called the Fall Line Zone. The zone extends along the western edge of the Coastal Plain. In the zone, erosion accelerates where streams change gradient as they pass from the Piedmont to the Coastal Plain. The accelerated erosion has produced rapids and small waterfalls which were used in colonial times to produce power for small industries.

Phosphate Deposits on the Ocean Floor

The sediments of early Miocene time were deposited about twenty million years ago. As the sea reinvaded the Coastal Plain unique conditions developed in the area that is now Beaufort County. In the crustal rocks beneath the Coastal Plain, a hinge-like fault trended east-northeast, dividing the ocean floor into two distinct regions. The ocean floor on the landward side of the fault was almost flat, with a gently rolling character. East of the fault, the bottom sloped slowly toward the deep ocean. The subsiding ocean floor west of the fault created a restricted basin into which nutrient-laden, deep ocean currents flowed from the north.

Single-celled plants and animals were abundant in the cool, relatively shallow waters, which ranged from 100 to 200 meters (330–660 feet) in depth. They flourished because of the nutrients carried into the basin by cold ocean currents. Some of the nutrients, including the element phosphorus, were precipitated as upwelling currents encountered warmer temperatures. With the passing of time, generations of single-celled organisms reproduced, and the dead remains of billions of minute plants and animals settled slowly toward the ocean floor. As they sank, the cells acted as nuclei around which the precipitating phosphate condensed. Still other organisms precipitated phosphate as part of their metabolic processes, adding to the volume of very fine, phosphate-rich particles.

Currents moving over the sloping bottom east of the fault swept some of the material out to the edge of the continental shelf. West of the fault, the phosphatic debris was trapped in the basin. The accumulating muds were reworked by marine worms and other bottom-dwelling organisms, resulting in even greater concentration of phosphate. Conditions on the floor of the basin caused the phosphate-laden deposits to accumulate in shallow troughs, while lime-rich layers developed on the slightly higher ridge areas. Scattered layers of clay carried out from the coast and very thin layers of volcanic ash, probably from eruptions far to the west, complete the mixture of sediments which make up the Pungo River Formation (plate 43) (see Appendix B).

Today, the Pungo River Formation is completely buried beneath younger sediments of the Coastal Plain. The deposits range in depth from 12 meters (39 feet) below sea level near the town of Washington to more than 70 meters (230 feet) below sea level in the northeastern portion of Beaufort County. Near Washington the deposits are only a meter or two thick, but the unit averages about 12 meters (39 feet) in thickness and reaches a maximum thickness of more than 36 meters (118 feet). The Pungo River Formation is being mined along the banks of the Pamlico River near Aurora, in Beaufort County, and is a major source of fertilizer for agriculture (plate 44). The open-pit mines have created an important new source of income in the region and opened a window into the past. Paleontologists use fossils from the Pungo River Formation to study the ancient environments of Miocene time. [245,305–316]

About thirteen million years ago, the sea once again withdrew from the Coastal Plain and streams began carving channels into the surface of the recently deposited Pungo River Formation. West of Beaufort County, streams carved the surface of the Castle Hayne Formation. Along the Coastal Plain's western edge, destruction was proceeding rapidly, leaving only scattered remnants of limestone in depressions on the land surface. In the east, where the formation was too thick to be destroyed, streams eroded channels in the limestone while ground water dissolved small sinkholes in the upper surface of the unit. Today, the erosional features are clearly visible in the limestone's surface where they have been protected by overlying sedimentary deposits.[239,241,285]

During middle Miocene time, about eleven million years ago, the ocean returned, covering the land in what is now southeastern Virginia. North of the North Carolina border, sediments which make up the Clairmont Member of the Eastover Formation were deposited in a shallow basin that was open to the sea (see Appendix B). After more than a million years, the sea withdrew. When ocean waters reflooded the land about nine million years ago, the shoreline shifted southward and water covered the eastern portion of North Carolina's Coastal Plain. During that time, the Cobham Bay Member was deposited in the northeastern portion of the state.

Fine, tan sands were deposited in a shallow open environment where a semitropical climate and an abundant food supply allowed large numbers of mollusks to form extensive shell beds on the sea floor. After some 400,000 years, the sea again withdrew and erosion continued over much of the Coastal Plain for the remainder of the Miocene epoch and into the beginning of Pliocene time. [317]

Erosion Continues on the Piedmont and Blue Ridge

By the beginning of the Pliocene epoch, erosion had produced a surface in the Piedmont and Blue Ridge provinces that was very similar to the one on which Carolinians live today. Streams had eroded the Schooley surface in different ways on either side of the Eastern Continental Divide. Streams flowing

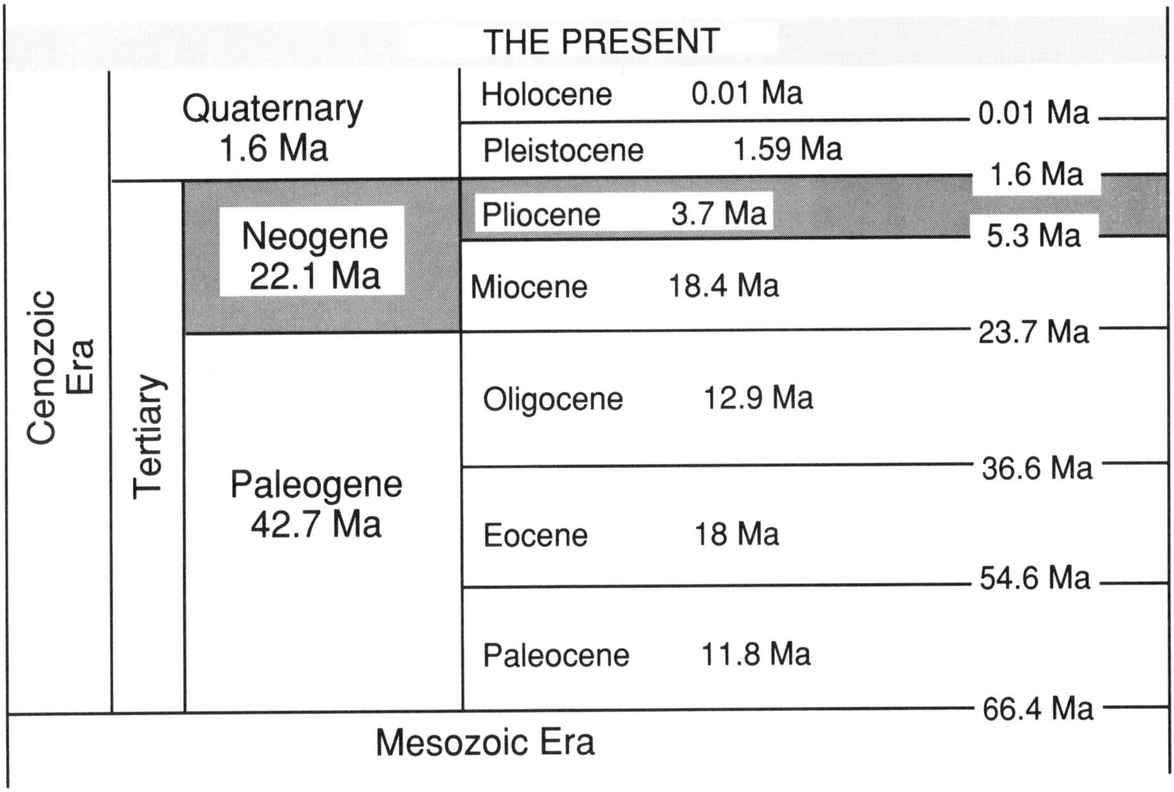

THE PRESENT			
Quaternary 1.6 Ma	Holocene	0.01 Ma	0.01 Ma
	Pleistocene	1.59 Ma	1.6 Ma
Neogene 22.1 Ma	Pliocene	3.7 Ma	5.3 Ma
	Miocene	18.4 Ma	23.7 Ma
Paleogene 42.7 Ma	Oligocene	12.9 Ma	36.6 Ma
	Eocene	18 Ma	54.6 Ma
	Paleocene	11.8 Ma	66.4 Ma

(Cenozoic Era, Tertiary; Mesozoic Era)

Figure 15–5: Geologic time column showing the Pliocene epoch in relation to the Cenozoic era (Ma = Million years).

west from the developing divide had managed to carve the land only slightly, widening and entrenching river channels like those of the New and French Broad rivers (figure 15–6).

East of the Continental Divide, steeper gradients produced by the shorter distance to the sea resulted in more rapid erosion. The rushing waters had almost destroyed the gently rolling surface of the old Schooley Peneplain. As they eroded the land, the streams produced a new surface called the Harrisburg Peneplain. Here and there, erosional remnants of the old Schooley surface still dot the Harrisburg surface in the Piedmont. Today, people recognize names like Pilot Mountain (plate 45), Hanging Rock, Crowder's Mountain, and Kings Mountain, but few realize that these landmarks are not mountains but rather erosional remnants of the older and higher land surface of early Miocene time. The largest area of such erosional remnants covers parts of Stanly, Montgomery, and Moore counties. The region, known as the Uwharrie Mountains, has been mistakenly described as the "oldest mountains in North America." While the rocks of the Uwharries are Precambrian in age, the erosion that created today's land surface is very young in geologic terms. [318]

The rolling surface of the Piedmont and stream valleys west of the Continental Divide in the Blue Ridge Province make up the Harrisburg erosional surface. In the Piedmont, the surface may be seen by standing on the crest of any exposed hill. The tops of all the surrounding hills are remnants of the Harrisburg erosional surface. The stream valleys were formed by erosion which has taken place during the nearly eighteen million years since that time. [3,281,282,303,304,318]

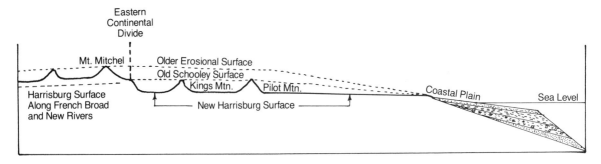

Figure 15–6:   By the beginning of Pliocene time, streams had remodeled the land surface, leaving the ancient Schooley Peneplain as mountain tops in the Blue Ridge and monadnocks in the Piedmont.

During Pliocene time, caverns began forming in areas where layers of limestone ($CaCO_3$) or dolomite ($MgCO_3$) had been deposited millions of years earlier. Rain, which had dissolved carbon dioxide from the air as it fell to earth, formed weak carbonic acid. As the water moved down through cracks in the rock, the weak acid dissolved carbonate minerals. Where streams eroded the land surface, they also lowered the water table, allowing air to replace the water in the caverns. Then, with the passage of time, more carbonate-saturated water formed stalactites and other familiar features in the caverns. Today, visitors to Linville Cavern in McDowell County take guided tours to see the natural "wonders" preserved in this cavern (plate 46). Meanwhile, **speleologists** are busy mapping and describing the almost 900 other caverns known to exist within the state. [319]

Among the more interesting of their discoveries is the existence of numerous "caverns" in igneous and metamorphic rock units. These "caverns" formed when tectonic forces shifted large blocks of rock, opening spaces between the walls of existing fractures. The largest of these tectonic "caverns" is Bat Cave in Henderson County. Bat Cave has mapped passages extending nearly 1.5 kilometers (1.4 miles) and includes one "room" that is 100 meters (330 feet) long and as much as 26 meters (85 feet) high. [320]

Fossil-Rich Deposits on the Coastal Plain

About five million years ago, erosion came to an end as the sea again moved west, covering the entire eastern half of the Coastal Plain. The water was shallow, ranging from a depth of about 15 meters (49 feet) to roughly 30 meters (98 feet). The first layers deposited by the returning sea were sandy beds formed in an open, continental-shelf environment. Later, conditions changed and a large, shallow basin formed that was protected from the ocean by a barrier island system. The shallow open-water areas were probably similar to the modern-day lagoons we know as **sounds**. In the protected basin, fresh water from the land became brackish where it mingled with salty ocean water. The climate also changed from cool-temperate to arid-temperate. The yearly cycle seems to have included a short rainy season producing an environment in which grasslands flourished in the Piedmont. As the shallow, brackish water warmed, the resulting environment promoted the growth of an abundant and varied animal community. [317,321–323]

The sedimentary unit which was deposited in these sounds is known to geologists as the Yorktown Formation (see Appendix B). The unit covers most of the northern portion of the Coastal Plain east of a line through today's towns of Wilson, Rocky Mount, and Roanoke Rapids. The sediments which form the Yorktown Formation include interbedded layers of sand, bluish clay, and shell-marl similar to those being formed in the brackish waters of our modern sounds.

The Yorktown Formation is famous throughout the world for the abundance and variety of fossils found in its layers (plates 47a & b). Dozens of different invertebrate forms, including gastropods, pelecypods, and ostracods, virtually cover the freshly mined land surface of the Lee Creek Mine at Aurora. The sands and sandy clays which surround the fossils include untold numbers of microfossils along with minute worm tube casings and bryozoans. Numerous shark teeth, whale bones and skulls, skate teeth, walrus tusks, and the bones of hundreds of different species fish and birds round out the fossil assemblage. [245,324–330]

The shark teeth range in size from several millimeters to teeth of the great white shark, *Carcharodon*, which are as much as 20 centimeters (8 inches) high. *Carcharodon* was largest shark known to have lived in these waters and is thought to have grown up to 13 meters (43 feet) in length. [331] The bones of birds also vary in size, ranging from those of tiny, sparrow-sized species to the one-meter-long wing bones of huge "false-toothed pelicans" (*Pseudodontornis*), which had wing spans of as much as 6 meters (20 feet). These giant sea birds weighed up to 40 kilograms (88 pounds) and used their jagged jawbones to chew up fish. [332]

West of the line through Wilson and Roanoke Rapids, the Yorktown Formation takes on a beach-like character with interbedded layers of fine sand that contain small flakes of mica and rounded quartz pebbles. [333] In such layers, near the town of Enfield in Halifax County, men digging a septic tank pit discovered the bones of *Pliohippus*. [334] Studies of vertebrate fossils from these Pliocene deposits in other southern states suggest that this ancestor of the modern horse roamed the grasslands along with rhinoceros, mammoths, mastodons, and other modern animals not found in North America today. [335]

In an area near the town of Benson in Johnston County, layers of well-rounded quartz pebbles are overlain by layers of silty sand. The fossils in these sediments match those found in Yorktown sediments farther north and east. Geologists working on this unit have named it the Macks Formation (figure 15–7) and suggest that it represents the remains of deposits laid down near the westernmost edge of the Yorktown Sea (see Appendix B). [327,336–337]

South of the Neuse River, sediments similar in age and character to those of the Yorktown Formation have been mapped in Robeson, Bladen, and Columbus counties. The same sediments also cover large sections of the Coastal Plain in South Carolina and Georgia. While the sediments reflect brackish and marine conditions similar to those found in the Yorktown deposits, the species of invertebrate fossils are distinctly different. Some geologists think a gentle upwarping occurred in the crustal rocks beneath the Coastal Plain. They believe the upwarping formed a low ridge on the ocean floor somewhere near the present course of the Neuse River. The ridge seems to have served as a barrier, separating the invertebrate animals living on the bottom into two groups. As a result, the fossils found in the Duplin Formation represent different species from those that lived in the area where the Yorktown Formation was being deposited (see Appendix B). [337]

Deposition of the Yorktown and Duplin formations continued on the Coastal Plain until about three million years ago when the land rose and the ocean once again retreated. For the next 500,000 years, the surface of the Yorktown Formation was carved by erosion. In places the streams cut channels up to 15 meters (49 feet) deep in the Yorktown beds. The deepest of those channels may have determined the eventual location of Ocracoke and Hatteras islands and the adjoining sounds by directing later flow in the estuaries. [337,338]

When the sea returned it filled the channels and covered the wide, flat surface. The rising ocean created beach and near-shore deposits of sandy clays in what is now the northeastern portion of the Coastal Plain. The climate was tropical and a variety of cor-

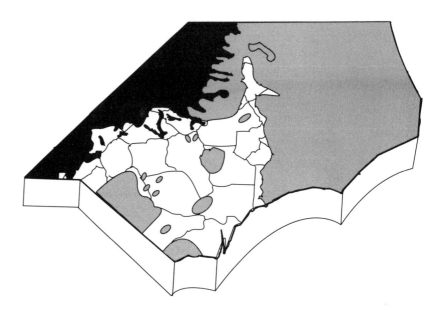

Figure 15–7:   Yorktown and Duplin formations were deposited in the eastern portion of the Coastal Plain while the Macks Formation represents beach deposits further west. The Yorktown and Duplin formations contain similar but different populations of invertebrate fossils, suggesting that the deposits were separated by a topographic feature that kept the two populations from intermingling.

als and other invertebrates flourished on the shoaling bottom. Today, excellent fossils may be collected from this unit known as the Chowan Formation (see Appendix B). Some of the best sites exist along the banks of the Chowan River in Bertie County and on the Tar River, just north of Greenville in Pitt County. [245,340–342]

Farther south, similar conditions existed along the present border between North and South Carolina. Deposits of lime-cemented sands and silts reflect slightly deeper water and quieter continental-shelf conditions. In shallower waters near what is now Elizabethtown in Bladen County, waves and longshore currents mixed vertebrate bones and other fossils from the older Black Creek Formation with this unit known as the Bear Bluff Formation (plates 48a & b) (see Appendix B). [245,343,344]

About 1.9 million years ago, the deposition of both the Chowan and Bear Bluff formations was interrupted by a brief period of erosion. The lowering of sea level was caused by a worldwide cooling and growth of glacial ice near the North and South poles. After a period of about 100,000 years, the climate warmed and global sea levels rose, causing the ocean to reflood the eastern Coastal Plain. The sediments deposited during the following years reflect considerably cooler conditions. Along the banks of the Neuse River in Craven County, bluish gray, lime-rich clays and sands may be seen that are characteristic of the James City Formation.

The unit varies in character from east to west. Lagoonal sands and muds much like those being deposited in today's sounds may be seen along the banks of the Neuse River below New Bern and in Green and Pitt counties. Evidence suggests that the water was about 6 meters (20 feet) deep and varied in salinity depending upon the amount of rainfall. Farther north and east, fossils from the Lee Creek Mine at Aurora reflect a more open continental-shelf environment. [245,337,345–347]

In the southern portion of North Carolina, this time is marked by deposits which occurred in southeastern Bladen, Columbus, and Brunswick counties. The deposits of the Waccamaw Formation were laid down very close to shore in environments which were also like those found in today's sounds. More than 500 different species of brackish and fresh water invertebrate animals lived in the shallow waters (see Appendix B). [245,348–352]

The deposition of James City and Waccamaw sediments continued in the eastern Coastal Plain until after the beginning of the Pleistocene epoch. The deposition, which seems to have ended about 1.2 million years ago, served as prelude to the final chapter of the state's geologic history.

16
NORTH CAROLINA IN THE "ICE AGE"

The most recent period of earth history, known as Quaternary time, is divided into two epochs. The first, the Pleistocene epoch, began some 1,590,000 years ago and lasted until the beginning of **Holocene** time 100,000 years ago. Holocene time includes the development of human civilization and is unique in that it is the one part of earth history that has not ended.

Erosion Forms the "Sand Hills"

As Pleistocene time began, deposition continued on the eastern Coastal Plain while streams eroded the Piedmont and Blue Ridge. In the southwestern portion of the North Carolina Coastal Plain, weathering and ground water combined to produce a unusual deposit. Where erosion had earlier carved rolling hills, water seeped down through the unconsolidated sediments. The water slowly transformed the sandy clays of the Cretaceous Middendorf Formation and smaller overlying remnants of the Castle Hayne and Duplin formations. The water seeped downward, carrying clay minerals from surface layers to lower levels and leaving unconsolidated sands behind. Prevailing winds, blowing mainly from the west, picked up some of the surface sand and piled it in small dunes on the sheltered sides of the hills. While none of the wind-formed deposits are more than 7 meters (23 feet) high, the rolling hills and unconsolidated nature of the sandy soil have led people to refer to the region as the "Sand Hills" (plate 49). [262,353,354]

		THE PRESENT		
	Quaternary 1.6 Ma	Holocene	0.01 Ma	0.01 Ma
		Pleistocene	1.59 Ma	1.6 Ma
	Neogene 22.1 Ma	Pliocene	3.7 Ma	5.3 Ma
		Miocene	18.4 Ma	23.7 Ma
Cenozoic Era / Tertiary	Paleogene 42.7 Ma	Oligocene	12.9 Ma	36.6 Ma
		Eocene	18 Ma	54.6 Ma
		Paleocene	11.8 Ma	66.4 Ma

Mesozoic Era

Figure 16–1:   Geologic time column showing the Pleistocene epoch in relation to the Cenozoic era (Ma = Million years)

Beach Scarps Form on the Coastal Plain

A little more than two million years ago, the sea finally withdrew from the eastern counties and a short period of erosion began. Then the climate warmed around the world, causing the polar ice caps to melt and release enormous amounts of water. As a result, the sea level rose to a point more than 91 meters (300 feet) above its present stand. During that time, waves and currents carved an erosional escarpment from Georgia through South Carolina and into North Carolina. The Orangeburg Escarpment enters North Carolina in Scotland County just west of the town of Laurel Hill and can be traced northwestward through Hoke County to Cumberland County where it disappears. [355,356]

While the escarpment is not a continuous feature, in places it produces a significant change in elevation. For example, where the Cape Fear River flows just east of the escarpment through Fayetteville in Cumberland County, the change in elevation is often as much as 46 meters (150 feet). The resulting geography was at least partly responsible for the settlement and development of the colonial towns of Campbellton and Cross Creek which later became Fayetteville.

In South Carolina and Georgia, sediments of the Duplin Formation taper to a feather edge just east of the escarpment, suggesting that the feature might have existed prior to the high sea-level stand which produced the Yorktown and Duplin formations. While the escarpment was certainly formed by erosion, there is presently no evidence to suggest which of the early high stands of sea level created the escarpment. [355,356]

North of Cumberland County, the beach created by this high stand of sea level forms a gentle sandy sloping feature known as the Coats Scarp. The scarp has been mapped in Harnett, Johnston, Wilson, and Nash counties. In southern Harnett and northern Cumberland counties, the feature connects with the Orangeburg Escarpment.

East of the Coats Scarp, a complex of sands and gravels was deposited on the sea floor. This series of unconsolidated sediments forms a deposit known as the Brandywine Terrace. The Brandywine Terrace was the first of at least six such terrace features which would be formed during the Pleistocene. The terrace deposits do not have formation names because they are neither large enough nor sufficiently well-defined to be referred to as formations. [346,360,367]

About 1.7 million years ago the sea once again withdrew from the Coastal Plain, beginning new cycles of advance and withdrawal that were caused by major climatic changes in other parts of the world. In the upper latitudes of the northern and southern hemispheres, sheets of glacial ice the size of continents were beginning a series of advances and retreats. As the Ice Age progressed, glacial activity north and west of the Carolinas completely reshaped the land surface.

While the continental glaciers never advanced as far south as the Carolinas, their effect on the climate was profound (figure 16–2). During glacial advances, the large amount of water tied cup in the ice caused the sea level to drop around the world. Dur-

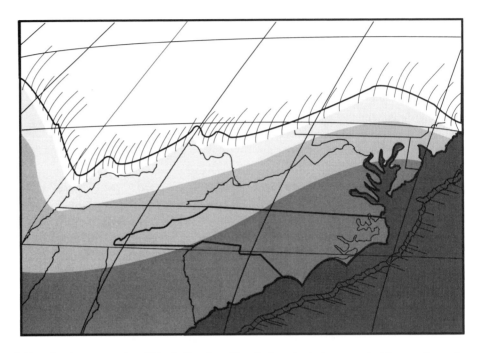

Figure 16–2:   Continental ice sheets never entered North Carolina. The darker shaded area probably experienced near-arctic climatic conditions while the lighter-gray areas were subjected to a climate more like that of modern-day Maine or Vermont.

ing glacial retreats, referred to as **interglacial periods**, the ice sheet melted even farther than at present, releasing enormous quantities of water and causing the sea level to rise to elevations far above the present-day sea level stand. The changing sea level created a series of beach scarps and terraces which cover the Coastal Plain from the Piedmont's edge to the present coastline and beyond. [368]

The first major glacial advance of the Ice Age is known as the Nebraskan Glaciation. The event began about 2.1 million years ago and caused the sea level to drop radically. During the Nebraskan Event, the shoreline retreated eastward to a point that is thought to have been east of the present coastline.

Then, after a period of some 380,000 years, the global climate warmed and the continental ice sheets melted, causing the sea level to rise. During this time, referred to as the Aftonian Interglacial Event, the rising sea moved the coastline westward to a point in Johnston County near the town of Wilson's Mills. There, waves of the advancing ocean created a second beach scarp, while the sediments of the Coharie Terrace were deposited to the east (figure 16–3). [355]

The advance of continental ice some 1.7 million years ago during the Kansan Glacial Event caused the sea to again withdraw from the Coastal Plain. In turn, the retreat of the Kansan ice sheets caused another rise in sea level, pushing the coastline west to a point in southern Johnston County. There, during the Yarmouth Interglacial Event, the Kenly Scarp and Wicomico Terrace were built.

The Surry Scarp and Talbot Terrace deposits were apparently formed about 800,000 years ago during the first portion of the Yarmouth, or "great," Interglacial Event. [366,367] The sediments underlying the surface of the Talbot Terrace are exposed in much of the southeastern part of the state. The unconsolidated sediments reflect their formation in very shallow water. The deposits, which are known as the Flanner Beach Formation (plate 50), include open-bay deposits of shelly pebbly-sands which accumulated behind barrier bars. The deposition took place under conditions much like those which exist in the modern open waters of Pamlico Sound. Overlying layers of mud with the shells of brackish water invertebrates, layers of sand that formed bars in the shallow water, and beds of peat with the stumps of cypress trees that grew in the swampy areas represent much quieter lagoonal environments. Today the stumps of trees that grew in the swamps can be seen in the banks of Albemarle, Pamlico Core, and Bogue sounds (see Appendix B). [245,337,347,360,361]

Sand and shell layers of approximately the same age are exposed at Snow's Cut just north of Carolina Beach and on the

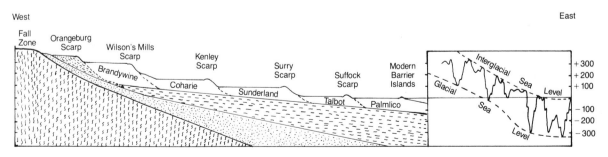

Figure 16–3: This cross section shows the author's interpretation of the general relationship between global glacial sea levels and the beach scarps which formed on the North Carolina Coastal Plain. Several problems, including a simplified sea level curve and the tectonic movement of the crust beneath the Coastal Plain, make this a very general representation of events.

present beach at Fort Fisher, in New Hanover County. The crossbedded layers of cemented shell fragments were formed when extensive shell beds were reworked by waves and currents (plate 51). The sediments are referred to as the Canepatch Formation (see Appendix B). The beds reflect a variety of environments ranging from quiet freshwater swamps and cypress groves to open bays, beaches, and ocean floors near shore. [245,337,362,363]

The Suffock Scarp is the easternmost in the sequence of visible beach scarps and terrace surface units. The beach was formed during the latter portion of the Yarmouth Interglacial Event about 600,000 years ago. The scarp is easily seen on satellite photographs and can be recognized on the ground as a low ridge. The ridge seems to begin just inland of the town of Salter Path in Carteret County and can be traced north from that point. The scarp, which is often interrupted by erosion, is marked by North Carolina state roads 306 and 32 as it stretches northward, passing near the towns of Aurora, Plymouth, and Edenton before entering Virginia.

The beds of the Pamlico Terrace resemble the Flanner Beach Formation of the Talbot Surface. Recent research has revealed several smaller scarps and old beaches within the present barrier island system. These features suggest that a number of different barrier island systems have existed during the past 100,000 years. [349,351] Probable storm beach ridges of sand, like the Arapahoe Ridge and fragments of barrier islands at Wrightsville Beach in Brunswick County; Morehead City, Beaufort, Harker's Island, Atlantic, and Cedar Island in Carteret County; and Waterlilly in Currituck County reflect the fluctuating sea level. Ancient stream channels, like those of the Neuse River through Morehead City and the Cape Fear River off Carolina Beach, along with submerged barrier island fragments on the continental shelf off Hatteras, provide ample evidence of activity during lower stands of sea level. Similar features may have existed on other terraces, but erosion has apparently destroyed them. [347,356–365]

The overall pattern of terraces throughout the Pleistocene indicates that widening of the ocean basins, or changes in their depth, were responsible for a slow but consistent drop in the average sea level. As a result, each successively younger terrace occupies a lower elevation on the Coastal Plain. [376,367]

Erosion Puts the Final Touches to the Piedmont and Blue Ridge

During the Pliocene and Pleistocene epochs, streams carved today's valleys into the almost flat Harrisburg Peneplain surface in the Piedmont and Blue Ridge. In the Piedmont, headward erosion on Triassic rocks north of Robbins in Moore County caused the Haw River to capture portions of the Deep and Rocky rivers. [368] In Wake County, the Neuse River continued cutting downward into the rocks of the Piedmont surface, completing entrenchment of old meanders in its river channel. In Moore County, an entrenched meander of the Cape Fear River is marked by the House in the Horseshoe State Historic Site. There, the river created an erosional landform that took on strategic importance during the Revolutionary War. West of the continental divide, the New and French Broad rivers carved new channels into the smaller flood plain surfaces of the Harrisburg surface they had created in earlier times within the river valleys (plate 52).

On the western portions of the Coastal Plain, rivers left deposits of gravel marking their channels. Today, these "High Terrace Gravels" may seen along U.S. Highway 74 near Lilesville, in Anson County, where they were deposited by the flowing water of the ancient Pee Dee River. Other deposits near the towns of Lillington (plate 53) and Buies Creek, in Harnett County, are thought to mark old channels of the Cape Fear River. [353–355]

The cooling of the global climate that produced the continental ice sheets in other areas of the world also had a profound effect on North Carolina. The least affected areas of the North Carolina Coastal Plain were more than 640 kilometers (400 miles) from the southern edge of the continental ice fields. Near the ocean, the forests were primarily made up of white pines, with a mixture of some spruce reflecting a cooler climate. In the northern and western Coastal Plain, mixed spruce and fir forests were common, indicating that the weather was much colder than it is today. During more recent times (10,000–15,000 years ago) the composition of the forests slowly changed. Oak and hickory became more prevalent as the white pine, spruce, and fir stands receded west toward the crest of Roan Mountain, Grandfather Mountain, and Mount Mitchell.

Additional evidence of the recent nature of the climatic change is provided by microclimatic floral assemblages on the north side of the Sauratown Mountains in Stokes and Surry Counties, along with the north-facing slopes of the Eno River Gorge in Durham County, and the Hemlock Bluffs in Wake County. Taken together, the character of the plant community suggests that the climate was much cooler as recently as 15,000 years ago. The evidence indicates that the temperatures ranged from a maximum of 10°C (14°F) to a minimum of − 10°C (− 50°F). [369–377]

In the highest of the state's mountain regions the slopes and valleys facing north may have briefly harbored small tongues of ice. Although none of the ice masses was large enough to leave easily discernable scars, polished surfaces, or striations typical of glaciers, careful study of higher valleys in the area around Mount Mitchell and Grandfather Mountain reveals a number of features that might have been formed by masses of ice or very small valley glaciers. Several valleys have the U-shape profiles formed by moving ice. Near the head of one or two valleys vague **cirque-like forms** suggest that ice plucked rocks and carried them away, leaving a bowl-shaped depression. In other places, piles of boulders that may have been transported by moving ice fill valley floors (plate 54). While none of the evidence is conclusive, the various features suggest the presence of small ice masses, a cooler climate, and a lower tree line. Some researchers have suggested that modern-day mountain "balds" may represent **tundra**[1] that developed above the ancient tree line. Indeed, the presence of "ice-shifted?" large blocks which may have been shifted down the slopes of Pilot Mountain suggest that the winters were severe even in the central Piedmont. [378–384]

Animal remains, like those of the plant community, show signs of a transitional, near-glacial climate during Pliocene and Pleistocene times. Near Arapahoe, just north of the Neuse River's junction with Bairds Creek in Pamlico County, fossils of a Pleistocene horse (*Equus complicatus*), a mammoth (*Mammuthus imperator*) (figure 16–4), and an alligator provide additional evi-

---

1. The term tundra is applied to areas in regions with arctic climate. The terrain is treeless with a marshy surface covered with mosses, lichens, and a variety of low shrubs. Many theories have been proposed to account for the formation of the Appalachian "balds," but their general characteristics closely match the accepted definition for tundra.

Plate 29: This typical border conglomerate near the eastern edge of the Dan River basin illustrates the wide variety of sizes and types of rock found in such conglomerates.

Plate 30: An artist's conception of the general structure of a typical Triassic basin. Notice the uneven floor caused by faults within the basins. Border conglomerates mark points where streams flowed into the basin, while swamps and playa lakes provided the habitat necessary to support a variety of plant and animal life.

Plate 31: Diplurus, a lobe-finned fish known as a coelacanth, inhabited the basins along with a variety of ray-finned fish. (Courtesy of American Museum of Natural History, Smithsonian Institution.)

Plate 32: Phytosaurs (Rutidon carolinensis) lived in swampy terrain near the playa lakes of the Sanford and Durham Triassic basins.

Plates 33a & b: Dictyocephalus was a rather large flat-bodied amphibian.
Typothorax was a small armored reptile that was apparently about half a meter
long. (Courtesy of the Pennsylvania Museum of Natural History.) [229]

Plate 34: Placerias is an example of the heavier reptiles that lived in the Triassic basins. While their weight made them slower and more open to attack, their armor seems to have provided ample protection against predators. (Courtesy of American Museum of Natural History, Smithsonian Institution.)

Plate 36: A typical basaltic dike cutting through meta-morphic rocks in Guilford County.

Plate 35: Life as it might have appeared near the middle of a basin during Late Triassic time. (Courtesy of American Museum of Natural History, Smithsonian Institution.)

Plate 37: The dark rock exposed in this Durham County quarry is part of a very thick diabase sill. The magma was intruded between layers of Triassic age in the Durham portion of the Deep River Basin.

Plate 38: These petrified log fragments were removed from the banks of the Cape Fear River in Cumberland County. Similar wood fragments are common in the sandy deposits within the Cape Fear River Valley. (Courtesy of Richard Small.)

Plate 39: The Castle Hayne limestone is quarried in many locations across eastern North Carolina and used for a variety of purposes, from road construction to the building of sea walls.

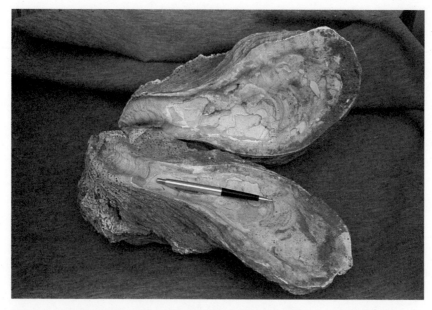

Plate 40: Crassostrea gigantissima grew in large numbers during the earliest portion of Miocene time. The shells formed bar deposits in channels carved in the Belgrade Formation.

Plate 41: Streams flowing east and west from a line near the present crest of the Blue Ridge produced an erosional divide. Later erosion by the eastward flowing streams produced the modern Appalachian Escarpment. (Courtesy of North Carolina Division of Travel and Tourism.)

Plate 42: Today the ancient Schooley Peneplain is represented by the tops of the general mountain surface in the Blue Ridge and farther east, by the tops of monadnocks including Kings Mountain and Pilot Mountain. (Courtesy of North Carolina Division of Travel and Tourism.)

Plate 43: The combination of a fault-generated basin with the metabolic processes of numerous small marine organisms served to concentrate phosphate-rich sands in what is now Beaufort County.

Plate 45: Pilot Mountain, in Surry County, is one of a number of erosionally resistant monadnocks standing on the Harrisburg Peneplain. (Courtesy of North Carolina Division of Travel and Tourism.)

Plate 44: The phosphate-rich sands of the Pungo River Formation are mined by the Texas Gulf Corporation near the town of Aurora in Beaufort County.

Plate 46:   Linville Cavern is the best-known natural cavern in North Carolina. This vertical cavern, which was formed by the solution of dolomitic limestone, is open to the public. (Courtesy of North Carolina High Country Host.)

Plates 47a & b: The fossils preserved in the sands and muds of the Yorktown Formation preserve evidence of an incredible variety of life forms. Sharks, walrus, seals, rays, and whales swam in the warm ocean while a variety of birds flew overhead. A similar variety of invertebrate animals of all sizes lived on the ocean floor. (Courtesy of Aurora Fossil Museum.)

Plates 48a & b: The Bear Bluff Formation includes a variety of invertebrate fossils.

Plate 49: The layer exposed in this borrow pit near Rockingham in Richmond County shows the effects of leaching by ground water. The crossbedded layers were formed as stream deposits. Leaching of clay from the upper layers by ground water destroyed the crossbeds, leaving loose sand which now forms the land surface.

Plate 50: The Flanner Beach Formation may be seen along the banks of the Neuse River below the city of New Bern. The deposits include interfingered layers of shells, sand, and clay with cypress stumps and beds of peat reflecting a swampy environment.

Plate 51: Crossbedded layers of coquina, or shell hash, formed in a high-energy beach environment. The deposit which outcrops on the beach at Fort Fisher is part of the Canepatch Formation. Other portions of the unit may be seen along the banks of Snow's Cut and in Carolina Beach State Park.

Plate 52: This incised meander loop of the New River occurs in Ashe County near the town of West Jefferson. The loop formed when the river was meandering on the nearly flat surface of the Schooley Peneplain. Later uplift caused the river to cut downward, incising the old meander loop.

Plate 53: These deposits of gravel near Lilesville, in Anson County, mark the course of the ancient Pee Dee River. The gravels were deposited as the river rolled and tumbled rocks in its channel. (Courtesy of North Carolina Division of Travel and Tourism.)

Plate 54: Block fields such as this one located in a tributary of Boone Fork suggest the existence of significant amounts of ice on the mountainsides during Pleistocene winters. The blocks range from 1.2 to 2.5 meters (4–8 feet) in length. [380]

Plate 55: This sinkhole is one of a group in a lense of Castle Hayne limestone near Magnolia in Duplin County. Sinkholes are collapse features that form due to solution of underlying rock in limestone formations. (Courtesy of Ms. Cindy Burnham.)

Plate 56: Aerial photograph of two typical Carolina Bays in Bladen County.

Plate 57:   This road has been cut through one of many vegetation-covered sand ridges which make up the Hoop Pole Woods area of Roosevelt Natural Area on Bogue Banks (see figure 17—6). [450]

Plate 58:   On this portion of Shackleford Banks, ocean sand dunes are slowly burying the maritime forest as the island slowly rolls over toward the mainland.

Plate 59:   An aerial view of the Outer Banks reveals how fragile the islands really are. Drum Inlet in the foreground shifts with every tide and storm.

Mastodon

Mammoth

Figure 16–4:   The climate in North Carolina during the Pleistocene time seems to have provided a transition zone where cold-climate animals, such as these mammoths, may have mingled with horses and other animals who lived in warmer climates farther south.

dence for a relatively temperate climate near the ocean. However, the presence of mammoth bones (*Mammuthus columbia*) from New Hanover County and mastodon fossils in Wayne County and near Winnebow, in Brunswick County, suggest that the climate was also much colder than the temperature range we consider normal. The presence on the Coastal Plain of a variety of animals that inhabited both warm and cold climates along with the floral changes indicate that southern North Carolina was probably a transition zone. For example, the discovery of a sea cow (*Manatee*) fossil in the **coquina**[2] at Fort Fisher (New Hanover County) suggests that animals normally found in warmer waters were venturing farther north during this time. [385–389]

Because of continuous erosion, no fossils have been found in the Blue Ridge or Piedmont, but in Tennessee, Kentucky, and southwestern Virginia, several Pleistocene fossil finds led to the conclusion that mammoth, mastodon, beaver, musk oxen, and several other cooler-climate mammals may have roamed freely over the inland portions of the Carolinas. [390–397]

---

2. Coquina is a sedimentary rock composed entirely of shell fragments cemented together by calcium carbonate.

17
THE "RECENT" PAST

Between 17,000 and 18,000 years ago the great ice fields of the last great glacial advance began melting. In North Carolina, the seas once again began rising from a low point about 122 meters (400 feet) below the present sea level while the climate began warming toward its present temperature level. [398]

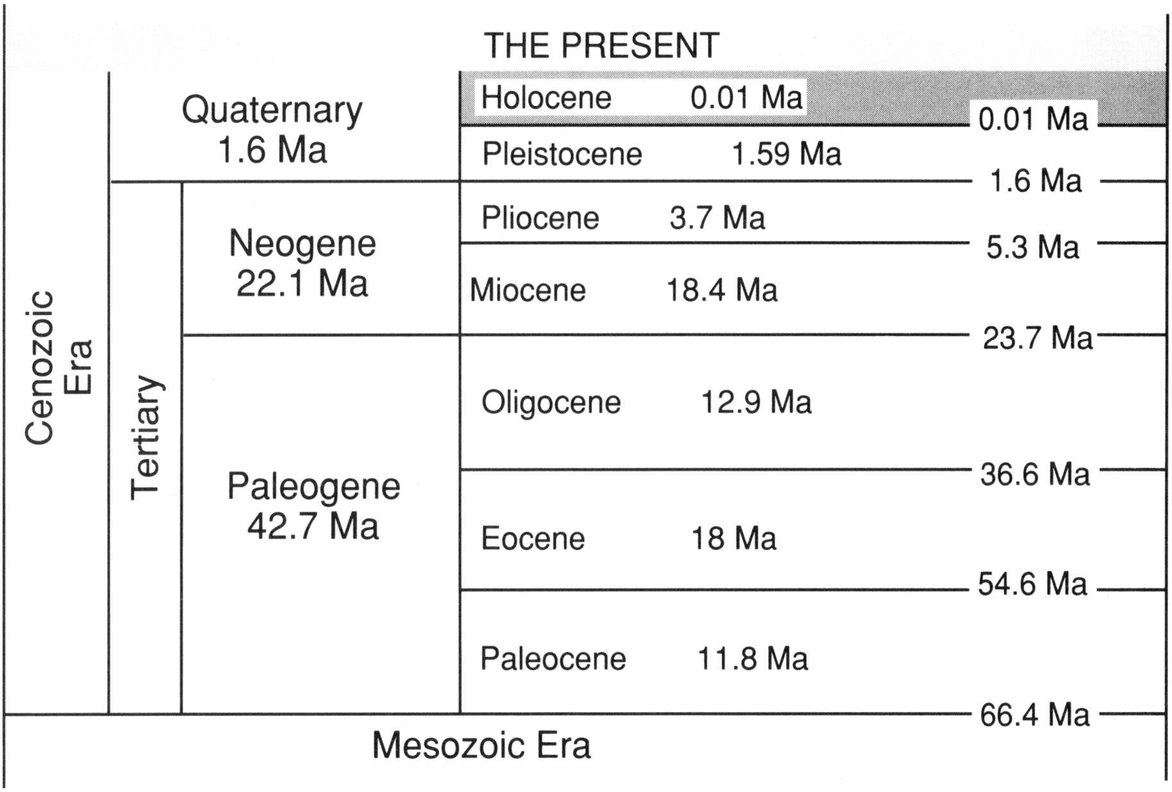

Cenozoic Era			THE PRESENT		
		Quaternary 1.6 Ma	Holocene	0.01 Ma	0.01 Ma
			Pleistocene	1.59 Ma	1.6 Ma
	Tertiary	Neogene 22.1 Ma	Pliocene	3.7 Ma	5.3 Ma
			Miocene	18.4 Ma	23.7 Ma
		Paleogene 42.7 Ma	Oligocene	12.9 Ma	36.6 Ma
			Eocene	18 Ma	54.6 Ma
			Paleocene	11.8 Ma	66.4 Ma
Mesozoic Era					

Figure 17–1: Geologic time column showing the Holocene epoch in relation to the Cenozoic era (Ma = Million years).

In the eastern portion of today's Coastal Plain, large swamps formed where generation after generation of plants died, were buried, and slowly changed to peat. [399–401] Near Magnolia, in Duplin County, ground water dissolved several large sinkholes in a large remnant of the Castle Hayne limestone. Other nearly flooded cavern systems, such as Rock House Cave in Onslow County and Old Blockhouse Cave in Jones County, suggest that small cavern systems may not be uncommon in limestones throughout the Coastal Plain (plate 55). [402, 405]

Streams also were at work in the western Costal Plain, but in some areas the land was so flat that a few inter-stream areas appear to have been temporarily protected from erosion. On one such inter-stream divide area, near the town of Benson, in Johnston County, evidence suggests that the land has remained essentially untouched by erosion for almost ten million years. [357]

Mysterious Depressions Called Carolina Bays

During this same time, shallow elliptical depressions were forming across the Coastal Plain. Today, these elliptical depressions usually contain swamps or lakes and are called Carolina Bays. The name Carolina Bay is taken from the fact that an evergreen plant known as Loblolly Bay (*Gordonia lasianthus*) is very common in the swampy depressions. The plants' green leaves often mark the presence of a swampy Carolina Bay in an otherwise brown winter landscape. Carolina Bays were first recognized in the nineteenth century and, since that time, research and debate concerning their origin has proceeded sporadically. More than 500,000 bays are now known to exist between southern New Jersey and northern Florida. The bays are found only on sandy Coastal Plain soils. They range in character from white sand-bottomed lakes to vegetation-filled swamps and vary in size from a few dozen meters to several kilometers in diameter. Often bays formed within bays, and in some areas, several bays intersect one another so that their rims cross. Throughout the length of the Atlantic Coastal Plain the bays are oriented with their long axes generally northwest-southeast (figure 17–2).[1]

At least fifteen different theories have been proposed to explain the origin of the Carolina Bays. The more prominent suggestions include artesian springs, wind-generated blowout basins, solution depressions, basins soured by gyroscopic eddies,

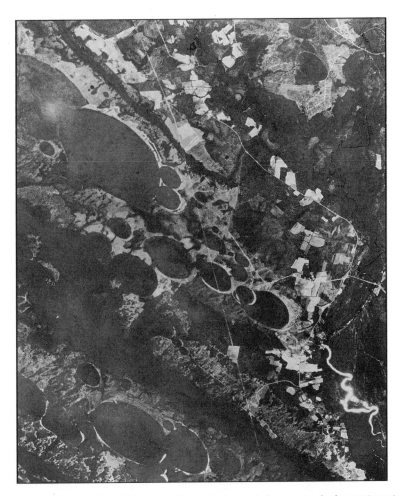

Figure 17–2:   The White Lake Orthophotoquad shows a typical assortment of Carolina Bay lakes and swamps. (Courtesy of United States Geological Survey.)

1. An orthophotoquad is a combination of a topographic map with a satellite or very high-altitude aerial photograph. The resulting map provides several kinds of information that are not available on each of the individual images.

sinkholes, and meteor craters. Many authors have supported the meteor swarm theory, which proposes that the elliptically shaped bays were created by a swarm of meteors or by a comet striking the earth. [406–433] Proponents of the meteor hypothesis cite the presence of small increases in the earth's magnetic field near several bays as evidence for meteorites. However, calculations by other investigators indicate that such meteorites would have had to range from 165 to 800 meters (540 to 2,624 feet) in diameter to produce the measured magnetic changes. Meteors of such size would almost certainly have produced massive craters rather than the relatively small Carolina Bays. In addition, cores from holes drilled in several bays and a seismic profile through Singletary Lake in Bladen County show little or no disturbance of the sedimentary layers beneath the bays (figure 17–3). [442]

Recent field studies of similar lakes in Alaska, Texas, and Chile, coupled with current measurements and wind tunnel studies, suggest a more feasible possibility. The investigators be-

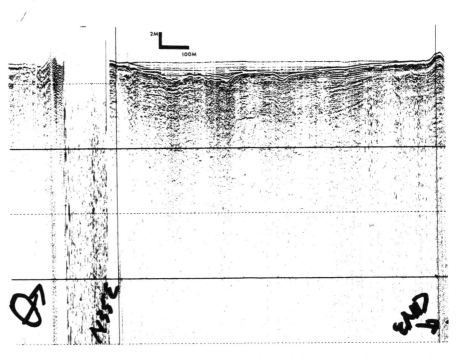

Figure 17–3:   Seismic profiles through the sediments below Singletary Lake show no disturbance of the sedimentary layers. (Courtesy of Dr. Jacob Kaczorowski.)[442]

lieve that the bays developed from natural depressions formed by current action on an emerging sea floor. In the Carolinas, the Coastal Plain region probably received enough rainfall to maintain water in the depressions. Prevailing winds, blowing from opposing directions, generated currents in the water-filled depressions. The currents moved sediment along the edges of the bays, converting the round or irregularly shaped depressions into elliptical bays with their long axes perpendicular to the direction of the prevailing winds (figure 17–4).

Varying conditions caused some lakes to fill with vegetation and turn into swamps, while others, such as White, Bladen, and Jones lakes in Bladen County remained open and water-filled. Apparently the most plausible sequence of events resembled the following pattern: After a depression formed, currents generated by prevailing winds changed the basin to an elliptical shape and produced a slightly raised sand rim. Later, minor climatic changes lowered the water level, allowing the development of smaller bays within bays. With the further lowering of water lev-

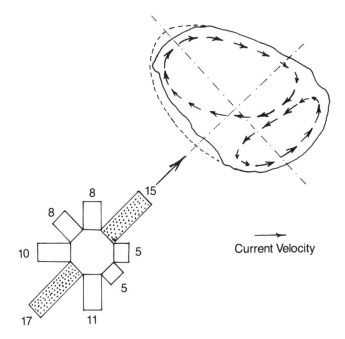

Current Velocity

Figure 17–4: Prevailing winds (blowing from the directions shown in the wind rose at left) generated currents in the water-filled bay lakes. The currents in turn produced the classic elliptical bay shape. [442]

els, swampy conditions caused some bays to fill with vegetation while others simply dried up. [436, 442]

Radiocarbon dating of peat deposits in the bays suggest that some began forming as many as 50,000 years ago, while others may be no more than 6,000 years old. Today, the question of the origin of Carolina Bays is still far from settled. Much more research will be needed to solve the riddle, but for the present, they pose an intriguing puzzle, both for geologists and the casually interested citizen (plate 56). [442,443]

Modern Barrier Islands

The most recently formed feature in North Carolina is the barrier island complex. The islands stretch along the eastern border of North Carolina from Corolla to Calabash. In one sense, the barrier is old because it formed during Pleistocene time. In another, the islands are the most contemporary of features because they are in a continuous state of change. The complex of sounds, rivers, islands, and the ocean form a fluctuating system that changes with every year and season. For most observers, however, the most obvious changes come with storms that overwash the islands, open and close inlets, and restructure the floors of the sounds. [444–448]

The process of island formation apparently began about 18,000 years ago as the sea rose in response to the warming climate. Where the rising waters surrounded a ridge on the land surface they created a low island by cutting the ridge off from the mainland. As water surged around each new island, currents swept sand along its length, first forming a beach and later building low **spits** and **bars** which extended the island in the direction of the current.

The original modern barrier probably formed far out on what is now the continental shelf and most, if not all, of its remnants have been swept away. However, we can see the same process at work on today's barrier where spits are being built from the ends of islands. The spits are slowly closing inlets or causing them to migrate along the barrier island chain (figure 17–5).

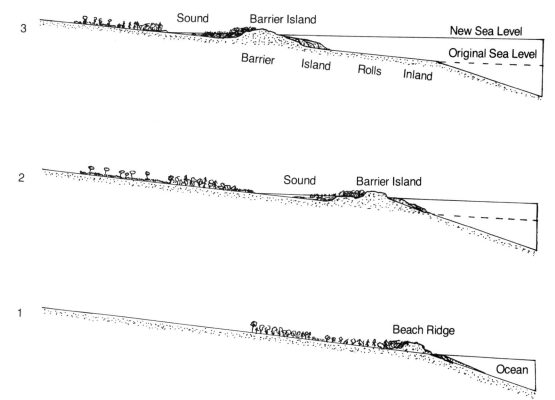

Figure 17—5:   A rising sea level is thought to have created barrier islands by surrounding and isolating high points on the flat Coastal Plain surface. [448]

With the passage of time, dunes formed on the islands. As the height of the barrier island increased, salt-tolerant plants took hold, eventually covering the spits and helping build dunes. Today, sand ridges can be seen from Cape Henry in Virginia south to Fort Caswell, in Brunswick County (figure 17—6 and plate 57). In many places, a dozen or more plant-covered spits form ridges which may be traced along the entire length of an island.

In scattered areas, like those around the towns of Atlantic and Newport in Carteret County, recently formed Carolina Bays transect the ridges, indicating that both the ridge- and bay-forming processes have been common in the region for several thousand years. [449, 450]

Along the lower portions of recently formed islands, the rising sea level caused the ocean to overwash portions of the islands on

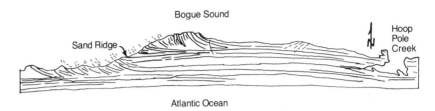

Figure 17–6:   Sand ridges form along Bogue Sound. (See also plate 57.)

a regular basis. During storms, surges overwashed higher areas, carrying sand from the beach over to the sound side of the islands. Where such overwash processes have been common, the islands are slowly "rolling themselves over" and moving toward the mainland. As a result, layers of peat that formed the salt marshes and stumps of trees which grew in maritime forests are being uncovered along modern beaches as the islands continue their steady march toward the land (plate 58). [451–459]

Today, remnants of old barrier islands that have run ashore in years past, may be seen along the stretch of land called Currituck at the villages of Waterlilly, Adlette, and Poplar Branch. Farther south, Roanoke Island may be part of the same island. In Carteret County, the towns of Cedar Island, Atlantic, Harkers Island, Beaufort, and Morehead City sit on another old island that has run ashore.

Other signs of constant change may be seen nearly everywhere along the coast. A walk along the wooded trails of the Roosevelt Natural Area reveals low ridges of sand built as the island was extended by longshore currents. At Nags Head, Hatteras, Fort Macon, or Fort Caswell, a walk along the seaward edge of the maritime forests reveals large dunes slowly covering the trees. In such cases, shifting winds are slowly moving sand, causing the islands to migrate toward the mainland.

Along the present barrier island chain, inlets open and close with some regularity. In some areas they seem to open and close with no pattern, while others, such as the Ocracoke inlet, have been open throughout recorded history. Each inlet provides a passage through which ocean waters can mix with those of the rivers flowing from the land (plate 59). The result is an environment of incredible biological abundance and diversity. [460]

Everywhere along the coast, new land is being built as it has been for millions of years across the Coastal Plain. Daily surges of wind and tide, along with the superimposed results of periodic storms, are molding the sediment brought by streams from the mainland into new bars, spits, and islands. Even offshore, the ancient channels carved by the Neuse and Cape Fear rivers during the lower sea levels of glacial advances are being filled with mud and sand by longshore currents. [461]

Erosion destroys a portion of one island and deposits the sand and mud in some other location. In the sounds, the rising of sea level causes accelerated erosion of shorelines and slow, but inexorable flooding of low-lying areas. For as long as the climate continues to grow warmer, sea level will continue rising, the shoreline will migrate slowly westward, and barrier islands will move toward the mainland.

One has only to walk the beaches, watch the tidal surge of water through an inlet, or observe the effect of a single storm to understand why the shoreline of the Carolinas is a place of change. Today's islands are different only in detail from yesterday's and will be changed by the next major storm. The combination of sand, wind, currents, and tides, punctuated by hurricanes and northeasters, make the North Carolina coast one of the most dynamic geological environments on earth. [448]

18
THE PRESENT

The present in North Carolina is the time of man. We tend to regard our planet using a time scale counted in days, months, and years rather than the broader scope of geologic time. Within such an abbreviated frame of reference little geologic activity can be detected. To be sure, streams may be seen carrying sand and mud toward the sea. Freezing and thawing processes may be seen to shift, or perhaps break, a rock. Waves and wind can be seen shifting dunes and inlets. But the slower, more subtle changes being caused by geologic processes are for the most part beyond our comprehension. Still, there are signs of activity in the earth.

In 1886, a major earthquake centered near Charleston, South Carolina, rocked the entire Atlantic Coast. During the following twenty years at least 400 smaller tremors announced movement in the shifting crust or sediment settling. [462] Today, an occasional minor earthquake still indicates instability, but other evidence suggests that more significant events are occurring. Very careful surveying shows that the Coastal Plain surface is sinking in one area and rising in another. In the northeastern counties—from the Virginia state line south to the city of New Bern—the crust is apparently sinking about 5 millimeters every year (1 inch every 5 years). The slowly melting glaciers and ice fields of the polar regions, coupled with the crustal sinking, are producing a slow rise in the sea level. This causes the waters of the sounds to invade the land which was only recently lifted from the sea. The results may spell trouble for coastal towns such as Elizabeth City, Manteo, Edenton, and Washington if the changes are as rapid as early measurements suggest. [463,464]

Farther south and west the same measurements indicate that the land is rising. The rate varies from about 5 millimeters per year near Raleigh and Wilmington to a maximum of 6.5 millimeters every year or about 1 inch every four years. [465] At first glance, such a slow rise appears reassuring, but some seismologists believe that any uplift is an indication that earthquakes may occur in years to come. [466]

The human race, with its limited perspective, has used and misused the land in the Carolinas. The paths that Native Americans and settlers followed along ridge lines and through mountain passes were created millions of years earlier by the erosive forces of running water. Even in our "modern" time, many of our highways follow these "paths of least resistance." Towns were settled where ridge lines intersected, mountain pass trails met, or water power was available along the fall zone. Similarly, settlements along the coast grew up at natural ports or near inlets to the sea. Only in the last two or three decades has man's technology outstripped the land, allowing the location of towns, highways, and industries to be based on criteria other than the lay of the land.

The mining industry still draws on mineral wealth concentrated during the Grenville mountain uplift of late Precambrian time and in the ancient island arc that forms today's "slate belt." Feldspar, mica, lithium, tungsten, pyrophyllite, phosphate, limestone, and crushed stone are just a few of the important minerals that add millions of dollars to the state's economy every year. Tourists come to admire the scenery of North Carolina's mountains and Piedmont and to collect some of the hundreds of different minerals that can be found within our borders. Travelers also come in droves to enjoy the sand and surf along the recently created Outer Banks.

North Carolinians and their guests are demonstrating a blatant disregard for the land that nurtures them. New construction fills streams with silt, while sewage fouls fishing grounds in the estuaries. Pollution and chemical spills contaminate cropland and water supplies. Trash blights the landscape, destroying its beauty and creating health problems. Unbridled and poorly planned development disregards natural processes and invites disaster. Only an informed and active citizenry can prevent the destruction of the land. [467]

If you walk the beaches of our state through a dozen or so seasons, hike the stream valleys, or climb the mountains you will discover that the billion-year-old processes which created the land are still at work. We are the ephemeral portion of our partnership with the earth. If we ignore the lessons our geologic heritage teaches, we are the ones who will suffer. The rocks and hills of the Carolinas have a message for us. They are saying, "We were millions of years in the making and we will be here long after the last human is gone. Take care how you treat us, lest you shorten your stay on this planet and become extinct before your time."

GEOLOGIC TIME TABLE Appendix A

ERA	PERIOD		EPOCH	DURATION		BEGINNING
CENOZOIC	Quaternary		Holocene	1.6	0.01	0.01
			Pleistocene		1.59	1.6
	TERTIARY	Neogene	Pliocene	64.8	3.7	5.3
			Miocene		17.9	23.7
		Paleogene	Oligocene		12.9	36.6
			Eocene		18	54.6
			Paleocene		11.8	66.4
MESOZOIC	Cretaceous			178.5	77.5	144
	Jurassic				64	208
	Triassic				37	245
PALEOZOIC	Permian			32.5	41	245
	Carboniferous (Pennsylvanian)				34	286
	Carboniferous (Mississippian)				40	320
	Devonian				48	408
	Silurian				30	438
	Ordovician				67	505
	Cambrian				65	570
PROTEROZOIC				1,930		2,600
ARCHEOZOIC						4,000+

GEOLOGIC COLUMN FOR THE NORTH CAROLINA COASTAL PLAIN

Geologic time		This column includes only those formations described in chapters 15-20
Epochs	Ma	NORTH SOUTH

Epochs	Ma	
Holocene		Unnamed surficial soils
	0.01	Flanner Beach Fm. Canepatch Fm.
Pleistocene		
	1.6	James City Fm. Waccamaw Fm.
Pliocene		Chowan River Fm. Bear Bluff Fm.
		Macks Fm.
		Yorktown Fm. Duplin Fm.
	5.3	Eastover Fm.
Miocene		Pungo River Fm.
	23.7	Belgrade Fm.
Oligocene		River Bend Fm.
	36.6	Castle Hayne Fm.
Eocene		
	54.6	Beaufort Fm.
Paleocene		
	66.4	- - - - - - - MESOZOIC - CENOZOIC BOUNDARY - - - - - - - - -
Upper Portion of Cretaceous Period		Peedee Fm.
		Black Creek Fm.
		Middendorf Fm.
		Cape Fear Fm.
	97.5	

Fm. = Formation

Adapted from Reference 245

Notes

1. King, P. B., and Beikman, H. M., 1974, Geologic Map of the United States. U.S. Geological Survey, Reston, Virginia, 4 sheets.
2. Brown, P. M., Parker, J. M., III, Burt, E. R., III, Carpenter, A. P., III, Enos, R. M., Flynt, B. J., Jr., Gallagher, P. E., Hoffman, C. W., Merschat, C. E., and Wilson, W. F., 1985, Geologic Map of North Carolina. Raleigh, Department of Natural Resources and Community Development, Division of Land Resources, 1 sheet.
3. Stuckey, J. L., 1965, North Carolina: Its Geology and Mineral Resources. Raleigh, North Carolina Department of Conservation and Development, 550 pp.
4. Hatcher, R. D., Jr., 1972, Developmental Model for the Southeastern Appalachians. Geological Society of America Bulletin, v. 83, n. 7, pp. 2735–2760.
5. Williams, H. and Hatcher, R. D., Jr., 1982, Suspect Terranes and Accretionary History of the Appalachian Orogen. Geology, v. 10, pp. 530–536.
6. Hatcher, R. D., Jr., 1987, Tectonics of the Southern and Central Appalachian Internides. Annual Review of Earth and Planetary Geosciences, v. 15, pp. 377–361.
7. Rodgers, J., 1970, The Tectonics of the Appalachians. New York, Wiley-Interscience Publishers, 271 pp.
8. Seyfert, C. K., and Sirkin, L. A., 1973, Earth History and Plate Tectonics, An Introduction to Historical Geology. New York, Harper and Row Publishers, 504 pp.
9. Dunbar, C. O., and Waage, K. M., 1969, Historical Geology. New York, John Wiley and Sons, 3rd. ed., 556 pp.
10. Levin, H. L., 1988, The Earth Through Time. Philadelphia, Saunders College Publishing, 593 pp.
11. Detrich, R. V., 1970, Geology and Virginia. Charlottesville, The University Press of Virginia, 213 pp.
12. Cameron, A. G. W., 1975, The Origin and Evolution of the Solar System. Scientific American, v. 233, n. 3, pp. 32–41.
13. Ringwood, A. E., 1975, Composition and Petrology of the Earth's Mantle. New York, McGraw-Hill Book Company, 239 pp.
14. Sevier, R., 1975, The Earth. Scientific American, v. 233, n. 3, pp. 83–90.
15. Mason, B., and Moore, C. B., 1982, Principles of Geochemistry, fourth edition. New York, John Wiley and Sons, 344 pp.
16. Moorbath, S., Allaart, J. H., Bridgewater, D., and McGregor, V. R., 1977, U-Pb Ages of Early Archean Supracrustal Rocks and Amitsoq Gneisses at Isua. Nature, v. 270, pp. 43–45.

17. Folinsbee, R. E., et al., 1968, A Very Ancient Island Arc *in* Knopff, L., Drake, C. L., and Hart, P. J., eds., The Crust and Upper Mantle of the Pacific Area. American Geophysical Union Monograph 12, 441 pp.

18. Catazaro, E. J., and Kulp, J. L., 1964, Discordant Zircons from Little Belt (Montana), Beartooth (Montana), and Santa Catalina (Arizona) Mountains. Geochemical and Cosmochemical Acta, v. 28, 87 pp.

19. Heimlich, R. A., and Banks, P. O., 1968, Radiometric Age Determinations, Bighorn Mountains, Wyoming. American Journal of Science, v. 266, 180 pp.

20. Rankama, K., ed., 1963, The Precambrian. New York, Wiley-Interscience Publishers, v. 1, 279 pp.

21. Schopf, J. W., and Barghoorn, 1967, Algae-like Fossils from the Early Precambrian of South Africa. Science, v. 156, pp. 508–512.

22. Schwartzbach, M., 1963, Climates of the Past, An Introduction to Paleoclimatology. New York, D. Van Nostrand Company Ltd., 213 pp.

23. Lindsay, D. A., 1966, Sediment Transport in a Precambrian Ice Age: the Huronian Gowganda Formation. Science, v. 154, p. 1442.

24. Young, G. M., 1970, An Extensive Early Proterozoic Glaciation in North America? Paleogeography, Paleoclimatology, Paleoecology, v. 7, p. 85.

25. Schmus, R. V., 1965, The Geochronology of the Blind River– Bruce Mines Area, Ontario, Canada. Journal of Geology, v. 73, p. 755.

26. Maxson, J. H., 1961, Geologic Map of Bright Angel Quadrangle, Grand Canyon National Park. Grand Canyon Natural History Association.

27. Zion Natural History Association, 1971, Geologic Cross Section of the Cedar Breaks-Zion-Grand Canyon Region. Springdale, Utah, Zion Natural History Association, Zion National Park, 1 sheet.

28. Dewit, M. J., 1970, Evidence for Salt Deposits in the Appalachian/Caledonian Orogen. Nature, v. 227, p. 829.

29. Kish, S. A., Merschat, C. E., Mohr, D. W., and Wiener, L. S., 1975, Guidebook to the Geology of the Blue Ridge South of the Great Smoky Mountains, North Carolina. Raleigh, Carolina Geological Society Annual Fieldtrip Guidebook, 49 pp.

30. Fullagar, P. D., and Bartholomew, M. J., 1983, Rubidium-Strontium Ages of the Watagua River, Cranberry, and Crossing Knob Gneisses, Northwestern North Carolina *in* Geologic Investigations in the Blue Ridge of Western North Carolina. Raleigh, Carolina Geological Society Field Trip Guidebook, pp. 1–24.

31. Odom, A. L., and Fullagar, P. D., 1971, Rb-Sr Whole-Rock Ages of the Blue Ridge Basement Complex (abs.). Abstracts with Programs, Southeastern Section, Geological Society of America, v. 3, n. 5, p. 336.

32. Fullagar, P. D., Hatcher, R. D., Jr., and Merschat, C. E., 1979, 1200 M. Y.-Old Gneisses in the Blue Ridge Province of North and South Carolina. Southeastern Geology, v. 20, n. 2, pp. 69–78.

33. Dietz, R. S., 1972, Geosynclines, Mountains, and Continent Building *in* Wilson, J. T., ed., 1973, Continents Adrift—Readings From Scientific American. San Franscisco, W. H. Freeman & Company, pp. 124–133.

34. Faucet, P. D., and Williams, R. T., 1988, Basement Beneath the Blue Ridge and Inner Piedmont in Northeastern Georgia and the Carolinas. A Preserved, Late Proterozoic, Rifted Continental Margin. Geological Society of America Bulletin, v. 100, n. 12, pp. 1999–2007.

35. Rankin, D. W., 1975, The Continental Margin of Eastern North America in the Southern Appalachians. The Opening and Closing of the Proto-Atlantic Ocean. American Journal of Science, v. 275-A, pp. 298–336.

36. Rankin, D. W., 1976, Appalachian Salients and Recesses. Late Precambrian Continental Breakup and the Opening of the Iapetus Ocean. Journal of Geophysical Research, v. 81, n. 32, pp. 5606–5619.

37. Fichter, L. S., and Diecchio, R. J., 1986, Stratigraphic Model for Timing the Opening of the Proto-Atlantic Ocean in Northern Virginia. Geology, v. 14, pp. 307–309.

38. Dennison, J. M., 1977, Effect of Late Precambrian Lineaments on Paleozoic Deposition and Subsequent Deformation of the Appalachian Basin (abs.). Abstracts with Programs, Southeastern Section, Geological Society of America Bulletin, v. 9, n. 3, pp. 254–255.

39. Odom, A. L., and Fullagar, P. D., 1973, Geochronology and Tectonic Relationships Between the Inner Piedmont, Brevard Zone, and Blue Ridge Belts, North Carolina. American Journal of Science, v. 273-A, pp. 133–149.

40. Stoddard, E. F., Farrar, S. S., Horton, J. W., Jr., Butler, J. R., and Druhan, R. M., 1988, The Eastern Piedmont of North Carolina in The Geology of the Carolinas, Golden Anniversary Volume of the Carolina Geological Society. 23 pp. In Press

41. Farrar, S. S., 1984, The Goochland Granulite Terrane: Remobilized Grenville Basement in the Eastern Virginia Piedmont. Geological Society of America, Special Paper 194, pp. 215–227.

42. Stoddard, E. F., Horton, J. W., Jr., Wylie, A. S., Jr., and Blake, D. E., 1986, The Western Edge of the Raleigh Belt Near Adam Mountain, Wake County, North Carolina. Geological Society of America, Centennial Field Guide—Southeastern Section, pp. 223–226.

43. Parker, J. M., 1978, The Geology and Mineral Resources of Wake County, North Carolina. Raleigh, North Carolina Department of Natural and Economic Resources, Division of Earth Resources, 122 pp.

44. Harrington, J. W., 1947, The Origin and Importance of the Raleigh (N.C.) Graphite. Journal of Geology, v. 56, n. 6, pp. 516–521.

45. Espenshade, G. H., Rankin, D. W., Shaw, K. W., and Newman, R. B., 1975, Geologic Map of the East Half of the Winston-Salem Quadrangle, North Carolina-Virginia. Reston, Virginia, United States Geological Survey, Misc. Invs. Series Map 1-709-B, 1 sheet.

46. Rankin, D. W., Espenshade, G. H., and Newman, R. B., 1972, Geologic Map of the West Half of the Winston-Salem Quadrangle, North Carolina-Virginia. Reston, Virginia, United States Geological Survey, Misc. Invs. Series Map 1-709-A, 1 sheet.

47. Butler, J. R., and Dunn, D. E., 1968, Geology of the Sauratown Mountains Anticlinorium and Vicinity, North Carolina. Southeastern Geology, Special Publication 1, pp. 19–47.

48. Hatcher, R. D., Jr., McConnell, K. I., and Heyn, T., 1983, Preliminary Results from Detailed Geologic Mapping Studies in the Western Sauratown Mountains Anticlinorium, North Carolina, *in* Geologic Investigations in the Blue Ridge of Western North Carolina. Carolina Geological Society Field Trip Guidebook, 7 pp.

49. Hatcher, R. D., Jr., 1988, Structure of the Sauratown Mountains Window, North Carolina. Raleigh, North Carolina Geological Survey, Carolina Geological Society Guidebook, 104 pp.

50. Hatcher, R. D., Jr., 1988, Sauratown Mountains Window—Problems and Regional Perspective *in* Hatcher, R. D., Jr., ed., Structure of the Sauratown Mountains Window, North Carolina. Raleigh, North Carolina Geological Survey, Carolina Geological Society Field Trip Guidebook, pp. 1–19.

51. McConnell, K. I., 1988, Geology of the Sauratown Mountains Anticlinorium: Vienna and Pinnacle 7.5 Minute Quadrangles *in* Hatcher, R. D., Jr., ed., Structure of the Sauratown Mountains Window, North Carolina. Carolina Geological Society Field Trip Guidebook, Raleigh, North Carolina Geological Survey, pp. 51– 66.

52. Walker, D., 1988, Paleogeographic Significance of the Quartzite on Pilot Mountain, Surry County, North Carolina, *in* Hatcher, R. D., Jr., ed., Structure of the Sauratown Mountains Window, North Carolina. Carolina Geological Society Field Trip Guidebook, Raleigh, North Carolina Geological Survey, pp. 67– 76.

53. Walker, D., Driese, S. G., and Hatcher, R. D., Jr., 1989, Paleotectonic Significance of the Quartzite of the Sauratown Mountains Window, North Carolina. Geology, v. 17, pp. 913–917.

54. Schwab, F. L., 1986, Upper Precambrian-Lower Paleozoic Clastic Sequences, Blue Ridge and Adjacent Areas, Virginia and North Carolina: Initial Rifting and Continental Margin Development, Appalachian Orogen *in* Textoris, D. A., ed, SEPM Field Guidebook. Society of Economic Paleontologists and Mineralogists, Third Annual Midyear Meeting, pp. 1–42.

55. Kline, S. W., 1987, The Catoctin Formation in the Eastern Blue Ridge of Virginia: Evidence for Submarine Volcanism (abs.). Abstracts with Programs, Southeastern Section, Geological Society of America, v. 19, n. 2, p. 93.

56. Brown, W. R., 1970, Investigations of the Sedimentary Record in the Piedmont and the Blue Ridge of Virginia *in* Fisher, G. W., et al., eds., 1970, Studies of Appalachian Geology, Central and Southern. New York, Wiley-Interscience Publishers, pp. 335–350.

57. Blackburn, W. H., 1976, Petrochemical Evidence Relating the Catoctin Volcanic Series to Late Precambrian Continental Separation (abs.). Northeastern and Southeastern Sections, Geological Society America Bulletin, v. 8, n. 2, p. 136.

58. Lowry, W. D., ed., 1971, Guidebook to Appalachian Tectonics and Sulfide Mineralization of Southwest Virginia. Blacksburg, Virginia Polytechnic Institute and State University, Department of Geological Science, Guidebook Number 5, 178 pp.

59. Bryant, R., and Reed, J. C., Jr., 1970, Geology of the Grandfather Mountain Window and Vicinity, North Carolina and Tennessee. Reston, Virginia, United States Geological Survey, Professional Paper 615.

60. Goldsmith, R., and Hadley, J. B., 1955, Pre-Ocoee Erosion Surface in the Great Smoky Mountains, North Carolina (abs.). Geological Society of America Bulletin, v. 66, n. 12, pt. 2, pp. 1687–1688.

61. King, P. B., Neuman, R. B., and Hadley, J. B., 1968, Geology of the Great Smoky Mountains National Park, Tennessee and North Carolina. Washington, United States Geological Survey, Professional Paper 587, 23 pp.

62. Rast, N., and Kohles, K. M., 1986, The Origin of the Ocoee Supergroup. American Journal of Science, v. 286, pp. 593–616.

63. Spence, W. H., and Carpenter, P. A., III, 1976, Metalogenic Zonation and a Model for the Development of the Piedmont of Eastern North Carolina (abs.). Northeastern and Southeastern Sections, Geological Society of America Bulletin, v. 8, n. 2, p. 273.

64. Dewey, J. F., and Byrd, J. M., 1970, Mountain Belts and the New Global Tectonics. Journal of Geophysical Research, v. 75, n. 14, pp. 2625–2647.

65. Bird, J. M., and Dewey, J. F., 1970, Lithosphere Plate Continental Margin Tectonics and the Evolution of the Appalachian Orogen. Geological Society of America Bulletin, v. 81, n. 4, pp. 1031–1060.

66. Secor, D. T., Sampson, S. L., Snoke, A. W., and Palmer, A. R., 1983, Confirmation of the Carolina Slate Belt as an Exotic Terrane. Science, v. 221, pp. 649–651.

67. Sundelius, H. S., 1970, The Carolina Slate Belt in Fisher, G. W., et al., eds., 1970, Studies of Appalachian Geology Central and Southern. New York, Wiley-Interscience Publishers, pp. 351–368.

68. Butler, J. R., 1986, Volcaniclastic Rocks of the Carolina Slate Belt, Central North Carolina in Textoris, D. A., ed., Society of Economic Paleontologists and Mineralogists, Field Guidebooks, Southeastern United States, Third Annual Meeting, pp. 44–51.

69. Butler, J. R., 1986, Carolina Slate Belt Near Albemarle, North Carolina. Geological Society of America, Centennial Field Guide—Southeastern Section, pp. 235–237.

70. Horton, J. W., Jr., 1986, The Roanoke Rapids Complex of the Eastern Slate Belt, Halifax and Northhampton counties, North Carolina. Geological Society of America, Centennial Field Guide—Southeastern Section, pp. 217–222.

71. LeHuray, A. P., 1987, U-Pb and Th-Pb whole-rock isochrons from metavolcanic rocks of the Carolina Slate Belt. Geological Society of America Bulletin, v. 99, pp. 345–361.

72. Newton, M. C., III, 1983, A Late Precambrian Resurgent Cauldron in the Carolina Slate Belt of North Carolina, U.S.A. Unpublished master's thesis, Blacksburg, Virginia Polytechnic Institute and State University, 111 pp.

73. Wright, J. E., 1974, Geology of the Carolina Slate Belt in the Vicinity of Durham, North Carolina. Unpublished master's thesis, Blacksburg, Virginia Polytechnic Institute and State University, 78 pp.

74. McConnell, K. I., 1974, Geology of the Late Precambrian Flat River Complex and Associated Volcanic Rocks Near Durham, North Carolina. Unpublished master's thesis, Blacksburg, Virginia Polytechnic Institute and State University, 64 pp.

75. Council, R. J., 1954, Commercial Rocks of the Volcanic-Slate Belt Series, North Carolina. Raleigh, North Carolina Department of Conservation and Development, Division of Mineral Resources, Information Circular 12, 30 pp.

76. Spence, W. H., 1975, A Model for the Origin of the Pyrophyllite Deposits in the Carolina Slate Belt (abs.). Abstracts with Programs, Southeastern Section, Geological Society of America Bulletin, v. 7, n. 4, p. 536.

77. McDaniel, R. D., 1976, Application of a Hot Spring-Fumerole Alteration Model to the Genesis of the Pyrophyllite Deposits of the Carolina Slate Belt. Raleigh, North Carolina State University, Department of Geosciences, 75 pp.

78. Cloud, P., Wright, J., and Glover, L., III, 1976, Traces of Animal Life From 620 Million-Year-Old Rocks in North Carolina. American Scientist, v. 64, n. 3, pp. 396–406.

79. Glaessner, M. F., 1971, Geographic Distribution and Time Range of the Edicaria Fauna. Geological Society of America Bulletin, v. 82, n. 2, p. 3160.

80. Glaessner, M. F., 1961, Precambrian Animals. Scientific American, v. 204, n. 3, pp. 72.

81. St. Jean, J., 1973, A New Cambrian Trilobite from the Piedmont of North Carolina. American Journal of Science, v. 273-A, pp. 196–216.

82. Teeter, S. A., 1984, First Confirmed Ediacarian Fossil from the Carolina Slate Belt. Unpublished master's thesis, University of North Carolina at Charlotte, 74 pp.

83. Gibson, G. G., Teeter, S. A., and Fedonkin, M. A., 1984, Ediacarian Fossils From The Carolina Slate Belt, Stanly County, North Carolina. Geology, v. 12, pp. 387–390.

84. Dott, R. H., and Batten, R. L., 1988, Evolution of the Earth. New York, McGraw-Hill Book Company, 643 pp.

85. Gibson, G. G., 1989, Trace Fossils from the Late Precambrian Carolina Slate Belt, South-Central North Carolina. Journal of Paleontology, v. 63, n. 1, pp. 1–10.

86. Harris, C. W., and Glover, L., III, 1985, Field Trip Guide, Carolina Geological Society, The Virgilina Deformation: Implications of Stratigraphic Correlation in the Carolina Slate Belt. Charlottesville, Virginia Division of Mineral Resources, 60 pp.

87. Harris, G. W., and Glover, L., III, 1988, The Regional Extent of the 600 MA Virgilina Deformation: Implications for Stratigraphic Correlation in the Carolina Terrane. Geological Society of America Bulletin, v. 100, pp. 200–217.

88. Seiders, V. M., and Wright, J. E., 1977, Geology of the Carolina Volcanic Slate Belt in the Asheboro, North Carolina, Area *in* Burt, E. R., ed., Field Guides for Geological Society of America, Southeastern Sec-

tion Meeting, Winston-Salem, North Carolina. Division of Earth Resources, N. C. Department of Natural and Economic Resources, pp. 1–34.

89. Randazzo, A. F., 1972, Petrography and Stratigraphy of the North Carolina Slate Belt, Union County, North Carolina. Raleigh, North Carolina Department of Natural and Economic Resources, Office of Earth Resources, Special Publication 4, 38 pp.

90. Black, W. W., 1976, Avalonian Ages of Metavolcanics and Plutons of the Carolina Slate Belt Near Chapel Hill, N.C. (abs.) Abstracts with Programs, Northeastern and Southeastern Sections, Geological Society of America, v. 8, n. 2, p. 136.

91. Fullagar, P. D., 1976, Radiometric Ages in the Southeastern United State (abs.). Abstracts with Programs, Northeastern and Southeastern Sections, Geological Society of America Bulletin, v. 8, n. 2, p. 311.

92. Skelly, R. L., and Driese, S. G., 1987, Sedimentary Environments of a Fluvial-to-marine Transition: The Lower Cambrian Chilhowee Group, Southeastern Tennessee (abs.). Southeastern Section, Geological Society of America Bulletin, v. 19, n. 2, p. 129.

93. Simpson, E. L., and Sundberg, F. A., 1987, Early Cambrian Age for Synrift Deposits of the Chilhowee Group of Southwestern Virginia. Geology, v. 15, pp. 123–126.

94. Rudwick, M. J. S., 1964, The Infra-Cambrian Glaciation and the Origin of the Cambrian Fauna in Nairn, A. E. M., ed., Problems in Paleoclimatology. New York, Wiley-Interscience Publishers, pp. 150–154.

95. Hutchinson, G. E., 1930, Restudy of Some Burgess Shale Fossils. Washington, United States National Museum Proceedings, v. 78, n. 1, 24 pp.

96. Morris, S. C., and Wittington, H. B., 1979, The Animals of the Burgess Shale. Scientific American, v. 241, n. 1, pp. 112–135.

97. Oriel, S. S., 1950, Geology and Mineral Resources of the Hot Springs Window, Madison County, North Carolina. Raleigh, North Carolina Department of Conservation and Development, Division of Mineral Resources, Bulletin 60, 70 pp.

98. Bartlett, C. S., and Kopp, O. C., 1971, A Linguloid Brachiopod from the Upper Precambrian (?) Mount Rogers Volcanic Group in Washington County, Virginia (abs.). Abstracts with Programs, Southeastern Section, Geological Society of America Bulletin, v. 3, n. 5, p. 293.

99. Blondeau, K. M., and Lowe, D. R., 1972, Upper Precambrian Glacial Deposits of the Mount Rogers Formation, Central Appalachians, U.S.A. Gardenvale, Quebec, Harpell's Press Cooperative, 24th International Geological Congress, Section 1.

100. Rogers, J., 1968, The Eastern Edge of the North American Continent During the Cambrian and Early Ordovician in Zen, et al., eds., Studies of Appalachian Geology. Northern and Maritime. New York, Wiley-Interscience Publishers, pp. 141–150.

101. Pfeil, R. W., and Read, J. F., 1977, Platform and Platform Margin Carbonate Facies, Cambrian Shady Dolomite, Virginia in Burt, E. R., ed., Field Guides for Geological Society of America, Southeastern Section

Meeting, Winston-Salem, North Carolina. Division of Earth Resources, N. C. Department of Natural and Economic Resources, pp. 35–75.

102. Power, W. R., and Forrest, J. T., 1973, Stratigraphy and Structure of the Murphy Marble Belt. American Journal of Science, v. 273, pp. 698–711.

103. Horton, J. W., Jr., and Butler, J. R., 1977, Guide to the Geology of the Kings Mountain Area, North Carolina and South Carolina *in* Burt, E. R., ed., Field Guides for Geological Society of America, Southeastern Section Meeting, Winston-Salem, North Carolina. Division of Earth Resources, N. C. Department of Natural and Economic Resources, pp. 76–149.

104. Goldsmith, R. Milton, D. J., and Horton, J. W., Jr., 1988, Geologic Map of the Charlotte 1° × 2° Quadrangle, North Carolina and South Carolina. Reston, United States Geological Survey, Miscellaneous Investigations Series, Map I-251-E, 2 sheets.

105. Horton, J. W., Jr., 1981, Geologic Map of the Kings Mountain Belt Between Gafney, South Carolina, and Lincolnton, North Carolina *in* Horton, J. W., Jr., Butler, J. R., and Milton, D. M., eds., 1981, Geological Investigations of the Kings Mountain Belt and Adjacent Areas in the Carolinas. Columbia, South Carolina Geological Survey, Carolina Geological Society Field Trip Guidebook, pp. 6–18.

106. Murphy, C. F., and Butler, J. R., 1981, Geology of the Northern Half of the Kings Creek Quadrangle, South Carolina *in* Horton, J. W., Jr., Butler, J. R., and Milton, D. M., eds., 1981, Geological Investigations of the Kings Mountain Belt and Adjacent Areas in the Carolinas. Columbia, South Carolina Geological Survey, Carolina Geological Society Field Trip Guidebook, pp. 49–64.

107. Butler, J. R., 1981, Geology of the Blacksburg South Quadrangle, South Carolina *in* Horton, J. W., Jr., Butler, J. R., and Milton, D. M., eds., 1981, Geological Investigations of the Kings Mountain Belt and Adjacent Areas in the Carolinas. Columbia, South Carolina Geological Survey, Carolina Geological Society Field Trip Guidebook, Columbia, pp. 65–71.

108. France, N. A., and Brown, H. S., 1981, A Petrographic Study of Kings Mountain Belt Metaconglomerates *in* Horton, J. W., Jr., Butler, J. R., and Milton, D. M., eds., 1981, Geological Investigations of the Kings Mountain Belt and Adjacent Areas in the Carolinas. Columbia, South Carolina Geological Survey, Carolina Geological Society Field Trip Guidebook, pp. 91–99.

109. Moss, B. G., 1981, "The Old Iron District"—A Legacy of Iron Mining and Manufacturing in South Carolina *in* Horton, J. W., Jr., Butler, J. R., and Milton, D. M., eds., 1981, Geological Investigations of the Kings Mountain Belt and Adjacent Areas in the Carolinas. Columbia, South Carolina Geological Survey, Geological Society Field Trip Guidebook, pp. 110–119.

110. Sharpe, W. E., 1981, The Barite Deposit at Kings Creek, South Carolina *in* Horton, J. W., Jr., Butler, J. R., and Milton, D. M., eds., 1981,

Geological Investigations of the Kings Mountain Belt and Adjacent Areas in the Carolinas. Columbia, South Carolina Geological Survey, Carolina Geological Society Field Trip Guidebook, pp. 120–129.

111. Posey, H. H., 1981, A Model for the Origin of the Metallic Mineral Deposits in the Kings Mountain Belt *in* Horton, J. W., Jr., Butler, J. R., and Milton, D. M., eds., 1981, Geological Investigations of the Kings Mountain Belt and Adjacent Areas in the Carolinas. Columbia, South Carolina Geological Survey, Carolina Geological Society Field Trip Guidebook, pp. 130–141.

112. White, J. S., 1981, Mineralogy of the Foote Mine, Kings Mountain, North Carolina *in* Horton, J. W., Jr., Butler, J. R., and Milton, D. M., eds., 1981, Geological Investigations of the Kings Mountain Belt and Adjacent Areas in the Carolinas. Columbia, South Carolina Geological Survey, Carolina Geological Society Field Trip Guidebook, pp. 39–48.

113. Horton, J. W., and Butler, J. R., 1986, The Kings Mountain Belt and Spodumene Pegmatite District, Cherokee and York Counties, South Carolina, and Cleveland County, North Carolina. Geological Society of America, Centennial Field Guide—Southeastern Section, pp. 239–244.

114. Butler, J. R., 1984, Geologic History of the Charlotte Belt at the Old Pineville Quarry, Northeastern York County, South Carolina. South Carolina Geology, v. 27, nos. 1 & 2, pp. 13–24.

115. Butler, J. R., 1980, Review of Potential Host Rocks for Radioactive Waste Disposal in the Piedmont Province of North Carolina. Department of Energy, Dupont Publication 1526, 47 pp.

116. Colton, G. W., 1970, The Appalachian Basin—Its Depositional Sequences and their Geologic Relationships *in* Fisher, G. W., Pettijohn, F. J., Reed, J. C., Jr., and Weaver, K. N., eds., Studies of Appalachian Geology: Central and Southern, New York, Interscience Publishers, pp. 5–48.

117. Farrar, S. S., 1985, Tectonic Evolution of the Easternmost Piedmont, North Carolina. Geological Society of America Bulletin, v. 96, pp. 362–380.

118. Bova, J. A., and Read, J. F., 1987, Incipiently drowned facies within a cyclic peritidal ramp sequence, Early Ordovician Chepultepec interval, Virginia Appalachians. Geological Society of America Bulletin, v. 98, pp. 714–727.

119. McSween, H. Y., Jr., Abbott, R. N., and Raymond, L. A., 1989, Metamorphic Conditions in the Ashe Metamorphic Suite, North Carolina Blue Ridge. Geology, v. 17, pp. 1140–1143.

120. Diecchio, R. J., 1986, Upper Ordovician and Silurian Stratigraphy of the Virginia and West Virginia Valley and Ridge: Sedimentary and Structural Effects of the Taconic Orogeny *in* Textoris, D. A., ed., SEPM Field Guidebook. Society of Economic Paleontologists and Mineralogists, Third Annual Midyear Meeting, pp. 217–252.

121. Wiener, L. S., 1979, Rate of Mid-Paleozoic Orogenic Uplift in the Southern Appalachians. Southeastern Geology, v. 21, n. 1, pp. 91–101.

122. Butts, C., 1940, Geology of the Appalachian Valley in Virginia. Charlottesville, Virginia Geological Survey, Bulletin 52, pts. 1 and 2, 568 pp. and 271 pp.

123. Dennison, J. M., 1976, Gravity Tectonic Removal of Cover of Blue Ridge Anticlinorium to From Valley and Ridge Province. Geological Society of America Bulletin, v. 87, n. 10, pp. 1470–1476.

124. Kulander, B. R., and Dean, S. L., 1986, Structure and Tectonics of Central and Southern Appalachian Valley and Ridge and Plateau Provinces, West Virginia and Virginia. The American Association of Petroleum Geologists Bulletin, v. 70, n. 11, pp. 1674–1684.

125. McSween, H. Y., Jr., Speer, J. A., and Fullagar, P. D., 1988, Plutonic Rocks of the Carolinas in The Geology of the Carolinas, Golden Anniversary Volume of the Carolina Geological Society, 20 pp. In Press.

126. Kish, S. A., 1983, A Geochemical Study of Deformation in the Blue Ridge and Piedmont of the Carolinas. Unpublished doctoral dissertation, Chapel Hill, University of North Carolina at Chapel Hill, 202 pp.

127. Butler, J. R., and Ragland, P. C., 1969, A Petrochemical Survey of Plutonic Intrusions in the Piedmont, Southeastern Appalachians, U.S.A. Contributions to Mineralogy and Petrology, v. 24, pp. 164–190.

128. Harper, S. B., and Fullagar, P. D., 1981, Rb-Sr Ages of Granite Gneisses of the Piedmont Belt of Northwestern North Carolina and Southwestern South Carolina. Geological Society of America Bulletin, pt. 1, v. 92, pp. 864–872.

129. Farrar, S. S., Russell, G. S., Russell, C. W., and Glover, L., III, 1981, Alleghenian Deformation and Metamorphism in the Eastern Piedmont of North Carolina: New Evidence from Rb-Sr Whole Rock and Biotite Ages (abs.). Geological Society of America Abstracts with Programs, v. 13, n. 7, pp. 449–450.

130. Carpenter, P. A., III, 1976, Metallic Mineral Deposits of the Carolina Slate Belt, North Carolina Slate Belt, North Carolina. Raleigh, North Carolina Department of Natural and Economic Resources, Division of Resource Planning and Evaluation, Mineral Resources Division, Bulletin 84, 166 pp.

131. Roberts, B., 1971, The Carolina Gold Rush. Charlotte, McNally and Loftin Publishers, 80 pp.

132. Carpenter, A. P., III, 1972, Gold Resources of North Carolina. Raleigh, North Carolina, Department of Natural Resources, Office of Earth Resources, Information Circular 21, 56 pp.

133. Knapp, H. P., 1975, Golden Promise in the Piedmont: The Story of John Reed's Mine. Raleigh, North Carolina Department of Cultural Resources, Division of Archives and History, 27 pp.

134. Saunders, J. A., 1989, Hydrogeochemical Aspects of Gold in the Weathering Environment: Implications for Possible Secondary Concentration in the Coastal Plain Sediments of South Carolina. Southeastern Geology, v. 29, n. 3, pp. 129–142.

135. Olsen, N. K., 1988, Geologic Activities in South Carolina in 1987. South Carolina Geology, v. 32, n. 1 and 2, pp. 27–34.

136. Wilson, W. F., and McKensie, B. J., 1978, Mineral Collecting Sites in North Carolina. Raleigh, North Carolina Department of Natural Re-

sources and Community Development, Geological Survey Section, Information Circular 24, 122 pp.

137. Weiner, L. S., and Merschat, C. E., 1975, Field Guide to the Geology of the Central Blue Ridge of North Carolina and the Spruce Pine Mining District. Raleigh, North Carolina Department of Natural and Economic Resources, Association of American State Geologists, Annual Meeting, 49 p.

138. Olsen, J. C., 1944, Economic Geology of the Spruce Pine Pegamitite District, North Carolina. Raleigh, North Carolina Department of Conservation and Development, Division of Mineral Resources, Bulletin 43, pts. 1 and 2, 178 pp.

139. Misra, K. C., and McSween, H. Y., Jr., 1984, Mafic Rocks of the Southern Appalachians: A Review. American Journal of Science, v. 284, n. 5/6, pp. 294–318.

140. McSween, H. Y., Jr., Sando, T. W., Clark, S. R., Harden. J. T., and Strange, E. A., 1984, The Gabbro-Metagabbro Association of the Southern Appalachian Piedmont. American Journal of Science, v. 284, n. 5/6, pp. 437–461.

141. McSween, H. Y., Jr., 1986, The Concord Gabbro-Syenite Complex, North Carolina. Geological Society of America, Centennial Field Guide—Southeastern Section, pp. 231– 233.

142. Hatcher, R. D., Jr., Hooper, R. J., Petty, S. M., and Willis, J. D., 1984, Structure and Chemical Petrology of Ultramafic Complexes and Their Bearing upon the Tectonics of Emplacement and Origin of Appalachian Ultramafic Bodies. American Journal of Science, v. 284, pp. 484–506.

143. Hoge, H. P., and Berkheiser, S. W., 1975, Depositional Environments of Devonian Carbonates in Eastern Kentucky (abs.). Abstracts with Programs, Southeastern Section, Geological Society of America Bulletin, v. 7, n. 4, p. 501.

144. Dennison, J. M., and Textoris, D. A., 1970, Devonian Tioga Tuff in the North Eastern United States. Bulletin Volcanologique, v. 34, n. 1, pp. 289–294.

145. Dallmeyer, R. D., 1976, Thermal History of the Western Margin: Central and Southern Appalachians (abs.). Abstracts with Programs, Northeastern and Southeastern Sections, Geological Society of America Bulletin, v. 8, n. 2, p. 157.

146. Fenton, C. L., and Fenton, M. A., 1958, The Fossil Book. Garden City, New Jersey, Doubleday and Company, 482 pp.

147. Andrews, H. N., 1974, Paleobotany 1947–1972. Annals of the Missouri Botanical Garden, v. 61, n. 1, pp. 179–202.

148. Banks, H. P., 1975, Early Vascular Land Plants Proof and Conjecture, Bioscience, v. 25, n. 11, pp. 730–737.

149. Gensel, P. G., 1977, Morphologic and Taxonomic Relationships of the Psilotaceae Relative to Evolutionary Lines in Early Land Vascular Plants. Brittonia, v. 29, n. 1, pp. 14–29.

150. Gensel, P. G., Andrews, H. N., and Forbes, W. H., 1975, A New Species of Sawdonia With Notes on the Origin of Mycrophylls and Lateral Sporoangia. Botanical Gazette, v. 136, n. 1, pp. 50–62.

151. Andrew, H. N., and Kasper, A. E., 1970, Plant Fossils of the Trout Valley Formation *in* Shorter Contributions to Maine Geology. Augusta, Maine Geologic Survey, Department of Economic Development, Bulletin 23, pp. 3–16.

152. Englund, K. J., Cecil, C. B., Strickler, G. D., and Warlow, R. C., 1976, Carboniferous Stratigraphy of Southwestern Virginia and Southwestern West Virginia (abs.). Abstracts with Programs, Northeastern and Southeastern Sections, Geological Society of America, v. 8, n. 2, p. 136.

153. Dever, G. R., Jr., Ferm, J. C., Horne, J. C., Smith, G. E., and Whaley, P. W., 1971, Depositional Environments of Eastern Kentucky Coals. Kentucky Geological Survey, 22 pp.

154. Cardwell, D. H., 1975, Geologic History of West Virginia. Huntington, West Virginia Geological and Economic Survey, 64 pp.

155. Warne, G. A., and Dennison, J. M., 1988, Preliminary Stratigraphic Analysis of the Maccrady Formation, Central Appalachians *in* Shumaka, R. C., ed., Appalachian Basin Industrial Associates, Department of Geology and Geography, Morgantown, West Virginia University, v. 14, pp. 166–186.

156. Tidwell, W. D., 1975, Common Fossil Plants of Western North America. Provo, Brigham Young University Press, 197 pp.

157. Andrews, H. N., Jr., 1970, Ancient Plants and the World They Lived In. Ithica, New York, Cornell University Press, 279 pp.

158. Callahan, P. S., 1972, The Evolution of the Insects. New York, Holliday House, 192 pp.

159. Goldstein, A. G., 1989, Tectonic Significance of Multiple Motions on Terrane-Boundary Faults in the Northern Appalachians. Geological Society of America Bulletin, v. 101, pp. 927–938.

160. Bobyarchick, A. R., Edelman, S. H., and Horton, J. W., Jr., 1988, Field Trip 3, The Role of Dextral Strike Slip in the Displacement History of the Brevard Zone *in* Secor, D. T., ed., Southeastern Geological Excursions, Columbia, South Carolina Geological Survey, pp. 53–154.

161. Reed, J. C., Jr., and Bryant, B., 1964, Evidence for Strike-Slip Faulting Along the Brevard Zone in North Carolina. Geological Society of American Bulletin, v. 75, pp. 1177–1195.

162. Fullagar, P. D., and Butler, J. R., 1979, 325 to 265 m.y.-old Granitic Plutons in the Piedmont of the Southeastern Appalachians. American Journal of Science, v. 279, pp. 161–185.

163. Horton, J. W., Blake, D. E., Wylie, A. S., and Stoddard, E. F., 1986, Metamorphosed Mélange Terrane in the Eastern Piedmont of North Carolina. Geology, v. 14, n. 6, pp. 551–553.

164. Secor, D. T., Snoke, A. W., Bramlett, K. W., Costello, O. P., and Kimbrell, O. P., 1986, Character of the Alleghenian Orogeny in the Southern Appalachians: Part I. Alleghenian Deformation in the Eastern Piedmont of South Carolina. Geological Society of America Bulletin, v. 97, pp. 1319–1328.

165. Dallmeyer, R. D., Wright, J. E., Secor, D. T., and Snoke, A. W., 1986, Character of the Alleghenian Orogeny in the Southern Appalachians:

Part II. Geological Constraints on the Tectonothermal Evolution of the Eastern Piedmont in South Carolina. Geological Society of America Bulletin, v. 97, pp. 1329–1344.

166. Secor, D. T., Jr., Snoke, A. W., and Dallmeyer, R. D., 1986, Character of the Alleghenian Orogeny in the Southern Appalachians: Part III. Tectonic Relations. Geological Society of America Bulletin, v. 97, pp. 1345–1353.

167. Russel, G. S., Russell, C. W., and Farrar, S. S., 1985, Alleghenian Deformation and Metamorphism in the Eastern North Carolina Piedmont. Geological Society of America Bulletin, v. 96, pp. 381–387.

168. Horton, J. W., Jr., Sutter, J. F., Stern, T. W., and Milton, D. J., 1987, Alleghenian Deformation, Metamorphism, and Granite Emplacement in the Central Piedmont of the Southern Appalachians. American Journal of Science, v. 287, n. 6, pp. 635–660.

169. Cook, F. A., Brown, L. D., Kaufman, S. E., Oliver, J. E., and Peterson, T. A., 1981, COCORP Seismic Profiling of the Appalachian Orogen Beneath the Coastal Plain of Georgia. Geological Society of America Bulletin, v. 92, pp. 738–748.

170. Iverson, W. P., and Smithson, S. B., 1983, Reprocessed COCORP Southern Appalachian Reflection Data: Root Zone to Coastal Plain. Geology, v. 11, pp. 422–425.

171. Harris, L. D., and Bayer, K. C., 1979, Sequential Development of the Appalachian Orogen above a Master Decollement—a Hypothesis. Geology, v. 7, pp. 568–572.

172. Cook, F. A., Albaugh, D. S., Brown, L. D., Kaufman, S., Oliver, J. E., and Hatcher, R. D., Jr., 1979, Thin-Skinned Tectonics in the Crystalline Southern Appalachians. COCORP Seismic Reflection Profiling of the Blue Ridge and Piedmont. Geology, v. 7, pp. 563–567.

173. Costain, J. K., and Coruh, C., 1987, Regional Ramp in the Blue Ridge Master Decollement in Crystalline Rocks from Virginia to South Carolina from Reflection Seismic Data (abs.). Southeastern Section, Geological Society of America Bulletin, v. 19, n. 2, p. 80.

174. Nelson, K. D., Arnow, J. A., McBride, J. H., Willemin, J. H., Huang, J., Zheng, L., Oliver, J. E., Brown, L. D., and Kaufman, S., 1985, New COCORP Profiling in the Southeastern United States. Part I: Late Paleozoic Suture and Mesozoic Rift Basin. Geology, v. 13, pp. 714–718.

175. Schlee, J. S. and Klitgord, K. K., 1986, Structure of the North American Atlantic Continental Margin. Journal of Geological Education, v. 34, pp. 72–89.

176. Hatcher, R. D., Jr., Hooper, R. J., McConnell, K. I., Heyn, T., and Costello, J. O., Geometric and Time Relationships Between Thrusts in the Crystaline Southern Appalachians in Mitra, G., and Wojtal, S., eds., 1988, Geometries and Mechanisms of Thrusting, with Special Reference to the Appalachians. Geological Society of America, Special Paper 222, pp. 185–196.

177. Horton, J. W., Jr., and Butler, J. R., 1986, The Brevard Fault Zone at Rosman, Transylvania County, North Carolina. Geological Society of America, Centennial Field Guide—Southeastern Section, pp. 251–256.

178. Boyer, S. E., 1976, Formation of the Grandfather Mountain Window, North Carolina by Duplex Thrusting (abs.). Geological Society of America Annual Meeting, pp. 788–789.

179. Hatcher, R. D., Jr., and Butler, R. J., 1986, Linville Falls Fault at Linville Falls, North Carolina. Geological Society of America, Centennial Field Guide—Southeastern Section, pp. 229–230.

180. Bryant, B., and Reed, J. C., Jr., 1970, Structural and Metamorphic History of the Southern Blue Ridge *in* Fisher, G. W., et al., eds., Studies of Appalachian Geology, Central and Southern. New York, Wiley Inter-Science Publishers, pp. 213–226.

181. Hubbert, K. J., and Harris, L. D., 1961, Role of Fluid Pressure in Mechanics of Overthrust Faulting I. Mechanics of Fluid-Filled Porous Solids and Its Application to Overthrust Faulting. Geological Society of America Bulletin, v. 70, n. 2, pp. 115–166.

182. Miller, R. L., 1973, Where and Why of Pine Mountain and Other Major Fault Planes, Virginia, Kentucky, and Tennessee. American Journal of Science, v. 273-A, pp. 353–371.

183. Harris, L. D., 1970, Details of Thin-Skinned Tectonics in Parts of the Valley and Ridge and Cumberland Provinces of the Southern Appalachians *in* Fisher, G. W., et al., eds., Studies of Appalachian Geology, Central and Southern. New York, Wiley Inter-Science Publishers, pp. 161–174.

184. Evans, M. A., 1989, The Structural Geometry and Evolution of Foreland Thrust Systems, Northern Virginia. Geological Society of America Bulletin, v. 101, n. 3, pp. 339–354.

185. Gwinn, V. E., 1970, Kinematic Patterns and Estimates of Lateral Shortening, Valley and Ridge and Great Valley Provinces, Central Appalachians *in* Fisher, G. W., et al., eds., Studies of Appalachian Geology, Central and Southern. New York, Wiley Inter-Science Publishers, pp. 127–146.

186. Smith, M. D., Noyer, M. C., and Smith, G. E., 1967, Some Aspects of the Stratigraphy of the Pine Mountain Front Near Elkhorn City, Kentucky, With Notes on Pertinent Structural Features. Louisville, Geological Society of Kentucky, Annual Spring Field Conference, 24 pp.

187. Englund, K. J., and Harris, L. D., 1961, Geologic Features of the Cumberland Gap Area, Kentucky, Tennessee, and Virginia. Louisville, Kentucky Geological Survey, 30 pp.

188. McGrain, P., 1975, Scenic Geology of Pine Mountain in Kentucky. Lexington, Kentucky Geological Survey, 34 pp.

189. Strahler, A. N., 1977, Principles of Physical Geology. New York, Harper & Row Publishers Inc., 419 pp.

190. Dietz, R. S., and Holder, J. C., 1970, The Breakup of Pangaea *in* Readings From Scientific American—Continents Adrift. San Francisco, W. H. Freeman and Company, pp. 102–113.

191. Bain, G. L., 1973, Feasibility of East Coast Triassic Basins for Waste Storage (interim report). Washington, United States Geological Survey, Open File Report, 113 pp.

192. May, P. R., 1971, Pattern of Triassic-Jurassic Diabase Dikes Around the North Atlantic in the Context of Predrift Position of the Conti-

nents. Geological Society of America Bulletin, v. 82, n. 5, pp. 1285–1292.

193. Bain, G. L., 1977, Wrench-Fault Tectonic Origin of East Coast Triassic Basins (abs.). Southeastern Section, Geological Society of America Bulletin, v. 9, n. 2, p. 115.

194. Marine, I. W., and Siple, G. E., 1971, Buried Triassic Basin in the Central Savannah River Area, South Carolina and Georgia (abs.). Southeastern Section, Geological Society of America Bulletin, v. 3, n. 5, p. 328.

195. Marine, I. W., 1976, Structural Model of the Buried Dumbarton Triassic Basin in South Carolina and Georgia (abs.). Northeastern and Southeastern Sections, Geological Society of America Bulletin, v. 8, n. 2, p. 225.

196. Ceddes, W. H., and Thayer, P. A., 1971, Gravity Investigation of the Dan River Triassic Basin of North Carolina (abs.). Southeastern Section, Geological Society of America Bulletin, v. 3, n. 5, p. 312.

197. Black, W. T., and Stewart, D. M., 1973, A Seismic Estimate of Depth of Triassic Durham Basin, North Carolina. Southeastern Geology, v. 15, n. 2, p. 116.

198. Bain, G. L., 1977, Structural Reinterpretation of the Durham-Wadesboro Triassic Basin, North Carolina (abs.). Southeastern Section, Geological Society of America Bulletin, v. 7, n. 4, p. 467.

199. Bain, G. L., and Stewart, D. M., 1975, Three Seismic Reflection-Refraction Traverses in Durham Triassic Basin Near Cary, Green-Level, and Bonsal, N.C. (abs.). Southeastern Section, Geological Society of America Bulletin, v. 7, n. 4, p. 467.

200. Bain, G. L., and Harvey, B. W., 1977, Field Guide to the Geology of the Durham Triassic Basin. Raleigh, North Carolina Department of Natural Resources and Community Development, 83 pp.

201. Meyertons, C. T., 1963, Triassic Formations of the Dan River Basin. Charlottesville, Virginia Division of Mineral Resources, Report of Investigation 6, 65 pp.

202. Thayer, P. A., Kirsten, D. S., and Ingram, R. L., 1970, Stratigraphy, Sedimentology, and Economic Geology of the Dan River Basin, North Carolina. Raleigh, North Carolina Department of Natural and Economic Resources, Division of Mineral Resources, Carolinas Geological Society Guidebook, 42 pp.

203. Randazzo, A. F., and Copeland, R. E., 1976, The Geology of the Northern Portion of the Wadesboro Triassic Basin, North Carolina. Southeastern Geology, v. 17, n. 3, pp. 115–130.

204. Thayer, P. A., 1970, Geology of Davie County Triassic Basin, North Carolina. Southeastern Geology, v. 11, n. 3, pp. 187–198.

205. Thayer, P. A., 1970, Stratigraphy and Geology of Dan River Triassic Basin, North Carolina. Southeastern Geology, v. 12, n. 1, pp. 1–31.

206. Krynine, P. D., 1950, Petrology, Stratigraphy, and Origin of the Triassic Sedimentary Rocks of Connecticut. Connecticut Geological and Natural History Survey, Bulletin 73, 247 pp.

207. Randazzo, A. F., Swe, W., and Wheeler, W. M., 1970, A Study of Tectonic Influence of Triassic Sedimentation—The Wadesboro Basin,

Central Piedmont. Journal of Sedimentary Petrology, v. 40, n. 3, pp. 998–1006.

208. Arbogast, J. S., 1976, Fluvial Deposition of Triassic Red Beds: Durham Basin, North Carolina (abs.). Northeastern and Southeastern Sections, Geological Society of America Bulletin, v. 8, n. 3, p. 125.

209. Olsen, P. E., Remington, C. L., Cornet, B., and Thompson, K. S., 1978, Cyclic Change in Late Triassic Lacustrine Communities. Science, v. 201, n. 4357, pp. 729–733.

210. Wheeler, W. H., and Textoris, D. A., 1978, Triassic Limestone and Chert of Playa Origin in North Carolina. Journal of Sedimentary Petrology, v. 48, n. 3, pp. 765–776.

211. Gore, P. J., 1986, Depositional Framework of a Triassic Rift Basin: The Durham and Sanford Sub-Basins of the Deep River Basin, North Carolina in Textoris, D. A., ed., Society of Economic Paleontologists and Mineralogists, Field Guidebooks, Southeastern United States, Third Annual Meeting, pp. 55–115.

212. Gore, P. J. W., and Renwick, P. L., 1987, Paleoecology of Floodplain Lakes in the Durham Sub-Basin of the Deep River Basin (Late Triassic), North Carolina (abs.). Southeastern Section, Geological Society of America Bulletin, v. 19, n. 2, p. 86.

213. Olsen, P. E., 1984, Comparative Paleolimnology of the Newark Supergroup: A Study of Ecosystem Evolution. Unpublished Doctoral Dissertation, Yale University, 756 pp.

214. Reinemund, J. A., 1955, Geology of the Deep River Coal Field, North Carolina. United States Geological Survey, Professional Paper 246, 159 pp.

215. Berry, E. W., 1938, Triassic Coals (abs.). Elisha Mitchell Scientific Society Journal, v. 54, n. 2, p. 526.

216. Hope, R. C., and Patterson, O. F., III, 1962, Triassic Flora from the Deep River Basin, North Carolina. Raleigh, North Carolina Division of Mineral Resources, Special Publication 2, 23 pp.

217. Prouty, W. F., 1931, A Bituminous Fossil Plant from the Triassic of North Carolina. Science News Service, v. 72, n. 1873, pp. 526.

218. Delevoryas, T., 1970, Plant Life in the Triassic of North Carolina. Discovery, v. 6, n. 1, pp. 1–14.

219. Delevoryas, T., and Hope, R. C., 1971, A New Triassic Cycad and its Phyletic Implications. Yale University, Peabody Museum, Postilla, n. 150, pp. 1–18.

220. Delevoryas, T., and Hope, R. C., 1973, Fertile Coniferophyte Remains from the Late Triassic Deep River Basin, North Carolina. American Journal of Botany, v. 60, n. 8, pp. 1–12.

221. Schaeffer, B., 1954, "Pariostegus," A Triassic Coelacanth (N.C.). Philadelphia Academy of Natural Science, Notulae Naturae, n. 261, 6 pp.

222. Olsen, P. E., McCune, A. R., and Thompson, K. S., 1982, Correlation of the Early Mesozoic Newark Supergroup by Vertebrates, Principally Fishes. American Journal of Science, v. 282, n. 1, pp. 1–44.

223. Lull, R. S., 1953, Triassic Life of the Connecticut Valley. Connecticut Geological and Natural History Survey, Bulletin 81, 336 pp.

224. Olsen, P. E., 1979, A New Aquatic Eosuchian from the Newark Super-group (Late Triassic-Early Jurassic) of North Carolina and Virginia. Postilla, n. 176, 14 pp.

225. Colbert, E. H., 1947, Studies of the Phytosaurs Machaeroprosus and Rutidon. American Museum of Natural History Bulletin, v. 88, n. 2, pp. 53–96.

226. Osborn, H. F., 1986, Observations on the Upper Triassic Mammals Dromatherium and Microconodon. Proceedings of the Philadelphia Academy of Natural Science for 1986, pp. 359–363.

227. Colbert, E. H., and Imbre, J. 1956, Triassic Metoposaurid Amphibians. American Museum of Natural History Bulletin, v. 110, n. 6, pp. 263–274.

228. Colbert, E. H., 1970, Fossils of the Connecticut Valley, The Age of Dinosaurs Begins (rev. ed.). Hartford, State Geological and Natural History Survey of Connecticut, Department of Agriculture and Natural Resources, Bulletin 96, pp. 1–31.

229. Sawin, M. J., 1947, The Pseudosuchian Reptile Typothorax Meadei, New Species. Journal of Paleontology, v. 21, n. 3, pp. 359–363.

230. Parker, J. M., III, 1966, Triassic Reptilian Fossil From Wake County, North Carolina (abs.). Elisha Mitchell Scientific Society Journal, v. 82, n. 2, p. 92.

231. DeBoer, J., and Snider, F. G., 1979, Magnetic and Chemical Variations of Mesozoic Diabase Dikes from Eastern North America. Evidence for a Hotspot in the Carolinas? Geological Society of America Bulletin, v. 90, n.2, pp. 185–198.

232. Koch, H. F., 1967, Probable Flow-Structures of the Diabase of the Durham Triassic Basin, N.C. (abs.) Elisha Mitchell Scientific Society Journal, v. 83, n. 3, p. 176.

233. Justus, P. S., 1967, Evidence for Volcanism or Shallow Intrusion in the Triassic Pekin Formation of the Deep River Basin, North Carolina (abs.). Elisha Mitchell Scientific Society Journal, v. 83, n. 3, p. 176–177.

234. Furbish, W. J., 1976, The Origin of Calcium Silicate and Associated Minerals from a Sill Near Durham, North Carolina. Southeastern Geology, v. 17, n. 8, pp. 149–160.

235. LePichon, M., and Fox, P. J., 1971, Marginal Offsets, Fracture Zones, and the Early Opening of the North Atlantic. Journal of Geophysical Research, v. 72, n. 26, pp. 6204–6308.

236. LePichon, M., 1968, Sea-Floor Spreading and Continental Drift. Journal of Geophysical Research, v. 73, n. 12, pp. 3661–3699.

237. Heirtzler, J. R., Dickson, G. O., Herron, E. M., Pitman, W. C., III, and LePichon, M., 1968, Marine Magnetic Anomalies, Geomagnetic Field Reversals, and Motions of the Ocean Floor and Continents. Journal of Geophysical Research, v. 73, n. 6, pp. 2119–2136.

238. Hurley, P. M., 1968, The Confirmation of Continental Drift in Readings From Scientific American—Continents Adrift. San Francisco, W. H. Freeman and Company, pp. 57–67.

239. Brown, P. M., Miller, J. A., and Swain, F., 1972, Structural and Stratigraphic Framework, and Spatial Distribution of Permeability of the

Atlantic Coastal Plain, North Carolina to New York. United States Geological Survey, Professional Paper 796, 79 pp., 59 plates.

240. Maher, J. C., 1971, Geologic Framework and Petroleum Potential of the Atlantic Coastal Plain and Continental Shelf, With a Section on Stratigraphy. United States Geological Survey, Professional Paper 659, 96 pp.

241. Richards, H. G., 1950, Geology of the Coastal Plain of North Carolina. Philadelphia, Transactions of the American Philosophical Society, New Series, v. 40, n. 1, 83 pp.

242. Gohn, G. S., 1988, Late Mesozoic and Early Cenozoic Geology of the Atlantic Coastal Plain: North Carolina to Florida *in* Sheridan, R. E., and Grow, J. A., eds., The Geology of North America, v. 1–2, The Atlantic Continental Margin: U.S., Geological Society of America, pp. 107–130.

243. Soller, D. R., 1988, Geology and Tectonic History of the Lower Cape Fear River Valley, Southeastern North Carolina. Professional Paper 1466-A, U.S. Geological Survey, 60 pp.

244. Carter, J. G., 1984, Summary of Lithostratigraphy and Biostratigraphy for the Coastal Plain of the Southeastern United States. Biostratigraphy Newsletter, n. 2.

245. Carter, J. G., Valone, R. E., Gallagher, P. E., and Rossbach, T. J., with contributions by Gensel, P. G., Wheeler, W. H., and Whitman, D., 1987, Fossil Collecting in North Carolina. Raleigh, North Carolina Department of Natural Resources and Community Development, Division of Land Resources, Geological Survey Section, Bulletin 89, 89 pp.

246. Roper, P. J., 1977, Westward Movement of the North American Plate and Its Effects on the Passive Tectonics of Eastern North Carolina (abs.). Southeastern Section, Geological Society of America, n. 31, n. 9, p. 180.

247. Custer, E. S., Jr., 1981, Depositional Environments of the Subsurface Cretaceous Deposits of Southeastern North Carolina. Unpublished doctoral dissertation, University of North Carolina at Chapel Hill, 116 pp.

248. Christopher, R. A., Owens, J. P., and Sohl, N. F., 1979, Late Cretaceous Palynomorphs from the Cape Fear Formation of North Carolina. Southeastern Geology, v. 20, n. 3, pp. 145–160.

249. Bartlett, C. S., 1967, Geology of the Southern Pines Quadrangle, North Carolina. Unpublished master's thesis, University of North Carolina at Chapel Hill, 101 pp.

250. Sohl, N. F., 1976, Reinstatement of the Name Cape Fear Formation in North and South Carolina *in* Cohee, G. W., and Wright, W. R., 1976, Changes in Stratigraphic Nomenclature by the United States Geologic Survey. Reston, Geologic Survey Bulletin 1422-A, 63 pp.

251. Bell, H., III, Butler, R. J., Howell, D. E., and Wheeler, W. H., 1974, Geology of the Piedmont and Coastal Plain Near Pageland, South Carolina, and Wadesboro, North Carolina. Columbia, Division of Geology, State Development Board, 23 pp.

252. Heron, S. D., and Wheeler, W. H., 1959, Guidebook for Coastal Plain Fieldtrip Featuring Basal Cretaceous Sediments of the Fayetteville,

North Carolina, Area. Southeastern Section, Geological Society of America, 20 pp.

253. Kesler, T. L., 1963, Environment of the Cretaceous Kaolin Deposits of Georgia and South Carolina. Georgia Mineral Newsletter, v. 16, n. 1–2, pp. 3–11.

254. Goff, J. H., 1959, Thomas Griffith's "A Journal of the Voyage to South Carolina, 1767" To Obtain Cherokee Clay for Josiah Wedgewood, With Annotations. Georgia Mineral Newsletter, v. 12, n. 3, pp. 1–10.

255. Andrews, H. M. Jr., 1948, Fossil Tree Ferns of Idaho. Archeology, n. 1, n. 4, pp. 190–195.

256. Allen, E. P., 1976, A Newly Discovered Petrified Wood Locality Near Fayetteville, North Carolina (abs.). Elisha Mitchell Scientific Society Journal, v. 83, n. 3, pp. 168–179.

257. West, W. R., 1968, Petrified Wood in North Carolina. Carolina Biological Supply Company, Carolina Tips, v. 31, n. 9

258. West, W. R., 1977, Temskya in North Carolina. Lapidary Journal, February, pp. 2614–2618.

259. West, W. R., 1978, North Carolina Temskya Update. Lapidary Journal, January, pp. 2112–2116.

260. Zastrow, M. E., 1982, Stratigraphy and Depositional Environments of the Black Creek Formation along the Neuse River, North Carolina. Unpublished master's thesis, University of North Carolina at Chapel Hill, 137 pp.

261. Shew, R. D., 1979, Geology of the Area Between Fayetteville and Elizabethtown, North Carolina. Unpublished master's thesis, University of North Carolina at Chapel Hill, 101 pp.

262. Cabe, S., 1984, Cretaceous and Cenozoic Stratigraphy of the Upper and Middle Coastal Plain, Harnett County, North Carolina. Unpublished doctoral dissertation, University of North Carolina at Chapel Hill, 101 pp.

263. Owens, J. P., and Sohl, N. F., 1989, Campanian and Maastrichtian Depositional Systems of the Black Creek Group of the Carolinas. Carolina Geological Society Field Trip Guidebook, Raleigh, North Carolina Geological Survey, 23 pp.

264. Doyle, J. A., and Hickey, L. J., 1976, Pollen and Leaves from the Mid-Cretaceous Potomac Group and their Bearing on Early Angiosperm Evolution in Beck, C. B., ed., Origin and Early Evolution of Angiosperms, New York, Columbia University Press.

265. Doyle, J. A., 1969, Cretaceous Angiosperm Pollen on the Atlantic Coastal Plain and its Evolutionary Significance. Journal of the Arnold Arboretum, v. 50, n. 1, pp. 1–35.

266. Berry, E. W., 1950, A Cretaceous Log-Jam (abs.). Elisha Mitchell Scientific Society Journal, v. 66, n. 2, pp. 116.

267. Baird, D., and Horner, J. R., 1979, Cretaceous Dinosaurs of North Carolina. Brimleyana, Raleigh, North Carolina Museum of Natural History, n. 2, pp. 1–28.

268. Baird, D., 1988, personal communication. Department of Geological and Geophysical Sciences, Princeton University.

269. Miller, H. W., 1967, Cretaceous Vertebrates From Phoebus Landing, North Carolina. Proceedings of the Natural Science Society of Philadelphia, v. 19, n. 5, pp. 219–235.

270. Miller, H. W., 1966, Cretaceous Vertebrate Fauna from Phoebus Landing, North Carolina (abs.). Elisha Mitchell Scientific Society Journal, v. 82, n. 2, p. 93.

271. Wheeler, W. H., 1966, A Mosasaur Mandible from the Black Creek Formation, Cretaceous of North Carolina (abs.). Elisha Mitchell Scientific Society Journal, v. 32, n. 2, pp. 92–93.

272. Miller, H. W., 1968, Additions to the Upper Cretaceous Vertebrate Fauna of Phoebus Landing, North Carolina. Elisha Mitchell Scientific Society Journal, v. 84, pp. 467–471.

273. Swift, J. P., 1964, Origin of the Cretaceous Pee Dee Formation of the Carolina Coastal Plain. Unpublished doctoral dissertation, University of North Carolina at Chapel Hill, 151 pp.

274. Ferenczi, I., 1958, The Geology of Cliffs of the Neuse State Park and its Surrounding Area. Raleigh, North Carolina Department of Natural and Economic Resources, Division of State Parks, Unpublished research document, 24 pp.

275. Brett, C. E., and Wheeler, W. H., 1961, A Biostratigraphic Evaluation of the Snowhill Member, Upper Cretaceous of North Carolina. Southeastern Geology, v. 3, n. 2, pp. 49–132.

276. Shannon, S. W., 1974, Extension of the Known Range of the Pleisosauria in the Alabama Cretaceous. Southeastern Geology, v. 14, n. 4, pp. 193–200.

277. Wheeler, W. H., and Curran, H. A., 1974, Relation of Rocky Point Member (Peedee Formation) to Cretaceous-Tertiary Boundary in North Carolina. The American Association of Petroleum Geologists Bulletin, v. 58, n. 9, pp. 1751–1757.

278. Brown, P. M., Brown, D. L., Shufflebarger, T. E., Jr., and Sampair, J. L., 1977, Wrench-Style Deformation in Rocks of Cretaceous and Paleocene Age, North Carolina Coastal Plain. Raleigh, North Carolina Department of Natural and Economic Resources, Division of Earth Resources, 74 pp.

279. Brown, P. M., and Miller, J. A., 1986, Cretaceous-Paleocene Boundary, Lenoir County, North Carolina in Textoris, D. A., ed., SEPM Field Guidebook. Society of Economic Paleontologists and Mineralogists, Third Annual Midyear Meeting, pp. 119–128.

280. Harris, W. B., Baum, G. R., and Bottino, M. L., 1976, The Paleocene Beaufort Formation, North Carolina: Microfauna and Radiometric Age (abs.). Northeastern and Southeastern Sections, Geological Society of America, v. 8, n. 2, p. 191.

281. Wright, F. J., 1926, The Erosional History of the Blue Ridge. Dennison University Bulletin, v. 28, n. 10, pp. 321–344.

282. Thornbury, W. D., 1965, Regional Geomorphology of the United States. New York, John Wiley and Sons Inc., 609 pp.

283. Dennison, J. M., and Johnson, R. W., Jr., 1971, Tertiary Intrusions and Associated Phenomena Near the Thirty-Eighth Parallel Fracture

Zone in Virginia and West Virginia. Geological Society of America Bulletin, v. 82, n. 1, pp. 501–507.

284. Clark, B. W., Miller, B. L., Stephenson, L. W., Johnson, B. L., and Parker, H. N., 1912, The Coastal Plain of North Carolina. Raleigh, North Carolina Geological and Economic Survey, v. 3, 552 pp.

285. Baum, G. R., 1980, Petrology and Depositional Environments of the Middle Eocene Castle Hayne Limestone, North Carolina. Southeastern Geology, Southeastern Geology, v. 21, n. 3, pp. 175–196.

286. Kellum, L. R., 1926, Paleontology and Stratigraphy of the Castle Hayne Marls in North Carolina. United States Geological Survey, 56 pp.

287. Fallaw, W. C., and Wheeler, W. H., 1963, The Cretaceous-Tertiary Boundary at the Type Locality of the Castle Hayne Formation. Southeastern Geology, v. 5, n. 1, pp. 23–26.

288. Upchurch, M. L., 1973, Petrology of the Eocene Castle Hayne Limestone at Ideal Cement Quarry, New Hanover County, North Carolina. Unpublished master's thesis, University of North Carolina at Chapel Hill, 110 pp.

289. Sanders, A. E., 1974, A Paleontological Survey of the Cooper Marl and Santee Limestone near Harleyville, South Carolina. Columbia, South Carolina Division of Geology, Geologic Notes, v. 18, n. 1, pp. 4–12.

290. Baum, G. R., 1977, Stratigraphic Framework of the Middle Eocene to Lower Miocene Formations of North Carolina. Unpublished doctoral dissertation, University of North Carolina at Chapel Hill, 158 pp.

291. Baum, G. R., Harris, B., and Zullo, V., 1977, Stratigraphic Revision and Structural Setting of the Eocene to Lower Miocene Strata of North Carolina (abs.). Southeastern Section, Geological Society of America, v. 9, n. 2, p. 144.

292. Harris, W. B., Baum, G. R., Wheeler, W. H., and Textoris, Daniel A., 1977, Lithofacies and Structural Framework of the Middle Eocene Castle Hayne Limestone, North Carolina (abs.). Southeastern Section, Geological Society of America, v. 9, n. 2, p. 144.

293. Thayer, P. A., and Textoris, D. A., 1977, Faunal and Diagenic Controls of Porosity and Permeability in Tertiary Aquifer Carbonates, North Carolina. Raleigh, North Carolina Department of Natural and Economic Resources, Division of Earth Resources, Special Publication 7, 35 pp.

294. Upchurch, M. L., 1979, Sponge Bearing Hardgrounds in the Castle Hayne Limestone *in* Baum, G. R., Harris, W. B., and Zullo, V. A., eds. Structural and Stratigraphic Framework for the Coastal Plain of North Carolina. Raleigh, Department of Natural and Community Development, Geological Survey Section, Field Trip Guide Book for the Carolina Geological Society and Atlantic Coastal Plain Geological Society, pp. 59–64.

295. Curran, H. A., 1986, Trace Fossils from the Rocky Point Member of the Peedee Formation (Upper Cretaceous) and the Castle Hayne Limestone (Eocene) *in* Textoris, D. A., ed., Society of Economic Paleontologists and Mineralogists, Field Guidebooks, Southeastern United States, Third Annual Meeting. pp. 285–288.

296. Dockal, J. A., 1986, Cements and Related Diagenic Features of the Castle Hayne Limestone, East Coast Limestone Quarry, Pender County, North Carolina *in* Textoris, D. A., ed., Society of Economic Paleontologists and Mineralogists, Field Guidebooks, Southeastern United States, Third Annual Meeting, pp. 277–284.

297. Harris, W. B., Zullo, V. A., and Otte, L. J., 1986, Eocene Carbonate Facies of the North Carolina Coastal Plain *in* Textoris, D. A., ed., Society of Economic Paleontologists and Mineralogists, Field Guidebooks, Southeastern United States, Third Annual Meeting, pp. 255–276.

298. Worsley, T. R., and Laws, R. A., 1986, Valcareous Nannofossil Biostratigraphy of the Castle Hayne Limestone *in* Textoris, D. A., ed., Society of Economic Paleontologists and Mineralogists, Field Guidebooks, Southeastern United States, Third Annual Meeting, pp. 289–296.

299. Thayer, P. A., Harris, W. B., and Zullo, V. A., 1986, Bentonite fromm the Upper Castle Hayne Limestone *in* Textoris, D. A., ed., Society of Economic Paleontologists and Mineralogists, Field Guidebooks, Southeastern United States, Third Annual Meeting, pp. 307–332.

300. Smith, A. B., 1958, Paleoecology of the Trent Formation (Lower Miocene: North Carolina). Unpublished master's thesis, University of Michigan, 108 pp.

301. Baum, G. R., 1981, Lithostratigraphy, Depositional and Tectonic Framework of the Eocene New Bern Formation and Oligocene Trent Formation North Carolina. Southeastern Geology, v. 22, n. 4, pp. 177–191.

302. Lawrence, D. R., 1976, Paleoenvironmental Setting of Crassostrea gigantissima (finch) Communities, Coastal Plain of North Carolina. Southeastern Geology, v. 17, pp. 55–66.

303. Fenneman, N.M., 1933, Physiography of the Eastern United States. New York, McGraw-Hill Book Company Inc., 714 pp.

304. Harrington, C., 1977, personal communication. Raleigh, North Carolina State University, Department of Geosciences.

305. Kimery, J. O., 1965, Description of the Pungo River Formation in Beaufort County, North Carolina. Raleigh, North Carolina Department of Conservation and Development, Division of Mineral Resources, Bulletin 79, 131 pp.

306. Gibson, T. G., 1967, Stratigraphy and Paleoenvironment of the Phosphatic Miocene Strata of North Carolina. Geological Society of America Bulletin, v. 78, n. 5, pp. 631–650.

307. Rooney, T. P., and Kerr, P. F., 1967, Mineralogic Nature and Origin of the Phosphatic Miocene Strata of North Carolina. Geological Society of America Bulletin, v. 78, n. 6, pp. 731–748.

308. Gibson, T. G., 1968, Stratigraphy and Paleoenvironment of the Phosphatic Miocene Strata of North Carolina. Geological Society of America Bulletin, v. 79, n. 10, pp. 1437–1447.

309. Leutze, W. P., 1968, Stratigraphy and Paleoenvironment of the Phosphatic Miocene of North Carolina. Discussion, Geological Society of America Bulletin, v. 79, n. 10, pp. 1433–1436.

310. Miller, J. A., 1971, Stratigraphic and Structural Setting of the Middle Miocene Pungo River Formation of North Carolina. Unpublished doctoral dissertation, University of North Carolina at Chapel Hill, 104 pp.

311. Riggs, S. R., Lewis, D. W., Scarborough, A. K., and Snyder, S. W., 1982, Cyclic Deposition of Neogene Phosphorites in the Aurora Area, North Carolina, and their Possible Relationship to Global Sea-Level Fluctuations. Southeastern Geology, v. 23, n. 4, pp. 189–204.

312. Snyder, S. W., Riggs, S. R., Katrosh, M. R., Lewis, D. W., and Scarborough, A. K., 1982, Synthesis of Phosphate Sediment Faunal Relationships within the Pungo River Formation: Paleoenvironmental Implications. Southeastern Geology, v. 23, n. 4, pp. 233–245.

313. Snyder, S. W., Hine, A. C., and Riggs, S. R., 1982, Miocene Seismic Stratigraphy, Structural Framework, and Sea Level Cyclicity: North Carolina Continental Shelf. Southeastern Geology, v. 23, n. 4, pp. 247–266.

314. Scarborough, A. K., Riggs, S. R., and Snyder, S. W., 1982, Stratigraphy and Petrology of the Pungo River Formation, Central Coastal Plain of North Carolina. Southeastern Geology, v. 23, n. 4, pp. 205–215.

315. Gibson, T. G., 1983, Stratigraphy of Miocene Through Pleistocene Strata of the United States Central Atlantic Coastal Plain in Ray, C. E., ed., Geology and Paleontology of the Lee Creek Mine, North Carolina, I. Smithsonian Contributions to Paleobiology, No. 53, Washington, Smithsonian Institution Press, pp. 35–80.

316. McLellan, J. H., 1983, Phosphate Mining at Lee Creek in Ray, C. E., ed., Geology and Paleontology of the Lee Creek Mine, North Carolina, I. Smithsonian Contributions to Paleobiology, No. 53, Washington, Smithsonian Institution Press, pp. 25–33.

317. Ward, L. W., and Blackwelder, B. W., 1980, Stratigraphic Revision of Upper Miocene and Lower Pliocene Beds of the Chesapeake Group, Middle Atlantic Coastal Plain. Reston, U. S. Geological Survey, Bulletin 1482-D, 71 pp.

318. Kesel, R. H., 1974, Inselbergs on the Piedmont of Virginia, North Carolina, and South Carolina: Types and Characteristics. Southeastern Geology, v. 16, n. 1, pp. 1–30.

319. Brown, H. S., 1961, Linville Caverns Through the Ages, The Geological Story. N.C. State University, Raleigh, 22 pp.

320. Holler, C. O., Jr., 1981, North Carolina's Bat Caves, A Significant Region of Tectonokarst. Proceedings of the International Congress of Speleology, n. 8, pp. 190–191.

321. Hazel, J. E., 1971, Paleoclimatology of the Yorktown Formation (Upper Miocene and Lower Pliocene) of Virginia and North Carolina in Oertli, M. J., ed., Paleoecologie Ostracodes Pau 1970, Bulletin Sentre Rech-SNPA, pp. 361–375.

322. Abbott, W. H., 1975, Miocene Opal Phytoliths and Their Climatic Implications. Geologic Notes, v. 19, n. 2, pp. 43–47.

323. Bailey, R. H., 1987, Stratigraphy and Depositional History of the Yorktown Formation in Northeastern North Carolina. Southeastern Geology, v. 28, n. 1, pp. 1–19.

324. Prouty, W. F., 1934, Fossil Whales of the North Carolina Miocene (abs.). Elisha Mitchell Scientific Society Journal, v. 50, n. 1–2, p. 52.

325. Kellog, R., 1965, Fossil Marine Mammals From the Miocene Calvert Formation of Maryland and Virginia. United States National Museum Bulletin, v. 274, n. 1–2, pp. 1–63.

326. Bailey, R. H., 1973, Paleoenvironments, Paleoecology, and Stratigraphy of Molluscan Assemblages from the Yorktown (Upper Miocene-Lower Pliocene) of North Carolina. Unpublished doctoral dissertation, University of North Carolina at Chapel Hill, 110 pp.

327. Oaks, R. Q., Jr., and Dubar, J. R., 1974, Tentative Correlation of Post-Miocene Units, Central and Southern Atlantic Coastal Plain in Oaks, R. Q., Jr., and Dubar, J. R., eds., Post-Miocene Stratigraphy Central and Southern Atlantic Coastal Plain. Logan, Utah State University Press, pp. 232–245.

328. Gibson, G. G., 1983, Stratigraphy of Miocene through Lower Pleistocene Strata of the Unites States Central Atlantic Coastal Plain in Ray, C. E., ed., Geology and Paleontology of the Lee Creek Mine, North Carolina, I. Smithsonian Contributions to Paleobiology, No. 53, Washington, Smithsonian Institution Press, pp. 35–80.

329. Hazel, J. E., 1983, Age and Correlation of the Yorktown (Pliocene and Croatan (Pliocene and Pleistocene) Formations at the Lee Creek Mine in Ray, C. E., ed., Geology and Paleontology of the Lee Creek Mine, North Carolina, I. Smithsonian Contributions to Paleobiology, No. 53, Washington, Smithsonian Institution Press, pp. 81–200.

330. Gibson, T. G., 1987, Miocene and Pliocene Pectinidae (Bivalvia) from the Lee Creek Mine and Adjacent Areas in Ray, R. E., ed., Geology and Paleontology of the Lee Creek Mine, North Carolina, II. Smithsonian Contributions to Paleobiology, No. 61, Washington, Smithsonian Institution Press, pp. 31–112.

331. Randall, J. E., 1973, Size of the Great White Shark (Carcharodon). Science, v. 181, pp. 169–170.

332. Olsen, T., 1988, Personal Communication, Washington, D.C., Smithsonian Institution, American Museum of Natural History, Division of Paleobiology.

333. Gamble, E., 1977, personal communication. Raleigh, North Carolina State University.

334. Cobb, C., 1923, The Immediate Ancestor of Our Domestic Horse Found Fossil in Halifax County, North Carolina (abs.). Elisha Mitchell Scientific Society Journal, v. 29, n. 1–2, pp. 31–32.

335. Voorhies, M. R., 1974, Late Miocene Terrestrial Mammals Echols County, Georgia. Southeastern Geology, v. 15, n. 4, pp. 223–235.

336. Daniels, R. B., and Gamble, E. E., 1974, Surficial Deposits of the Neuse-Cape Fear Divide Above the Surry Scarp, North Carolina in Oaks, R. O., and Dubar, J. R., eds., 1974, Post–Miocene Stratigraphy Central and Southern Atlantic Coastal Plain. Logan, Utah State University Press, pp. 88–101.

337. Colquhoun, D. J., 1974, Cyclic Surficial Stratigraphic Units of the Middle and Lower Coastal Plain Central South Carolina in Oaks, R. O., and Dubar, J. R., eds., 1974, Post-Miocene Stratigraphy Central and Southern Atlantic Coastal Plain. Logan, Utah State University Press, pp. 179–190.

338. Welby, C. W., 1971, Post-Yorktown Erosional Surface, Pamlico River and Sound, North Carolina. Southeastern Geology, v. 13, n. 4, pp. 199–205.

339. Alt, D., 1974, Arid Climate Control of Miocene Sedimentation and Origin of Modern Drainage, Southeastern United States in Oak, R. O., Jr., and Dubar, J. R., eds., 1974, Post-Miocene Stratigraphy Central and Southern Atlantic Coastal Plain, Logan, Utah State University Press, pp. 21–29.

340. Blackwelder, B. W., 1979, Stratigraphy of Upper Pliocene and Lower Pleistocene Marine and Estuarine Deposits of Northeastern North Carolina and Southeastern Virginia. Reston, U.S. Geological Survey, Bulletin 1502-B, pp. B1– B17.

341. Bailey, R. H., 1977, Neogene Mulluscan Assemblages Along the Chowan River, North Carolina. Southeastern Geology, v. 18, n. 3, pp. 173–189.

342. Bailey, R. H., and Tedesco, S. A., 1986, Paleoecology of a Pliocene Coral Thicket from North Carolina: An Example of Temporal Change in Community Structure and Function. Journal of Paleontology, v. 60, n. 6, pp. 1159–1176.

343. Dubar, J. R., 1971, Neogene Stratigraphy of the Lower Coastal Plain of the Carolinas. Myrtle Beach, South Carolina, Atlantic Coastal Plain Geological Association, 12th Annual Field Conference, 128 pp.

344. Dubar, J. R., 1987, Geology of the Dongola 7.5-Minute Quadrangle, Horry amd Marion Counties, South Carolina. South Carolina Geology, v. 31, n. 1, pp. 1–15.

345. Dubar, J. R., and Soliday, J. R., 1963, Stratigraphy of the Neogene Deposits, Lower Neuse Estuary, North Carolina. Southeastern Geology, v. 4, n. 4, pp. 213–233.

346. Dubar, J. R., and Howard, 1969, Paleoecology of the James City Formation (Plio-Pleistocene ?), Neuse River Estuary, North Carolina (abs.). Geological Society of America, Abstracts with Programs, v. 4, p. 20.

347. Dubar, J. R., Solliday, J. R., and Howard, J. F., 1974, Stratigraphy and Morphology of Neogene Deposits, Neuse River Estuary, North Carolina in Oaks, R. O., and Dubar, J. R., eds., 1974, Post-Miocene Stratigraphy Central and Southern Atlantic Coastal Plain. Logan, Utah State University Press, pp. 102–122.

348. Dubar, J. R., 1975, A Waccamaw Faunal Assemblage, Longs Quadrangle, Horry County, South Carolina. Geologic Notes, v. 19, n. 2, pp. 32–42.

349. Wheeler, W. H., Daniels, R. B., and Gamble, E. R., 1983, The Post-Yorktown Stratigraphy and Geomorphology of the Neuse-Pamlico Area, Eastern North Carolina in Ray, C. E., ed., Geology and Paleontology of the Lee Creek Mine, North Carolina, I. Smithsonian Contributions to Paleobiology, No. 53, Washington, Smithsonian Institution Press, pp. 201–218.

350. Daniels, R. B., Gamble, E. E., Wheeler, W. H., and Holzhey, C. S., 1972, Carolina Geological Society and Atlantic Coastal Plain Geolog-

ical Society Fieldtrip Guidebook. Raleigh, North Carolina Department of Natural and Economic Resources, Division of Earth Resources, 36 pp.

351. Mixon, R. B., and Pilkey, O. N., 1976, Reconnaissance Geology of the Submerged and Emerged Coastal Plain Province Cape Fear to Cape Lookout Area, North Carolina. United States Geological Survey, Professional Paper 852, 45 pp.

352. Newton, C. R., 1978, Early Pleistocene (Calabrian) Age of the Wacamaw Formation at Walker's Bluff, Elizabethtown, N.C. (abs.). Southeastern Section, Geological Society of America, v. 10, n. 4, p. 194.

353. Bell, H., III, Butler, J. R., Howell, D. E., and Wheeler, W. H., 1974, Geology of the Piedmont and Coastal Plain Near Pageland, South Carolina, and Wadesboro, North Carolina. Carolina Geological Society Field Trip Guidebook, Columbia, South Carolina Geological Survey, 23 pp.

354. Cabe, S. D., 1980, Post-Eocene Stratigraphy of the Carthage and Southern Pines 7½° Quadrangles, North Carolina. Unpublished master's thesis, University of North Carolina at Chapel Hill, 97 pp.

355. Daniels, R. B., Gamble, E. E., and Wheeler, W. H., 1978, Upper Coastal Plain Surficial Sediments Between the Tar and Cape Fear Rivers, North Carolina. Southeastern Geology, v. 19, n. 2, pp. 69–81.

356. Johnson, H. S., and DuBar, J. R., 1964, Geomorphic Elements of the Area between the Cape Fear and Pee Dee Rivers, North and South Carolina. Southeastern Geology, v. 6, pp. 37–47.

357. Daniels, R. B., Gamble, E. E., Wheeler, W. H., and Nettleton, W. D., 1966, Coastal Plain Stratigraphy and Geomorphology Near Benson, North Carolina. Southeastern Geology, v. 18, n. 4, pp. 159–182.

358. Doering, J. A., 1960, Quaternary Surface Formations of the Southern Part of Atlantic Coastal Plain. Journal of Geology, v. 68, pp. 182–202.

359. Daniels, R. B., Gamble, E. E., and Nettleton, W. D., 1966, The Surry Scarp From Fountain to Potters Mill, North Carolina. Southeastern Geology, v. 7, n. 2, pp. 41–50.

360. Mixon, R. B., 1986, Depositional Environments and Paleogeography of the Interglacial Flanner Beach Formation, Cape Lookout Area, North Carolina in Neathery, T. L., ed., Geological Society of America Centennial Field Guide, Volume 6, Southeastern Section, pp. 315–320.

361. Keoughan, K. M., 1988, Stratigraphy of the Pliocene and Pleistocene Deposits of Cherry Point Marine Corps Air Station, North Carolina. Unpublished master's thesis, University of North Carolina at Chapel Hill, 71 pp.

362. Fallaw, W. C., 1965, The Pleistocene Neuse Formation in Southeastern North Carolina. Unpublished doctoral dissertation, University of North Carolina at Chapel Hill, 160 pp.

363. Fallaw, W. C., and Wheeler, W. H., 1969, Marine Fossiliferous Pleistocene Deposits in Southeastern North Carolina. Southeastern Geology, v. 10, n. 1, pp. 35–54.

364. Daniels, R. B., and Gamble, E. E., 1977, The Arapahoe Ridge—A Pleistocene Storm Beach. Southeastern Geology, v. 18, n. 4, pp. 231–247.

365. Daniels, R. B., Gamble, E. E., and Wheeler, W. H., 1971, The Goldsboro Ridge, an Enigma. Southeastern Geology, v. 12, n. 3, pp. 151–158.

366. Colquhoun, D. J., and Johnson, H. S., Jr., 1986, Tertiary Sea-Level Fluctuation in South Carolina. Paleography, Paleoclimatology, Paleoecology, v. 5, pp. 105–126.

367. Haq, B. U., Hardenbol, J., and Vail, P. R., 1987, Chronology of Fluctuating Sea Levels Since the Triassic. Science, v. 235, pp. 1156–1167.

368. Moore, W. W., 1972, Geomorphology of the Deep River Drainage Basin and Carthage Area, North Carolina. Unpublished master's thesis, University of North Carolina at Chapel Hill, 81 pp.

369. Richards, H. G., and Judson, S., 1965, The Atlantic Coastal Plain and the Appalachians in the Quaternary in Wright, H. E., Jr., and Frey, D. G., eds., The Quaternary of the United States. Princeton University Press, 129 pp.

370. Pierce, J. W., and Colquhoun, D. J., 1970, Holocene Evolution of a Portion of the North Carolina Coast. Geological Society of America Bulletin, v. 81, n. 12, pp. 3697–3714.

371. Whitehead, D. R., 1967, Studies of Full-Glacial Vegetation Climate in the Southeastern United States in Cushing, E. J., and Wright, M. E., eds., 1967, Volume 7 of the VII Congress of the International Association for Quaternary Research, pp. 237–248.

372. Whitehead, D. R., 1965, Palynology and Pleistocene Phytogeography of Unglaciated Eastern North America in Wright, H. E., and Frey, D. E., eds., The Quaternary of the United States, Part 1, Geology. Princeton, Princeton University Press, pp. 417–482.

373. Buell, M. F., 1945, Late Pleistocene Forests of Southeastern North Carolina. Torreya, v. 45, n. 4, pp. 12–28.

374. Frey, D. G., 1955, A Time Revision of the Pleistocene Pollen Chronology of Southeastern North Carolina. Ecology, v. 36, n. 4, pp. 762–763.

375. Frey, D. G., 1953, Regional Aspects of the Late-Glacial and Post-Glacial Pollen Succession North Carolina. Ecological Monographs, v. 23, n. 3, pp. 289–313.

376. Schroeder, R. A., and Bada, J. L., 1973, Glacial-Post-Glacial Temperature Differences Deduces From Aspartic Acid Racemization in Fossil Bones. Science, v. 132, pp. 479–482.

377. Whitehead, D. R., and Barghoorn, E. R., 1962, Pollen Analytical Investigations of Pleistocene Deposits From Western North and South Carolina. Durham, Duke University Press, Ecological Monographs, v. 32, pp. 347–369.

378. Michalek, D. D., 1960, Fanlike Features and Related Periglacial Phenomena of the Southern Blue Ridge. Unpublished doctoral dissertation, University of North Carolina at Chapel Hill, 215 pp.

379. Haselton, G. M., 1967, Wisconsin Glaciation in the Blue Ridge Province, Southern Appalachians, North Carolina (abs.). Northeastern and Southeastern Sections, Geological Society of America, v. 8, n. 2, p. 192.

380. Berkland, J. O., and Raymond, L. A., 1973, Pleistocene Glaciation in the Blue Ridge Province, Southern Appalachian Mountains, North Carolina. Science, v. 181, pp. 651–653.

381. Haselton, G. M., 1973, Possible Relict Glacial Features in the Black Balsam Knob and Richland Balsam Area, North Carolina. Southeastern Geology, v. 15, n. 3, pp. 119–125.

382. Berkland, J. O., 1974, North Carolina Glaciers: Evidence Disputed (Reply). Science, v. 184, pp. 89–91.

383. Carson, R. J., Beck, R. V., Chappelear, J. W., Lanier, M. D., McCurry, G. W., Neal, R. H., Stanley, L. G., Walker, R. G., and Wilson, J. R., 1974, Pseudo-Glaciation of Grandfather Mountain, North Carolina (abs.). Southeastern Section, Geological Society of America, v. 6, p. 340.

384. Raymond, L. A., 1977, Glacial, Periglacial, and Pseudo-Glacial Features in the Grandfather Mountain Area, North Carolina. Southeastern Geology, v. 18, n. 4, pp. 213–229.

385. Collection, Raleigh, North Carolina Museum of Natural History.

386. Mansfield, W. C., 1928, Notes of the Pleistocene Fauna From Maryland and Virginia and Pliocene and Pleistocene Faunas From North Carolina. United States Geological Survey, Professional Paper 150, 140 pp.

387. Funderberg, J. B., 1960, Fossil Manatee From North Carolina. Journal of Mammalogy, v. 41, n. 4, p. 521.

388. Fallaw, W. C., 1973, Depositional Environments of the Marine Pleistocene Deposits in Southeastern North Carolina. Geological Society of America Bulletin, v. 84, n. 1, pp. 257–268.

389. Campbell, L., Campbell, S., Colquhoun, D., Ernissee, J., and Abbott, W., 1975, Plio-Pleistocene Faunas of the Central Carolina Coastal Plain. Geologic Notes, v. 19, n. 3, pp. 51–124.

390. Miller, W., 1982, The Paleoecologic History of Late Pleistocene Estuarine and Marine Fossil Deposits in Dare County, North Carolina. Southeastern Geology, v. 23, n. 1, pp. 1–14.

391. Madden, C. T., 1985, On a Single Elephant Tooth: Most Primitive Mammoth from Coastal Plain of Southeastern United States. Southeastern Geology, v. 25, n. 4, pp. 207–211.

392. Hibbard, C. W., Ray, D. E., Savage, D. E., Taylor, D. W., and Guilday, J. E., 1965, Quaternary Mammals of North America in Wright, M. E., Jr., and Frey, D. G., eds., The Quaternary of the United States, Princeton, Princeton University Press, 509 pp.

393. Guilday, J. E., and McGrady, A. D., 1967, Vertebrate Fossils, Appalachian Caves and Their Implications to Pleistocene Geology (abs.). National Speleogical Society Bulletin, v. 29, n. 3, p. 105.

394. Ray, C. E., 1967, Pleistocene Mammals from Ladds, Bartow County, Georgia. Georgia Academy of Science Bulletin, v. 25, n. 3, pp. 120–150.

395. Schultz, C., Bertrand, T., Loyd, G., Whitmore, F. C., Ray, L. L., and Crawford, E. C., 1967, Big Bone Lick Kentucky—A Pictorial Story of the Famous Fossil Locality from 1962–1966. Lincoln, Nebraska University State Museum, Museum Notes number 33, v. 46, n. 22, p. 12.

396. Guilday, J. E., 1971, The Pleistocene History of the Appalachian Mammal Fauna in Holt, P. C., Patterson, R. A., and Hubbard, J. P., eds., The Distributional History of the Biota of the Southeastern Appala-

chians: Part III, Vertebrates. Blacksburg, Virginia Polytechnic Institute and State University, Research Division Monograph 4, pp. 233–262.

397. Lackey, L. E., 1977, Mastodon and Associated Full Glacial Fauna and Flora From Memphis, Tennessee (abs.). Southeastern Section, Geological Society of America Bulletin, v. 9, n. 2, p. 156.

398. Bellis, V., O'Conner, M. P., and Riggs, S. R., 1975, Estuarine Shoreline Erosion in the Albemarle-Pamlico Region of North Carolina. Raleigh, North Carolina State University, Sea Grant Publication UNC-SG-75-29, 67 pp.

399. Whitehead, D. R., 1972, Developmental and Environmental History of the Dismal Swamp. Ecological Monographs, v. 42, pp. 310–315.

400. Whitehead, D. R., and Campbell, S. K., 1976, Palynological Studies of the Bull Creek Peat, Horry County, South Carolina: Geomorphological Implications. Southeastern Geology, v. 17, n. 3, pp. 161–174.

401. Ingram, R. L., and Barnes, J. S., 1986, Fuel Grade Peat Deposits of Eastern North Carolina *in* Textoris, D. A., ed., SEPM Field Guidebook. Society of Economic Paleontologists and Mineralogists, Third Annual Midyear Meeting, pp. 375–379.

402. Maness, L. V., and Holler, C. O., 1979, North Carolina Coastal Plain Caves (abs.) *in* Abstracts of Papers 1978 Convention. The National Speleological Society Bulletin, v. 41, n. 4, p. 113.

403. McGowan, F. W., and McGowan, P. C., 1971, Flashes of Duplin's History and Government. Raleigh, Edwards and Broughton Company, 569 pp.

404. Gamble, E. E., Daniels, R. B., and McCracken, R. J., 1972, A,i2 Horizons of Coastal Plain Soils Pedogenic or Geologic Origin. Southeastern Geology, v. 11, n. 3, pp. 137–152.

405. Daniels, R. B., Gamble, E. E., and Wheeler, W. H., 1971, Stability of Coastal Plain Surfaces. Southeastern Geology, v. 13, n. 2, pp. 61–75.

406. Prouty, W. F., 1934, Carolina Bays and Elliptical-Like Basins. Journal of Geology, v. 34, n. 2, pp. 200–207.

407. MacCarthy, G. R., 1936, Magnetic Anomalies and the Geologic Structures of the Carolina Coastal Plain. Journal of Geology, v. 44, n. 3, pp. 396–406.

408. MacCarthy, G. R., 1936, Meteors and the Carolina Bays (abs.). Elisha Mitchell Scientific Society Journal, v. 50, n. 1–2, pp. 211.

409. MacCarthy, G. R., 1937, The Carolina Bays. Geological Society of America Bulletin, v. 48, n. 9, pp. 1211–1225.

410. Johnson, D. W., 1940, Mysterious Craters of the Carolina Coast, A Study in Methods of Research. Science in Progress, Yale University Press, American Scientist, v. 32, n. 1, pp. 1–22.

411. Johnson, D. W., 1942, The Origin of the Carolina Bays. New York, Columbia University Press, 314 pp.

412. Johnson, D. W., 1942, Rotary Currents and the Carolina Bays. Journal of Geomorphology, v. 4, n. 4, pp. 307–321.

413. Johnson, D. W., 1942, Rotary Currents and the Carolina Bays (Conclusion). Journal of Geomorphology, v. 5, n. 1, pp. 59–72.

414. Cooke, C. W., 1943, Elliptical Bays (North and South Carolina). Journal of Geology, v. 51, n. 6, pp. 419–427.

415. Prouty, W. F., 1943, The Carolina Bays. Compass, v. 23, n. 4, pp. 236–244.

416. Johnson, D. W., 1944, Role of Artesian Waters in Forming the Carolina bays. Science News Service, v. 86 pp. 255–258.

417. McCambell, J. C., 1945, Meteorites and the Carolina Bays. Journal of Geology, v. 53, n. 8, pp. 388–392.

418. McCambell, J. C., 1945, A Geomagnetic Study of Bladen County, North Carolina, "Carolina Bays." Journal of Geology, v. 53, n. 1, pp. 66–67.

419. McCambell, J. C., 1945, An Evaluation of the Artesian Hysis of the Origin of the Carolina Bays. Elisha Mitchell Scientific Society Journal, v. 60, n. 2, pp. 183–185.

420. Buell, M. F., 1946, Jerome Bog, A Peat Filled "Carolina Bay." Torrey Botanical Club Bulletin, v. 73, n. 1, pp. 24–33.

421. Buell, M. F., 1946, The Age of Jerome Bog, A "Carolina Bay." Science, v. 103, pp. 14–15.

422. Grant, C., 1948, Meteoritic Origin of the "Carolina Bays" Questioned. Popular Astronomy, v. 56, n. 10, pp. 511–527.

423. Prouty, W. F., 1948, Heart-Shaped Carolina Bays (abs.). Geological Society of America Bulletin, v. 59, n. 12, pt. 2, p. 1345.

424. Frey, D. G., 1949, Morphometry and Hydrography of Some Natural Lakes in the North Carolina Coastal Plain, The Bay Lake as a Morphologic Type. Elisha Mitchell Scientific Society Journal, v. 65, n. 1, pp. 1–37.

425. Cooke, C. W., 1950, Carolina Bays, Traces of Tidal Eddies (abs.). Geological Society of America Bulletin, v. 21, n. 12, pt. 2, p. 1452.

426. Frey, D. G., 1950, Carolina Bays in Relation to the North Carolina Coastal Plain. Elisha Mitchell Scientific Society Journal, v. 66, n. 1, pp. 44–52.

427. Johnson, W. R., Jr., Straley, H. W., III, and Straley, H. W., IV, 1950, Depth to Anomaly Source for Carolina Bays. Georgia Geological Survey Bulletin, n. 60, pp. 125–130.

428. Melton, F. A., 1950, The Carolina "Bays." Journal of Geology, v. 53, n. 2, pp. 123–134.

429. Prouty, W. F., 1950, Origin of Carolina Bays. Popular Astronomy, v. 58, n. 1, pp. 17–21.

430. Frey, D. G., 1951, Pollen Succession in the Sediments of Singletary Lake. Ecology, v. 32, n. 3, pp. 518–533.

431. Odum, H. T., 1952, The Carolina Bays and the Pleistocene Weather Map. American Journal of Science, v. 250, pp. 263–302.

432. Frey, D. G., 1953, Stages in the Ontogeny of the Carolina Bays. International Association Theoretical and Applied Limonology Congress (Great) Britain, Proceedings, v. 12, pp. 660–668.

433. Wells, B. W., and Bryce, S. G., 1953, Carolina Bays, Additional Data on their Origin, Age, and History. Elisha Mitchell Scientific Society Bulletin, v. 69, n. 2, pp. 119–141.

434. Cooke, C. W., 1954, Carolina Bays and The Shape of Eddies. United States Geological Survey, Professional Paper 254-1, pp. 195–204.

435. Frey, D. G., 1954, Evidence for the Recent Enlargement of the Bay Lakes of North Carolina. Ecology, v. 35, n. 1, pp. 78–88.

436. Carson, C. E., and Hussey, K. M., 1960, Hydrodynamics in three Arctic Lakes. Journal of Geology, v. 68, n. 6, pp. 535–600.

437. Preston, C. D., and Brown, C. Q., 1964, Geologic Section of a Carolina Bay, Sumpter County, South Carolina. Southeastern Geology, v. 6, n. 2, pp. 21–29.

438. Frink, J. W., and Murray, G. E., Jr., 1967, Elliptical "Bays" of "Craters" of the Southeastern United States. Compass, v. 17, n. 4, pp. 227–233.

439. Price, W. A., 1968, Carolina Bays in Fairbridge, R. W., ed., The Encyclopedia of Geomorphology. New York, Reinhold Book Corporation, pp. 102–109.

440. Thom, B. G., 1970, Carolina Bay, Genesis, Age. Geological Society of America Bulletin, v. 81, n. 3, pp. 783–813.

441. Gohn, G. S., Higgins, B. B., Owens, J. P., Schneider, R., and Hess, M. M., 1976, Lithostratigraphy of the Clubhouse Crossroads Core: Charlestown Project, South Carolina (abs.). Northeastern and Southeastern Section, Geological Society of America, v. 8, n. 2, p. 314.

442. Kaczorowski, R. T., 1977, The Carolina Bays: A Comparison With Modern Oriented Lakes. Columbia, University of South Carolina, Department of Geology, Coastal Research Division, Technical Report 13-CRD, 124 pp.

443. Savage, H., Jr., 1982, The Mysterious Carolina Bays. Columbia, University of South Carolina Press, 121 pp.

444. Pierce, J. W., and Colquhoun, D. J., 1970, Configuration of the Holocene Primary Barrier Island Chain, Outer Banks, North Carolina. Southeastern Geology, v. 11, n. 4, pp. 231–236.

445. Oaks, R. C., Cock, N. K., Sanders, J. E., and Flint, R. F., 1974, Post-Miocene Shorelines and Sea Levels Southeastern Virginia in Oaks, R. O., and Dubar, J. R., eds., Post-Miocene Stratigraphy Central and Southern Atlantic Coastal Plain, Logan Utah, Utah University Press, pp. 52–87.

446. Shepard, F. P., and Wanless, N. R., 1971, Our Changing Coastlines. New York, McGraw-Hill Publishing Company Inc., 539 pp.

447. O'Connor, M. P., and Riggs, S. R., 1977, Estuarine Shoreline Types and Erosional Processes of North Carolina (abs.). Southeastern Section, Geological Society of America, v. 9, n. 2, p. 172.

448. Pilkey, O. H., Jr., Neal, W. J., and Pilkey, O. H., Sr., 1978, From Currituck to Calabash: Living with North Carolina's Barrier Islands. Research Triangle Park, North Carolina Science and Technology Research Center, 228 pp.

449. Hennigar, H. F., 1977, Historical Evolution of Sand Dunes: Currituck Spit, Virginia/ North Carolina (abs.). Southeastern Section, Geological Society of America, v. 9, n. 2, p. 147.

450. Fisher, J. J., 1967, Development Pattern of Relict Beaches, Outer Bank Barrier Island Chain North Carolina. Unpublished doctoral dissertation, University of North Carolina at Chapel Hill, 250 pp.

451. Hoyt, J. M., 1967, Barrier Formation, Geological Society of America Bulletin, v. 78, pp. 1125–1136.

452. Riggs, S. R., and O'Connor, M. P., 1975, Evolutionary Succession of Drowned Coastal Plain—Bar-Built Estuaries (abs.). Geological So-

ciety of America Bulletin, Abstracts with Programs, v. 7, n. 7, pp. 1247–1248.

453. Moorefield, T. P., 1976, Geologic Processes of the Fort Fisher Coastal Area. Unpublished master's thesis, Greenville, East Carolina University, 100 pp.

454. Susman, K. R., and Heron, D., 1976, Post-Miocene Subsurface Stratigraphy of Shackleford Banks a Barrier Island Near Cape Lookout, N.C. (abs.) Northeastern and Southeastern Sections, Geological Society of America, v. 8, n. 2, pp.280–281.

455. Moslow, T. F., and Heron, D., 1977, Evidence of Relict in the Holocene Stratigraphy of Core Banks from Cape Lookout to Drum Inlets (abs.). Southeastern Section, Geological Society of America, v. 9, n. 2, p. 170.

456. Herbert, J. R., and Heron, S. D. Jr., 1978, Relict Inlets of Northern Core Bank: Evidence from Holocene Inlet Fill and Geometric Features (abs.). Southeastern Section, Geological Society of America, v. 10, n. 4, p. 172.

457. Hosier, P. E., and Cleary, W. J., 1978, Geomorphic and Vegetational Recovery Patterns Following Washovers in Southeastern North Carolina (abs.). Southeastern Section, Geological Society of America, v. 10, n. 4, p. 172.

458. Herron, S. D., Jr., Moslow, T. F., Berelson, W. M., Herbert, J. R., Steele, G. A., III, and Susman, K. R., 1984, Holocene Sedimentation of a Wave-Dominated Barrier Island Shoreline: Cape Lookout, North Carolina. Marine Geology, v. 60, pp. 413–434.

459. Dolan, R., and Lins, H., 1986, The Outer Banks of North Carolina. Washington, U.S. Geological Survey, Professional Paper, 1177-B, 47 pp.

460. Thurman, H. V., and Webber, H. H., 1984, Marine Biology. Columbus, Charles E. Merrill Publishing Company, 446 pp.

461. Newton, J., 1976, personal communication, Beaufort, Duke University Marine Laboratory.

462. Higgins, B. B., and Poenoe, P., 1974, A Geologic and Geophysical Study of the Charlestown, South Carolina Earthquake Zone. Earthquake Information Bulletin, v. 6, n. 6, pp. 16–23.

463. Brown, L. D., 1978, Recent Vertical Crustal Movement Along the East Coast of the United States. Tectonophysics, v. 44, n. 1, pp. 205–231.

464. Langfelder, J. S. D., and Amein, M., 1968, A Reconnaissance of Coastal Erosion in North Carolina. Raleigh, North Carolina State University, Department of Civil Engineering, 127 pp.

465. Balazs, E. I., 1974, Vertical Crustal Movements on the Middle Atlantic Coastal Plain and Indicated By Precise Leveling (abs.). Northeastern Section, Geological Society of America, v. 6., n. 1, p. 3.

466. Stewart, D. M., 1977, personal communication, University of North Carolina at Chapel Hill.

467. Kaufman, W., and Pilkey, O. H., Jr., 1983, The Beaches Are Moving: The Drowning of America's Shoreline. Durham, Duke University Press, 336 pp.

Index